THE POETICAL WORKS OF MARY HOWITT, ELIZA COOK, AND L. E. L.

A NEW EDITION.

BOSTON:
PHILLIPS, SAMPSON, & CO.,
110 WASHINGTON STREET.
1853.

ADVERTISEMENT.

The present volume is now issued, in accordance with a previously announced plan, of publishing a uniform and cheap edition of such of the poets as a discriminating public have sanctioned as standard. In this instance, as in some of the preceding volumes, abridgment was found necessary, to keep it within the plan originally adopted. In performing this delicate work, the proprietors have had such aid as they think will warrant them in saying, that, although the complete poetical productions of these celebrated writers is not comprised in this edition, yet it contains all that is material in preserving their high position as female poets.

STEREOTYPED BY
CHARLES W. COLTON.

CONTENTS.

HOWITT'S POEMS.

1*

LANDON'S POEMS.

THE

POETICAL WORKS

OF

MARY HOWITT.

A NEW EDITION.

BOSTON:
PHILLIPS, SAMPSON, & CO.,
110 WASHINGTON STREET.
1853.

HYMNS AND FIRE-SIDE VERSES.

L'ENVOI.

I HAVE indited thee with care and love,
  My little book; and now I send thee forth
On a good mission like the gentle dove,
  Bearing glad tidings with thee o'er the earth.

Thou wast not meant for riot and for jest,
  Dear little book, all simple as thou art;
But in sweet homes to be a loving guest;
  And find a place in many a guileless heart.

Have not a fear! I know that thou wilt find
  Thy journey pleasant as a path of flowers,
For pure and youthful hearts are ever kind,
  Glad to be pleased with labor such as ours.

Sit down with little children by the way,
  And tell them of sweet Marien, how she went
Over the dreary world from day to day,
  On Christian works of love, like thee, intent.

Tell them of Him who framed the sea, the sky;
  The glorious earth and all that dwell therein;
And of that Holy One made strong to die,
  Sinless himself, to save the world from sin.

And thou hast many a tale of wonder planned
  With various art, to make thy spirit wise
These have I given thee that thou may'st command
  Glad smiles at will, and pitying tears and sighs.

For thus, young, generous spirits would be won;
  And I have gifted thee to win them best;
Now go thou forth undaunted, gentle one,
  And trust thy cause to every youthful breast.

Go forth, and have thou neither fear nor shame;
  Many shall be thy friends, thy foes be few;
And greet thou those who love thee in my name,
  Yea, greet them warmly! Little book, adieu!

MARIEN'S PILGRIMAGE.

A FIRE-SIDE STORY.

Christianity, like a child, goes wandering over the world. Fearless in its innocence, it is not abashed before princes, nor confounded by the wisdom of synods. Before it the blood-stained warrior sheathes his sword, and plucks the laurel from his brow; — the midnight murderer turns from his purpose, and, like the heart-smitten disciple, goes out and weeps bitterly. It brings liberty to the captive, joy to the mourner, freedom to the slave, repentance and forgiveness to the sinner, hope to the faint-hearted, and assurance to the dying.

It enters the huts of poor men, and sits down with them and their children; it makes them contented in the midst of privations, and leaves behind an everlasting blessing. It walks through great cities, amid all their pomp and splendor, their unimaginable pride, and their unutterable misery, a purifying, ennobling, correcting, and redeeming angel.

It is alike the beautiful companion of childhood and the comfortable associate of age. It ennobles the noble; gives wisdom to the wise, and new grace to the lovely. The patriot, the priest, and the eloquent man, all derive their sublime power from its influence.

Thanks be to the Eternal Father, who has made us one with Him, through the benign Spirit of Christianity!

PART I.

Through the wide world went Marien,
  On a holy mission sent,
A little child of tender years,
  Throughout the world she went.

And ever, as she went along,
  Sweet flowers sprang 'neath her feet
All flowers that were most beautiful,
  Of virtues strong and sweet.

And ever, as she went along,
  The desert beasts grew tame
And man, the savage, dyed with blood,
  The merciful became.

Now, if you will attend to me,
  I will, in order, tell
The history of this little child,
  And what to her befell.

No friend at all had Marien,
  And at the break of day,
In a lonesome place within the world,
  In quiet thought she lay.

The stars were lost in coming morn,
  The moon was pale and dim,
And the golden sun was rising
  Over the ocean's rim.

With upturned eye lay Marien; —
  "And I am alone," said she,
"Though the blackbird and the nightingale
  Sing in the forest-tree:

"Though the weak woodland creatures
  Come to me when I call,
And eat their food from out my hand;
  And I am loved by all:

"Though sun, and moon, and stars come out,
  And flowers of fairest grace,
And whate'er God made beautiful,
  Are with me in this place:

"Yet I am all alone, alone,
  Alone both night and day!
So I will forth into the world,
  And do what good I may:

"For many a heart is sorrowful,
  And I that heart may cheer; —
And many a weary captive pines
  In dungeons dark and drear; —
And I the iron bonds may loose, —
  Then why abide I here?

"And many a spirit dark with crime
  Yet longeth to repent;
And many a grievous wrong is done
  To the weak and innocent; —
And I may do the injured right,
  May save the penitent!

"Up, I will forth into the world!"
  And, thus as she did say,
Sweet Marien from the ground rose up,
  And went forth on her way.

Through the wood went Marien,
  The thick wood and the green!
And not far had she traveled, ere
  A cruel sight was seen.

Under the green and leafy boughs
  Where singing birds were set;
At strife about their heritage,
  Two ruffian brothers met.

"Thou shalt not of our father's land,"
  The elder said, "have part!"
The younger brother spoke no word,
  But stabbed him to the heart.

Then deep into the forest dark
  With desperate speed he ran,
And gentle Marien stood beside
  The bleeding, murdered man.

With pitying tears that would not cease,
  She washed his wounded side,
And prayed him to have faith in Him
  Who for the sinner died.

But no sign made the murdered man,
  There stiff in death he lay; —
And Marien through the forest wild
  Went mourning on her way.

Ere long, as she went wandering on,
  She came to where there sat,
With folded arms upon her breast,
  A woman desolate.

Pale was she as the marble stone,
  And steadfast was her eye;
She sat enchained, as in a trance,
  By her great misery.

"What ails thee, mother?" Marien said,
  In a gentle voice and sweet;
"What aileth thee, my mother?"
  And knelt down at her feet.

"What aileth thee, my mother?"
  Kind Marien still did say;
And those two words, *my mother*,
  To the lone heart found their way.

As one who wakeneth in amaze,
  She quickly raised her head;—
And, "Who is't calls me mother?"
  Said she, "my child is dead!"

"He was the last of seven sons —
  He is dead — I have none other;—
This is the day they bury him;—
  Who is it calls me mother?"

"'Tis I," said gentle Marien,
  "Dear soul, be comforted!"
But the woman only wrung her hands,
  And cried, "My son is dead!"

"Be comforted," said Marien,
  And then she sweetly spake
Of Jesus Christ, and how he came
  The sting from death to take.

She told of all his life-long love,
  His soul by suffering tried:
And how at last his mother stood
  To see him crucified.

Of the disciples' broken hearts
  She told, of pangs and pain;
Of Mary at the sepulchre,
  And Christ arisen again.

"Then sorrow not," she said, "as though
  Thou wert of all bereft;
For still, though they beloved are not,
  This blessed faith is left.—

"That when thy dream of life is o'er,
  Thou shalt embrace thy seven,
More beautiful than earthly sons,
  With our dear Lord in heaven!"

Down on her knees the woman fell,
  And "blessed be God," said she,
"Who in my sorest need hath sent
  This comforter to me!"

PART II.

Now Marien in the woman's house
Abode a little space,
And comfort to the mother came;
And a dear daughter's place
Had Marien in the woman's heart,
Doing the while a daughter's part.

But now 'twas time that she must go;
For Marien's duty was not there,
Now grief was past, and wo was done;
So, with the rising of the sun,
She rose up forth to fare.

"Nay, bide with me," the woman said,
Or, if as thou dost say,
Duty forbids that this may be,
I a day's journey go with thee,
To speed thee on the way."

So forth the loving pair set out,
The woman and the child;
And first they crossed the desert heath,
And then the mountains wild.

And in the woman's arms she lay,
That night within the forest hoar,
And the next morn, with loving heart,
They said farewell, as those who part
To meet on earth no more.

Upon her way went Marien,
  From morn till set of day,
And the peace of God that passeth word,
  Upon her spirit lay,
And ofttimes she sang aloud
  As she went on her way.

The joyfulest song sang Marien
  That e'er left human tongue ;
The very birds were mute, to hear
  The holy words she sung.

But now the darksome night came on,
  And Marien lay her down
Within a little way-side cave,
  On mosses green and brown.

And in the deepest hush of night
  Rude robbers entered in ;
And first they ate and drank, then rose
  To do a deed of sin.

For with them was a feeble man,
  Whom they had robbed, and they
Here came to foully murder him,
  And hide him from the day.

Up from her bed sprang Marien,
  With heavenly power endued ;
And in her glorious innocence,
  Stood 'mong the robbers rude.

"Ye shall not take the life of man!"
  Spake Marien low and sweet ;

"For this will God take strict account,
  Before his judgment-seat!"

Out from the cave the robbers fled,
  For they believed there stood
A spirit stern and beautiful,
  Nor aught of flesh and blood.

And two from out the robber-band
  Thenceforward did repent,
And lived two humble Christian men,
  On righteous deeds intent.

When from the cave the robber-band
  Had fled, the aged man
Rose from the floor where he was laid,
  And marveling much, began.—

"Who art thou child? and those few words
  Of might which thou hast spoken,
What may they be? My foes have fled—
  And lo! my bonds are broken;
At thy few words my foes have fled,
  My rigid bonds have broken!"

Then Marien 'gan to tell him how
  Through her God's power had wrought;
And him from peril, nigh to death,
  Thus wondrously had brought.

She told him how holy Daniel's faith
  The caged beasts disarmed;
How the three righteous children walked
  Through raging fire unharmed.

She told how Peter, bound with chains,
Lay in the prison-ward,
How God's good angel freed him straight,
And the strong prison's iron gate
Oped of its own accord.

"God knows our wants," said Marien,
"And in our sorest need,
Puts forth his arm to rescue us,
For he is merciful, and thus
It is that thou art freed."

"Let us go hence!" the old man said,
And o'er the forest sod,
They, hand in hand, with quiet steps,
Went forward, praising God.

Ere noontide, to a forest grange
They came, a sylvan place,
Where trooped, no longer fearing man,
The forest's native race,
The white doe and the antlered stag,
And every beast of chase.

'Twas joy to see them drawing near
The old man as he came;
And this he stroked, and that he called
By some familiar name.

'Twas joy unto the little child
This pleasant place to see;
"This is my home," he said, "and here
Thou shalt abide with me."

"I have no child to be mine heir,
  And I am growing old;—
Thou shalt be heir to all my lands,
  And heir of all my gold.

"Thou shalt be comfort to mine age,
  And here within this wood,
'Mongst faithful, gentle things, shalt thou
  Grow up to womanhood!"

There dwelt the lovely Marien.
  Within the forest wild;
And she unto the lone old man
  Was dearer than a child.

There dwelt the lovely Marien,
  Yet not long dwelt she there;—
The old man died;—and then came forth
  A kinsman for the heir.

A lean and rugged man of pelf,
  In wickedness grown old;
From some vile city-den he came,
  And seized upon the gold;—
He slew the tamed forest-beasts,—
  The forest-grange he sold.

And with hard speeches, coarse and rude,
  Away the child he sent;
Meek Marien answered not a word,
  But through the forest went.

PART III.

THROUGH the wild wood went Marien,
For many a weary day;
Her food the forest-fruits, and on
The forest-turf she lay.

The wildern wood was skirted
By moorlands dry and brown;
And after them came Marien
Into a little town.

At entrance of the little town
A cross stood by the way;
A rude stone cross, and there she knelt
A little prayer to say.

Then on the stone steps sate her down;
And soon beside her crept,
A pale child with a clasped book,
And all the while he wept.

"Why weep you child," asked Marien
"What troubleth you so sore?"
At these words spoken tenderly,
The child wept more and more.

"I have not heard," at length he said,
"Kind words this many a year;
My mother is dead — and my father
Is a hard man and severe.

"I sit in corners of the house
  Where none can see me weep;
And in the quiet of the day,
  'Tis here I often creep.

"The kid leaps by his mother's side,
  The singing birds are glad:
But when I play me in the sun,
  My heart is ever sad.

"They say this blessed book can heal
  All trouble, and therefore
All day I keep it in my sight;
I lay it 'neath my head at night,
But it doth bring no cure to me:—
I know not what the cause may be,
  For I of learning have no store!"

Thereat, like to a broken flower,
  The child drooped down his head;
Then Marien took the clasped book,
  And of the Saviour read.

She read of him, the humble child
  Of poverty and scorn;
How holy angels sang for him
  The night that he was born.

How blessed angels came from heaven
  To hail the Christmas night,
And shepherd people with their flocks
  Beheld the glorious sight.

Then read she how, a growing youth,
His parents he obeyed,
And served, with unrepining will,
St. Joseph at his trade.

Then how he grew to man's estate,
And wandered up and down,
Preaching upon the lone sea-side,
And in the busy town.

Of all his tenderness, his love,
Page after page she read;
How he made whole the sick, the maimed,
And how he raised the dead.

And how he loved the children small,
Even of low degree;
And how he blessed them o'er and o'er,
And set them on his knee.

When this the little child had heard,
He spoke in accents low,
"Would that I had been one with them
To have been blessed so!"

"Thou shalt be blessed, gentle one!"
Said Marien kind and mild,
"Christ, the Great Comforter, doth bless
Thee, even now, poor child!"

So conversed they of holy things
Until the closing day;
Then Marien and the little child
Rose up to go their way.

As to the town they came, they passed
An ancient church; and "here
Let us go in!" the pale child said,
"For the organ pealeth over head,
And that sweet strain of holy sound
Like a heavenly vesture wraps me round,
And my heavy heart doth cheer."

So Marien and the little child
Into the church they stole;
And many voices rich and soft
Rose upward from the organ loft,
And the majestic instrument
Pealed to an anthem that was sent
To soothe a troubled soul.

Anon the voices died away,
The pealing organ ceased,
And through the church's ancient door
Passed chorister and priest.

And Marien and the little child
Went forward hand in hand
Adown the chancel aisle, and then
At once they made a stand.

Over the altar hung a piece
With holy influence fraught,
A work divine of wondrous skill
By some old painter wrought.

The gracious Saviour breathing love,
Was there like life expressed,
And round his knees the children small
Were thronging to be blessed.

Down dropped the child upon his knees,
  And weeping, tenderly
Cried "bless me, also, poor and weak,
  Or let me go to thee!"

Anon his little head dropped low,
  And his white lips 'gan to say,
"Oh kiss me gentle one, for now
  Even I am called away —
The blessed mother's voice I hear,
  It calleth me away!"

So died the child; — and Marien laid
  His meek arms on his breast,
With the clasped book between his hands: —
  Thus God had given him rest!

And Marien, weeping holy tears,
  Sate down beside the dead,
And slept that night within the church,
  As in a kingly bed.

Scarce from the church had Marien passed,
  When came the father there,
As was his wont, though fierce and bad,
  To say a morning prayer!

Not seven paces had he gone,
  When, heart-struck, he surveyed
Before his feet, that little child,
  In his dead beauty, laid.

At once as by a lightning stroke
  His softened soul was torn

With a deep sense of all the wrong
  That little child had borne.

And then came back the timid voice,
  The footstep faint and low,
The many little arts to please,
  The look of hopeless wo,
And many a shuddering memory
  Of harsh rebuke and blow.

No prayer of self-approving words,
  As was his wont, he said,
But humbled, weeping, self-condemned,
  He stood before the dead.

PART IV.

Ten long days' travel Marien went,
  O'er woodland and o'er wold,
Teaching and preaching by the way,
  Like Jesus Christ of old.

Sometimes within the baron's hall
  A lodging she would find,
And never went she from the door
  But blessings staid behind;
Proud foes forgiven, revenge withheld,
  And plenteous peace of mind.

With shepherd people on the hills;
With toiling peasant men
She sate; with women dwelling lone,
On mountain or in glen.

By wayside wells she sate her down,
With pilgrims old and bent;
Or, hand in hand, with children small,
To the village school she went.

She made them spare the singing birds
All in their leafy bowers;
She made them love all living things;
And praise God for the flowers.

But now she came to where there raged
Wild war throughout the land;
She heard the vexed people's cry;
She saw the ravaged corn-fields lie;
The hamlets smoking to the sky;
And everywhere careering by
The spoiler's savage band.

All hearts were changed. Like ravening wolves
Men preyed upon each other;
Dead children lay on the bloody mould;
And pitiless had grown, and cold,
The heart of many a mother.

Wild shouts and horrid shrieks around
Filled all the air; the earth
Reeked with the blood that had been spilt;
And man made mockery and mirth
Of agony and mortal wo: —
Yet through all this did Marien go.

Outraged of heart, the child went on,
  Weeping upon her way;
And now she soothed a dying wretch,
Then for another ran to fetch
  Water; and every day
Did deeds of mercy good and mild: —
Thus journeyed on the pitying child.

On went she, — and as she went on,
  Men grew ashamed of blood,
So beautiful did mercy seem;
  And the wild soldier rude
Slunk back as slinks a noisome beast;
  And to their homes once more
Came mothers with their little ones;
  And old men, weak and hoar,
Sate in the sun as they had wont,
  Unfearing at the door.

On went the child, — and as she went,
  Within the Baron's hall,
Were hung up helm, and mail, and sword,
  To rust upon the wall.

On went she, — and the poets sung
  No longer war's acclaim,
But holy hymns of love and joy,
  To hail her as she came.

On went she, like an angel good;
  With bounding steps she went,
Day after day, until she came
  To the great Conqueror's tent.

There sat he, a strong man of blood,
  Steel-mailed and scarfed with blue,
Poring o'er charts of distant lands,
  For new lands to subdue.

Beside him stood the gentle child;
  And now he traced with care,
Measuring from river unto sea,
  A fertile region fair.

"'Tis a good land," said Marien,
  "From river unto sea;
And there a quiet people dwell,
  Who never heard of thee.

"They feed their flocks and herds in peace;
  The fruitful vine they till;
The quiet homes their fathers built,
  They and their children fill.

"Even now their happy children's joy
  Thee and thy will condemn;
Wherefore should'st thou possess that land?
  God gave it unto them!"

Into her face the proud man looked,
  Amazed at what he heard;
Then turned unto his charts again,
  And answered never a word.

Another land among the hills
  He measured with his eye;
"'Tis a stern land," said Marien
  "A land of liberty!

"There fled the Christians in old time,
  And built their churches there:
And bells, upon the sabbath morn,
  Call all that land to prayer.

"Would'st thou God's people tribulate?
  A cursed thing it were
To make that Christian land of love
  A bloody sepulchre!"
The proud man turned him round about,
  And fiercely gazed at her.

"Rivers of blood have flowed for thee!"
  Unblenching Marien said,
"And many a Christian land hast thou
  With Christian blood made red.

"Up, sin no more! 'Tis coming now,
  The day thou canst not flee,
When all the thousands thou hast slain
  God will require of thee!

"Thou man of blood, repent, repent,
  Repent whilst yet you may,
And store up deeds of love and peace
  Against that awful day!"

Up from his seat the Conqueror rose,
  And paced the uneasy tent,
And ground his teeth and groaned aloud,
  As one that doth repent.

Forth from the tent sped Marien;
  And many a summer's day
Throughout a blessed land of peace
  She journeyed on her way.

PART V.

At length, after long travel past,
  She came, as it grew late,
Along a beaten road, that led
  To a vast city gate.

A vast and populous city, where
  Rose dome, and tower, and spire,
And many a gilded pinnacle,
Far-seen, as the bright sunset fell,
  Like glittering points of fire.

A city vast and populous,
  Whose thronging multitude
Sent forth a sound afar-off heard,
  Strong as the ocean-flood.

A strong, deep sound of many sounds,
  Toil, pleasure, pain, delight,
And traffic, myriad-wheeled, whose din
  Ceased not by day or night.

And through the city gate a throng
  Passed ever, never spent;
A busy mingling human tide
  Of those who came and went.

'Twas a proud city and a rich;
  A city fair and old;
Filled with the world's most costly things,--
  Of precious stones and gold;
Of silks, fine woods, and spiceries;
  And all that's bought and sold.

Thither came homeless Marien,
  Came there as it grew late,
Foot-sore and weary, friendless, poor,
  Unto the city gate.

There found her a poor carpenter
  Returning from his trade,
And he, with pitying countenance,
  Her weary form surveyed.

"Come!" said he, "thou unto my house
  Shalt go; and of my bread,
And of my cup, thou shalt partake;
Shalt bide with me!" and as he spake,
  Her weary steps he led.

Unto an humble place that stood
  'Mong dwellings of the poor
He brought her; bade her welcome thrice
  Unto his lowly door.

The good-wife met her with like cheer:
  "And though our fare is scant,
Fear not," she said, "whilst we have food,
  It is not thou shalt want!"

So dwelt she with this humble pair
  In the great city, cherished so,
As parents cherish their first-born ·
  Nor would they let her go.

Thus for a year she dwelt with them;
  And that while their abode
Was blessed exceedingly; their store
  Grew daily, weekly, more and more;
And peace so multiplied around,
The very hearth seemed holy ground,
As if once more on earth was found
  The Paradise of God.

'Twas she that blessed the bread they ate,
  'Twas she soothed all their cares;
They knew not that they entertained
  An angel unawares.

With simple hearts that had no guile
  They of the Saviour heard;
And, weeping tears of joyful faith,
  Believed and blessed each word.

No more they marveled how their board
  With plenteous food was spread;
Five barley loaves dispensed by Christ
  The famished thousands fed.

With love that would not be repressed,
  Their kindling bosoms burned,
And 'mong their neighbors poor they went,
  To teach what they had learned.

To teach how Christ unto the poor,
  The sinner vile, was sent;
How Mary washed his feet with tears,
And wiped them with her golden hairs,
  A weeping penitent.

And how the sinful woman stood
  Unjudged before his face;
How the poor prodigal sped back
  Repentant to his place;

How to the thief upon the cross
  He said, thou art forgiven,
And thou shalt be with me this day
  In the paradise of heaven.

So preached the carpenter; and men
  Turned from their evil ways,
And Christian prayer was heard around,
  And Christian hymns of praise.

Strange seemed these things; and to the rich,
  And to the proud, 'twas told,
How many of the meaner sort
  Lived like the saints of old.

How holy, blameless, were their lives;
  And how poor craftsmen vile,

Amid their fellows, tool in hand,
  The gospel preached the while.

'Twas told of Marien, how she came
  A wanderer none knew whence;
Friendless and poor, of mind mature,
  A Child in innocence;
As thus 'twas told, some blessed God,
  But others took offence.

"Why," said they, "should this simple child,
  These men of low degree,
Thus preach and practice? what new faith
  Is there, or need there be?

"Bishops have taught a thousand years,
  And learned men are they;
These are mad doctrines, false, unfit,
  Devised to lead astray."

Therefore the simple people were
  To a full synod brought,
To answer for their altered lives,
  And for the faith they taught.

Much marveled all those learned men
  To see them fearless stand
Calm, unabashed; with ready wit,
  And language at command.

And to their taunt of low estate,
  They answered, "let alone
All pride of rank; Christ chose the poor,
  To make his gospel known.

" And what are we ? — Immortal souls,
  For whom Christ's blood was shed ;
Children of one great sire, with ye,
Co-heirs of Immortality ;
Alike you both in birth and death ;
Alone our lot so differeth,
  As God shall judge the dead ! "

Then were they questioned of old creeds,
  By sophistries perplexed ;
So that their artless lore might fail,
  Their simple souls be vexed.

But they were steadfast in the faith
  As taught the holy book ;
And thence it was adjudged a crime
  Upon its page to look.

And the grave synod rose in wrath,
  And they were judged blasphemers dire,
And doomed, their daring heresies
  To expiate in fire.

PART VI.

So perished, for their faith in Christ,
  This righteous couple; for their foes
Beseeching pardon; blessing God
  That they were reckoned among those
Worthy to die for Christ, whose place
Is with the Holiest face to face.

Beside the pile stood Marien
  Weeping sad human tears,
Yet strengthening, comforting the while,
  And soothing all their fears.

And as she spoke, her countenance
  With heavenly lustre beamed,
And all around her youthful form
  Celestial beauty streamed.

Men looked on her with wondering awe,
  As on an angel's face,
And pity, and love, and sweet remorse,
  In every heart had place.

Throughout the city rang the tale
  Of this divinest child;
And for her sake unto her faith
  Many were reconciled.

Unto the synod came these things;
  And "here let her be brought,

To answer for herself," they said,
"And suffer as she ought."

As Christ among the doctors stood,
So she among these men,
Stern, rugged-browed, and deeply versed
In parchment and in pen;
Meekly she stood; when they reviled,
Reviling not again.

Yet with sweet words and argument,
Rather of love than lore,
She pleaded for the faith, as ne'er
Pled youthful tongue before.

All were amazed who heard her words;
And straightway spoke each one
Unto his neighbor, "Through this child
May mighty things be done!"

Then threatening words anon grew soft,
"And thou with us shalt go,"
They said, "and with the poor and vile
No longer suffer wo.

"Thou shalt be clothed in purple robes,
In gold and linen fine;
Shalt eat the daintiest food; shalt drink
The spirit-gladdening wine.

"And with us in proud palaces,
A crowned queen shalt be;
Leave but these men, for they are poor,
And can do naught for thee!

"Behold the stake at which they burn —
The iron rack behold —
Are these the men to make thee rich
With silver and with gold.

"Come with us, glorious Marıen,
And in our places high,
We will exalt thee as a queen,
Will deck thee royally!"

"Nay," said sweet Marien, "as a queen
It is not I may bide;
I am not won with power nor gold,
Nor aught of human pride.

"Who clothes the lilies of the field,
Will clothe me, even as they;
Who hears the ravens when they cry,
Will feed me day by day!"

But still the tempters kept with her;
And "Come away," they said,
And she unto a sumptuous dome
With royal pomp was led.

They showed her all that palace proud;
They showed her store of gold;
They told her of a hundred realms,
And wealth a hundred-fold.

"And all this shall be thine," they said,
"All this be thine, and more,
So thou wilt bind thyself to us,
And leave the weak and poor!

"Thou that art weak and poor thyself,
  A crowned queen shalt be!"
Said Marien, "In the wilderness
  The Tempter came, and he
Offered to Jesus Christ such gifts
  As now ye offer me!"

Those rugged brows grew dark; "Come now
  With us," they fiercely said,
"And see what never daylight saw,
  The halls of dole and dread!"

Then unto chambers hidden, vast,
  Mysterious, far from view,
They led her; there was set the rack,
  The knotted cord, the screw,
And many a horrid instrument,
  Whose dark ensanguined hue
Told of their purpose; "These," said they,
  "Many strange wonders do!

"Look well; could'st thou endure these things?
  Strong men have died ere now
Under their torment; men were they,
  A little child art thou!"

Then Marien meekly answered, "What
  God suffereth you to dare,
He, to whom darkness is as light,
  Will strengthen me to bear!"

"Come onward yet," they said; and down
  Damp, broken stairs they went;
Down, down to hidden vaults of stone,
  Through vapors pestilent.

And then with sullen iron keys
  They opened doors of stone;
And heavy chained captives there
  They showed her, one by one.

Old, white-haired men; men middle-aged,
  That had been strong of limb;
But each, now pallid, hollow-eyed,
  Like spectres worn and dim.

And many, as the dull door oped,
  Ne'er lifted up the head; —
Heart-broken victims of long pain,
  Whose very hope was dead.

Others with feverish restlessness
  Sprang up, and with quick cry,
That thrilled the hearer to the soul,
  Demanded liberty.

With bleeding heart went Marien on;
  And her conductors spake,
"These are our victims; these await
  The rack, the cord, the stake.

"And as these are, so shalt thou be
  If thou our will gainsay;
Accept our service, pride, and power;
  Or, on this very day,
Racked, prisoned, poor, and miserable,
  Thou shalt be, even as they!"

Down on the floor sank Marien,
  And, "Oh, dear Lord!" she cried

"Assist thy poor and trembling one
  This awful hour to bide;
Let me be strong to do thy will,
  Like him who bowed, and died!"

"They took her:—of that prison-house
  The secrets who may say?—
Racked, fettered, captived, in their power,
  The gentle Marien lay;
Captive within their torture-halls
  A long night and a day!

PART VII.

Then forth they brought her; gave her wine
  And pleasant food to eat;
And "Rest thee, Marien, in our arms,"
  Sung syren voices sweet.

"Rest thee within our arms; refresh
  Thy fainting soul with wine;
Eat and be glad; forget the past,
  And make all pleasure thine!"

"Tempt me not!" said the feeble child,
  "Take hence your spiced bowl;
Is't not enough to rack my limbs,
  But you must vex my soul?

"Look at my flesh, which ye have torn;
  Look at your bloody rack;—
Take hence your gifts, and let me go
  To my own people back.

'To my own people let me go,
  A bruised and broken reed:
I for your purpose am unmeet;
  Let me go hence with speed."

So, in her weakness, prayed the child;
  But those remorseless men,
More dead than living, bore her back
  Unto their prison-den.

Into a noisome prison-house,
  With iron doors made fast,
'Mong felons and 'mong murderers,
  Was gentle Marien cast.

Upon the hard, cold prison floor,
  Sick unto death she lay,
As if God had forsaken her,
  For many a weary day.

She thought of her sweet forest life,
  And of those creatures small,
Weak, woodland creatures, tamed by love,
  That came unto her call.

She thought of him, the forest-lord,
  And of the forest-grange;
Of the delicious life she led,
  With liberty to range.

And as she thought, even as a child's,
  The ceaseless tears did flow,
For torturing pain and misery
  Had brought her spirit low.

When one from out the felon band
  Came softly to her side,
And "Do not weep, thou little child!"
  With pitying voice, he cried.

"At sight of thee, I know not why,
  My softened heart doth burn,
And the gone tenderness of youth
  Doth to my soul return.

"I think upon my early days,
  Like unto days of heaven;
And I, that have not wept for years,
Even as a child, shed ceaseless tears,
  And pray to be forgiven!"

"Blessed be God!" said Marien,
  And rose up from the floor;
"I was not hither brought in vain!
  His mercy I adore,
Who out of darkness brought forth light!"
  And thus she wept no more.

But ever of the Saviour taught;
  How he came down to win,
With love, and suffering manifold,
  The sinner from his sin.

How, not to kings and mighty men
He came, nor to the wise,
But to the thief and murderer,
And those whom men despise.

And how, throughout the host of heaven
Goes yet a louder praise
O'er one poor sinner who doth turn
From his unrighteous ways,
Than o'er a hundred godly men,
Who sin not all their days.

Thus with the felons she abode,
And that barred prison rude
Was as if angels dwelt therein,
And not fierce men of blood;
For God had her captivity
Turned into means of good.

Now all this while sweet Marien's friends,
Who in the town remained,
Of her took painful thought, resolved
Her freedom should be gained.

And at the last they compassed it,
With labor long and great;
And through the night they hurried her
Unto the city gate.

There many a mother stood, and child,
Weeping with friendly wo,
Thus, thus to meet, as 'twere from death.
And then to bid her go.

To bid her go, whom so they loved,
  Nor once more see her face;
To bid her go; to speed her forth
  To some more friendly place.

Thus, amid blessings, prayers, and tears,
  About the break of day,
She left the city, praising God
For her release; and swiftly trod
  Upon her unknown way.

PART VIII.

A BOW-SHOT from the city gate
  Turned Marien from the plain,
Intent by unfrequented ways
  The mountain land to gain.

With bounding step she onward went,
  Over the moorland fells;
O'er fragrant tracts of purple thyme,
  And crimson heather-bells.

Joyful in her release she went,
  Still onward yet, and higher;
Up many a mossy, stony steep,
Through many a flock of mountain sheep,

By the hill-tarns so dark and deep,
  As if she could not tire.

Onward and upward still she went
  Among the breezy hills,
Singing for very joyfulness
  Unto the singing rills.

The days of her captivity,
  The days of fear and pain,
Were past, and now through shade and shine,
  She wandered free again.

Free, like the breezes of the hill,
  Free, like the waters wild;
And in her fullness of delight,
Unceasingly from height to height
  Went on the blessed child.

And ever when she needed food,
  Some wanderer of the hill
Drew forth the morsel from his scrip,
  And bade her eat her fill.

For He who fed by Cherith-brook
  The prophet in his need,
Of this the wandering little one
  Unceasingly had heed.

And ever when she needed rest,
  Some little cove she found,
So green, so sheltered, and so still,
Upon the bosom of the hill,
  As angels girt it round.

Thus hidden 'mong the quiet hills,
  Alone, yet wanting naught,
She dwelt secure, until her foes
  For her no longer sought.

Then forth she journeyed. Soon the hills
  Were of more smooth descent;
And downward now, and onward still,
  Toward the sea she went.

Toward the great sea for many days;
  And now she heard its roar!
Had sunlit glimpses of it now,
  And now she trod the shore.

A rugged shore of broken cliffs,
  And barren wave-washed sand,
Where only the dry sea-wheat grew
  By patches on the strand.

A weary way walked Marien
  Beside the booming sea,
Nor boat, nor hut, nor fisherman
  Throughout the day saw she

A weary, solitary way;
  And as the day declined,
Over the dark and troubled sea
  Arose a stormy wind.

The heavy waves came roaring in
  With the strong coming tide;
The rain poured down, and deep dark night
  Closed in on every side.

There stood the homeless Marien
  With bare, unsandaled feet;
And on her form, with pitiless force,
  The raging tempest beat.

Clasping her hands, she stood forlorn,
  "In tempest, and in night:"
She cried, "Oh Lord, I trust in thee,
  And thou wilt lead me right!"

Now underneath a shelving bank
  Of sea-driving sand, there stood
A miserable hut, the home
  Of a poor fisher good,

Whose loving wife but yesternight
  Died in his arms, and he,
Since that day's noon, alone had been
  Casting his nets at sea.

At noon, he kissed his little ones,
  And would be back, he said,
Long ere night closed; but with the night
  Arose that tempest dread.

It was an old and crazy boat,
  Wherein the man was set,
And soon 'twas laden heavily
  With many a laden net.

"Oh sorrow, sorrow!" groaned he forth,
  As rose the sudden squall,
Thinking upon the mother dead,
  And on his children small.

"Oh sorrow, sorrow!" loud he cried,
  As the helm flew from his hand,
And he knew that the boat was sinking,
  But half a league from land.

"Oh sorrow, sorrow!" as he sank,
  Was still his wailing cry;
And Marien heard, amid the storm,
  That voice of misery.

Now all this while the children small
  Kept in their dreary place,
Troubled and sad, and half afeared
  Of their dead mother's face.

And when, to while the time, they played
  With shells beside the door,
They found they had not hearts for mirth,
  And so they played no more.

Yet keeping up, with forced content,
  Their hearts as best they might;
Still wishing afternoon were gone,
  And it was only night.

But when, hour after hour went on,
  And the night tempest black
Raged o'er the stormy sea, and still
  The father came not back;

It would have touched a heart of stone
  To see their looks of fear —
So young and so forlorn; — their words
  Of counsel small to hear.

And now they shouted through the storm;
  And then with bitter wit,
As they had seen their mother do,
  A fire of wood they lit,
That he might see the light afar,
  And steer his boat by it.

Unto this light came Marien;
  And ere her weary feet
Had reached the floor, the children ran
  With eager arms to meet
Their loving father, as they thought,
  And give him welcome sweet.

Alas! the father even then
  Had run his mortal race;
But God had sent his Comforter
  To fill his earthly place.

PART IX.

Woe's me, what secret tears are shed,
  What wounded spirits bleed;
What loving hearts are sundered,
  And yet man takes no heed!

He goeth on his daily course,
  Made fat with oil and wine,

And pitieth not the weary souls
  That in his bondage pine;
That turn for him the mazy wheel;
  That delve for him the mine.

And pitieth not the children small,
  In noisy factories dim,
That all day long, lean, pale, and faint,
  Do heavy tasks for him!

To him they are but as the stones
  Beneath his feet that lie:
It entereth not his thoughts that they
  From him claim sympathy.

It entereth not his thoughts that God
  Heareth the sufferer's groan,
That in his righteous eye, their life
  Is precious as his own.

This moves him not. But let us now
  Unto the fisher's shed,
Where sat his little weeping ones
  Three days beside the dead.

It was a solitary waste
  Of barren sand, which bore
No sign of human dwelling-place
  For miles along the shore.

Yet to the scattered dwellers there
  Sped Marien, and besought
That of the living and the dead
  They would take Christian thought.

So in the churchyard by the sea,
  The senseless dead was laid:
"And now what will become of us!"
  The weeping children said.

"For who will give us bread to eat?
  The neighbors are so poor!
And he, our kinsman in the town,
  Would drive us from his door.

"For he is rich and pitiless,
  With heart as cold as stone!
Who will be parents to us, now
  That ours are dead and gone?"

"Weep not," said faithful Marien,
  "Man's heart is not so hard,
But it your friendless misery
  Will tenderly regard!

"And I with you will still abide,
  Your friendless souls to cheer,
Be father and mother both to you:
  For this God sent me here.

"And to your kinsman in the town,
  Who hath such store of gold,
I will convey you: God can change
  His spirit stern and cold.

"And ye, like angels of sweet love,
  From earth his soul may win.
Fear not; and we with morning light
  The journey will begin."

They took their little worldly store;
  And at the break of day,
Leaving the lonesome sea-side shed,
  Set out upon their way.

'Mong sandy hills their way they wound;
  O'er sea-grass dusk and harsh;
By many a land-mark lone and still;
  Through many a salt-sea marsh.

And thus for twice seven days they went,
  A little roving band,
Walking along their weary way;
  Like angels, hand in hand.

And everywhere kind Christian folks
  They found, as Marien said,
Who gave them lodging for the night,
  And gave them daily bread.

And thus they pilgrimed, day by day,
  Alone yet not cast down,
Strengthened by Marien's company,
  Unto the seaport town.

A busy town beside the sea,
  Where men were all astir,
Buying and selling; eager-eyed,
Two different races, yet allied, —
  Merchant and mariner.

A place of ships, whose name was known
  Far oft, beyond the main;
A busy place of trade, where naught
  Was in repute but gain.

Thither they came, those children poor,
  About the eventide,
And where dwelt he, their kinsman rich,
  They asked on every side.

After long asking, one they found,
  An old man and a poor,
Who undertook to lead them straight
  Unto the kinsman's door.

But ever, as he went along,
  He to himself did say,
Low broken sentences, as thus,
  "Their kinsman! — well-a-way!"

All through a labyrinth of walls
  Blackened with cloudy smoke,
He led them, where was heard the forge
  And the strong hammer's stroke.

And beneath lofty windows dim,
  In many a dolefel row,
Whence came the jangle of quick looms,
  Down to the courts below.

Still on the children, terrified,
  With wildered spirits passed;
Until of these great mammon halls,
  They reached the heart at last, —
A little chamber, hot and dim,
  With iron bars made fast.

There sate the kinsman, shrunk and lean
  And leaden-eyed and old,

Busied before a lighted lamp
  In sealing bags of gold.

The moment that they entered in,
  He clutched, with pallid fear,
His heavy bags, as if he thought
  That sudden thieves were near.

"Rich man!" said Marien, "ope thy bags,
  And of thy gold be free,
Make gladsome cheer, for heaven hath sent
  A blessing unto thee!"
"What!" said the miser, "is there news
  Of my lost argosy?"

"Better than gold, or merchant-ships,
  Is that which thou shalt win,"
Said Marien, "thine immortal soul
  From its black load of sin."

"Look at these children, thine own blood,"
  And then their name she told;
"Open thine heart to do them good,
  To love them more than gold;—
And what thou givest will come back
  To thee, a thousand fold!"

"Ah," said the miser, "even these
  Some gainful work may do,
My looms stand still; of youthful hands
  I have not half enow;
I shall have profit in their toil;
  Yes, child, thy words are true!"

"Thou fool!" said Marien, "still for gain,
To cast thy soul away!
The Lord be judge 'twixt these and thee
Upon his reckoning day!

"These little ones are fatherless, —
He sees them day and night;
And as thou doest unto them,
On thee he will requite!"

Gave I not alms upon a time?"
Said he, with anger thrilled;
"And when I die, give I not gold,
A stately church to build?

"What wouldst thou more? my flesh and blood
I seek not to gainsay,
But what I give, is it unmeet
Their labor should repay!"

So saying, in an iron chest,
He locked his bags of gold,
And bade the children follow him.
In accents harsh and cold.

PART X.

"Oh leave us not, sweet Marien?"
  The little children spake;
"For if thou leave us here, alone,
  Our wretched hearts will break."

She left them not — kind Marien?
  And in a noisome room,
Day after day, week after week,
  They labored at the loom.

The while they thought with longing souls
  Upon the breezy strand,
The flying shuttles, to and fro,
  Passed through each little hand.

The while they thought with aching hearts,
  Upon their parents dear,
The growing web was watered
  With many a bitter tear.

And the sweet memory of the past, —
  The white sands stretching wide;
Their father's boat wherein they played,
  Upon the rocking tide;

The sandy shells; the sea-mew's scream;
  The ocean's ceaseless boom;
Came to them like a troubling dream,
  Within the noisy loom.

Wo-worth those children, hard bested,
  A weary life they knew;
Their hands were thin, their cheeks were pale,
  That were of rosy hue.

The miser kinsman in and out
  Passed ever and anon;
Nor ever did he speak a word,
  Except to urge them on.

Wo-worth those children, hard bested,
  They worked the livelong day;
Nor was there one, save Marien,
  A soothing word to say: —
So, amid toil and pain of heart,
  The long months wore away.

The long, the weary months passed on,
  And the hard kinsman told
Over his profits; every loom
  Increased the hoard of gold;
"'Tis well!" said he, "let more be spun,
  That more may yet be sold!"

So passed the time; and with the toil
  Of children weak and poor,
The sordid kinsman's treasure-hoards
  Increased more and more.

But ere a year was come and gone,
  The spirit of the boy
Was changed; with natures fierce and rude
  He found his chiefest joy.

The hardness of the kinsman's soul
  Wrought on him like a spell,
Exciting in his outraged heart,
  Revenge and hatred fell;
The will impatient to control;
  The spirit to rebel.

Hence was there warfare 'twixt the two,
  The weak against the strong;—
A hopeless, miserable strife
  That could not last for long;
How can the young, the poor, contend
  Against the rich man's wrong!

The tender trouble of his eye,
  Was gone; his brow was cold;
His speech, like that of desperate men,
  Was reckless, fierce, and bold.

No more he kissed his sister's cheek;
  Nor soothed her as she wept;
No more he said at Marien's knee
  His prayers before he slept.

But they, the solitary pair,
  Like pitying angels poured
Tears for the sinner; and with groans
  His evil life deplored.

Man knew not of that secret grief,
  Which in their bosoms lay;
And for their sinful brother's sin,
  Yet harder doom had they.

But God, who trieth hearts; who knows
The springs of human will;
Who is a juster judge than man,
Of mortal good and ill;

He saw those poor despised ones,
And willed them still to mourn;
He saw the wandering prodigal,
Yet bade him not return.

In his good time that weak one's wo,
Would do its work of grace;
And the poor prodigal, himself,
Would seek the father's face;—
Meantime man's judgment censured them,
As abject, mean, and base.

The erring brother was away,
And none could tell his fate;
And the young sister at the loom
Sate drooping, desolate.

She mourned not for her parents dead,
Nor for the breezy shore:
And now the weary, jangling loom
Distracted her no more.

Like one that worketh in a dream,
So worked she day by day,
Intent upon the loving grief,
Which on her spirit lay;
And as she worked and as she grieved,
Her young life wore away.

And they who saw her come and go,
  Oft said, with pitying tongue,
" Alas, that labor is the doom
  Of aught so weak and young!"

Alone the kinsman pitied not;
  He chid her, that no more
The frame was strong, the hand was swift,
  As it had been before.

— All for the child was dark on earth,
  When holy angels bright
Unbarred the golden gates of heaven
  For her one winter's night.

Within a chamber poor and low,
  Upon a pallet bed
She lay, and "Hold my hand, sweet friend,"
  With feeble voice she said.

"Oh hold my hand, sweet Marien,"
  The dying child spake low;
"And let me hear thy blessed voice,
  To cheer me as I go!

"'Tis darksome all — Oh, drearly dark!
  When will this gloom pass by?
Is there no comfort for the poor,
  And for the young who die!"

Down by her side knelt Marien,
  And kissed her fading cheek,
Then of the loving Saviour,
  In low tones 'gan to speak.

She told of Lazarus, how he lay,
A beggar mean and poor,
And died, in misery and want,
Beside the rich man's door.

Yet how the blessed angels came,
To bear his soul on high,
Within the glorious courts of heaven,
On Abraham's breast to lie.

She told how children, when they die,
Yet higher glory win,
And see the Father face to face,
Unsoiled by tainting sin.

"Blessed be God!" the child began,
"I doubt not, neither fear,
All round about the bed, behold,
The angel-bands appear!

"I go! — yet still, dear Marien,
One last boon let me win! —
Seek out the poor lost prodigal,
And bring him back from sin!

"I go! I go!" and angels bright,
The spirit bare away: —
On earth 'twas darksome, dreary night,
In heaven 'twas endless day!

— And now, upon that selfsame night,
Within a carved bed,
Lay the rich kinsman wrapt in lawn,
With pillows 'neath his head.

Scheming deep schemes of gold, he lay
  All in that lordly room;
Blessing himself that he had stores
  For many years to come.

Just then an awful form spake low,
  A form that none might see:
"Thou fool, this very night, thy soul
  Shall be required of thee!"

And when into that chamber fair
  Stole in the morning ray,
A lifeless corpse, upon his bed,
  The miser kinsman lay.

—Beside his door stood solemn mutes;
  And chambers high and dim,
Where hung was pall, and mourning lights
  Made show of grief for him.

Full fifty muffled mourners stood,
  Around the scutcheoned bed,
That held the corse, as if, indeed,
  A righteous man were dead.

Within a tomb, which he had built,
  Of costly marble-stone,
They buried him, and plates of brass
  His name and wealth made known.

A coffin of the meanest wood,
  The little child received;
And o'er that humble, nameless grave,
  No hooded mourner grieved.

Only kind Marien wept such tears,
  As the dear Saviour shed,
When in the house of Bethany
  He mourned for Lazarus dead.

PART XI.

Now from the miser kinsman's house
  Came many a jovial sound;
And lavish heirs had spent his gold,
  Ere twelve months had gone round.

That while within the busy town
  Dwelt Marien; and each day,
In some good deed of Christian love
  And mercy, passed away.

For many an abject dweller there,
  Grief-bowed and labor-spent,
Groaned forth, amid his little ones,
  To heaven his sad lament;
And unto such, to raise, to cheer,
  The sent of God, she went.

But she who, even as they, was poor,
  Failed not of daily bread;
A stranger, many took her in,
  And warmed, and clothed, and fed

And when a sickness sore befell,
  And nigh to death she lay,
Kind hearts there were who came to her,
  And watched her night and day.

And afterwards, when evil men
  Doomed her in bonds to lie,
Many a true, noble friend arose,
  Willing for her to die.

Oh, blessed Christian hearts, who thus
  Unto this little one
Did deeds of love ; for as to Christ
  These righteous works were done !
And they who blessed her, for themselves
  A tenfold blessing won !

Thus dwelt sweet Marien in the town
  For many a passing year ;
Yet of the poor, lost prodigal
  No tidings could she hear.

She found him not ; but yet she found
  Others who, even as he,
Had gone astray, and pined forlorn
  In hopeless misery.

To these repentant, outcast ones,
  She spake kind words of grace,
And led them back, with yearning hearts,
  To seek the father's face ;
To find forgiveness in His heart,
  And love in His embrace.

Oh blessed, blessed Marien!
  — But let us now recall
Whate'er had happed of change and wo
  Unto the prodigal.

He saw his little sister pine;
  He saw her silent wo;
He saw her strength decline, yet still
  Her weary labor grow.

As this he saw, yet more and more
  He hated that hard man,
With whom their cheerless misery,
  Their daily tasks began.

And even to true Marien,
  He bare an altered mind: —
Alas, that injuries should make
  Else loving hearts unkind!

But so it is! and when the twain
  To cheer his spirit strove,
His wrath arose, and he repelled
  Their patient deeds of love.

Then evil men assailed his youth;
  And he who was so frail
In suffering, 'gainst the tempter's might
  Was feeble to prevail.

He was their easy prey; their tool;
  And bravely clothed and fed;
In desperate scenes, 'mid desperate men,
  A lawless life he led.

Yet often to his soul came back
  Sweet memory of the time,
When he, a happy thoughtless child,
  Had knowledge of no crime.

And like a heavier, wearier wo,
  Than labor night and day,
The consciousness of evil deeds
  Upon his spirit lay.

He thought of slighted Marien,
  And of the sister meek;
Of the thin hands that plied the loom,
  And of the faded cheek;
Yet how he had deserted them,
  The faithful and the weak!

He heard his loving parent's voice
  Reproach him in his sleep;
And conscience, that stern bosom-guest,
  Ceaseless upbraidings keep.

Yet, for the hated kinsman's sake,
  Neither would he regard;
And, because man was hard to him,
  Made his own nature hard.

Thus doing outrage to his soul,
  By chance he went one day
Through the brown trodden churchyard, where
  The little sister lay.

A sexton there at work he found;
  And why he turned the mould

So carefully, he asked, since there
  No name the tenant told.

Replied he, "In this wide churchyard
  I know each separate mound;
Yet unto me that little grave
  Alone seems holy ground."

And then he told of Marien,
  And how she there had wept
Over the child, that 'neath the mould,
  In dreamless quiet slept.

"A little, friendless pauper child,
  She lieth here," said he;
"Yet not a grave in all the ground
  Like this affecteth me!"

Saying this, he wiped a tear aside,
  And turned him from the place;
And, in the skirts of his rich robe,
  The brother hid his face.

—He left the town; and in a ship,
  Bound for a far-off strand,
He took his voyage; but distress
  Pursued her from the land.

At first disease was 'mong her men;
  And suffering long and sore,
In midst of joyless, suffering mates,
  Forlorn and sad he bore.

Next mutiny brake forth; and then
  That miserable ship,
As if there were no port for her,
Without a wind the sails to stir,
  Lay moveless on the deep.

As Jonah, fleeing from the Lord,
  The soul-struck penitent
Lay self-condemned, believing all
  On his account were sent.

Anon a tempest rose, and drove
  The ship before the gale
For three long days; and bore away
  Her rudder, mast, and sail.

On the fourth night dark land appeared,
  And the strained vessel bore
Right on the rocky reef, and lay
  A wreck upon the shore.

At daybreak only he remained
  To note the vessel's fate:—
The Crusoe of a desert isle,
  Abject and desolate.

— The world went on as it was wont,
  And in the city street,
And in the busy market-place,
  Did thronging thousands meet.

Upon the hearths of poor men's homes
  Good neighbors met at night;
And kindness and companionship
  Made wo and labor light.

The loneliest hut among the hills
  To human hearts was known;
And even in kingly palaces,
  Men might not dwell alone.

The world went on as it was wont;
  And no man knew the while
Of that poor lonely prodigal,
  Upon his lonely isle.

He clomb the cliffs to look afar
  Over the distant sea;
If, please God, for his rescuing
  A coming sail might be.

He lit his beacon fires at night;
  He hoisted signals high; —
But the world went on as it was wont,
  And not a ship sailed by.

He was not missed among his kind, —
  Man had forgot his name;
But unto Him who cares for all,
Who sees the little sparrow fall,
  His lonely misery came.

God saw him; saw his broken heart,
  His cheerless solitude,
Saw how his human pride was gone,
  His human will subdued.

Saw him and loved him. Broken heart,
  Look up! the Father's voice
Calleth thee from thy depths of wo,
  And biddeth thee rejoice!

— Now Marien from the trading town
Had voyaged; sent of Heaven
She knew not whither; and the ship,
Which with long storm had striven,
At length upon a glorious isle
Amid the seas was driven;

Where dwelt a gentle race at rest
Amid their flowery wilds,
Unknown to all the world, with hearts
As simple as a child's.

With them abode sweet Marien:
But now it chanced one day,
As in a slender carved boat
Upon the shore she lay,
A strong wind came, and filled the sail,
And bare her thence away.

She had no fear, true Marien; —
That God was good, she knew,
And even then had sent her forth
Some work of love to do.

The prodigal upon his rock
Was kneeling, and his prayer
For confidence in heaven, arose
Upon the evening air,
Just as the little boat approached
The island bleak and bare.

The boat ran up a creek, as if
'Twere steered by angels good;
And ere the evening prayer was done
Beside the youth she stood.

The chiefest joy it hath not words
  Its deep excess to say;
And as if he had seen a sprite,
  His spirit died away.

Then with clasped hands, and broken speech,
  And tears that ceaseless flowed,
He poured forth from his full heart
  A fervent praise of God.

PART XII.

"But let us hence," said Marien;
  And with the earliest morn,
Within the slender carved boat,
  They left the isle forlorn.

A light breeze from the desert shore
  Over the waters blew,
And the little boat sailed on before,
  Till the isle was out of view.

As friends long parted, met once more,
  They sat; and of times gone,
And of the blessed dead conversed,
  As the slender boat sailed on,

And as they sailed, sweet Marien
  Over the Gospel bent,
And read of joy that is in heaven
  O'er sinners that repent:

And of the weary prodigal
  Returning, bowed with shame,
And the good father hastening forth
  To meet him as he came;

And how he bade the fairest robe
  Be brought; the golden ring;
Shoes for the feet; and music sweet,
  As if to hail a king.

"For this, my son," said he, "was dead,
  And is alive; is found,
Who was long lost; 'tis meet, therefore,
  That stintless joy abound!"

"Oh, child of wo," said Marien,
  "Look up, for thou art he;
And round about the father's throne
  Many rejoice for thee!"

"Oh Lord, I bless thee," said the youth,
  "That of thy mercy great,
Thou hast vouchsafed to rescue me
  From my forlorn estate!
And henceforth, to thy work of love
  Myself I dedicate!

"The meanest of thy creatures, low
  I bend before thy throne,

And offer my poor self, to make
  Thy loving kindness known!

"Oh father, give me words of power,
  The stony hearts to move;
Give me prevailing eloquence,
  To publish forth thy love!

"Thy love which wearieth not; which like
  Thy sun, on all doth shine!
Oh Father, let me worship Thee
Through life, by gladly serving Thee!
I love not life; I ask not wealth;
My heart and soul, my youth and health,
  My life, oh Lord, are thine!"

So spake the youth; but now the boat
  The glorious island neared,
Which, like a cloudland realm of bliss,
  Above the sea appeared.

Skyward rose sunny peaks, pale-hued
  As if of opal glow;
And crested palms, broad-leaved and tall,
  In valleys grew below.

A lovely land of flowers, as fair
  As Paradise, ere sin
And sorrow, that corrupting pair,
  With death had entered in.

A lovely land! — "And even now,"
  Cried Marien, "see they come,
Children of love, my brother, now
  To bid thee welcome home!

"For these, God kept thee in the wild,
 From sinful men apart!
For these, his people, through distress,
 Made pure thy trusting heart!

"Thy work is here! Go forth, 'mid these
 Meek children of the sun,
Oh servant of the Lord, and tell
 What He for thee hath done!"

Down to the shore the thousands came,
 A joyous, peaceful host,
To welcome Marien back, whom they
 Had sorrowed for as lost.

"And welcome to thee, little child!"
 They sang forth sweet and clear;
"And welcome to the stranger poor,
 Who cometh with thee here!"

And then they brought him silken cloth,
 Since he was meanly dressed;
And juicy, mellow fruits to eat,
And perfumed waters for his feet,
 And mats whereon to rest.

And ever as they served him,
 They sang forth sweet and low,
"Would this repose might solace thee,
 These apples cure thy wo!"

And though the twain knew not their speech,
 Yet well they understood
The looks of love that welcomed them,
 Their actions kind and good.

With them for many a year abode
  The youth, and learned their tongue;
And with the sound of Christian praise
  The hills and valleys rung.

Oh beautiful beyond all lands
  That lay beneath the moon,
Was that fair isle of Christian love,
  Of Christian virtues boon.

A joyful people there they dwelt,
  Unsuffering from their birth;
Of simplest life; benignly wise;
  As angels on the earth.

And with them dwelt the holy youth,
  Their chief, their priest, their friend,
Beloved and loving, for their sakes
  Willing himself to spend.

Like to some ancient church of Christ,
  From worldly taint kept free,
Lay this delicious isle of love
  Amid its summer sea.

But now the work he had to do
  Was done; and ere his day
Approached its noon, his strength, his life,
  Was wearing fast away.

They saw his cheek grow thin and pale;
  His loving eye grow dim;
And with surpassing tenderness
  They sorrowed over him

Old men, and youths, and women meek,
  And children wild and young,
Followed his steps with watchful care,
  And weeping round him hung.

In flowery thickets of the hills
  Sad mourners knelt in prayer,
That God this servant so revered,
  This friend beloved would spare.

And round about his feet they sat,
  Observant, meek, and still,
To gather up his latest words,
  To do his slightest will.

Now all this while good Marien
  Had wandered far and wide,
Through divers realms, for many a year,
  The hand of Heaven her guide.

And now unto the glorious isle
  She came; but on the shore
She saw no wandering company,
  As she had seen before.

'Twas Sabbath eve, and o'er the isle
  A solemn stillness lay;
A stillness, how unlike the calm
  Of many a Sabbath day;

A hush, as of suspended breath,
  Ere some great grief began;
For the mournful people silently
  Stood round the dying man.

Through the still vales went Marien,
And came at length to where,
'Mid flowering trees, knelt many a one
In agony of prayer.

Onward she went, not many steps,
With heart of mournful ruth,
When, like a dying angel laid,
She saw the holy youth.

With closed eyes and pallid lips
He lay, as one whose life
Meeteth with death, yet waiteth still
The last conflicting strife.

Beside him knelt she on the turf,
And spoke in accents low
Words of strong love, which like new life
Seemed through the frame to go.

He raised himself, and blessing God,
That He of him had care,
And now in his dark trial-hour,
Had sent his angel there;

With low-toned voice, more musical
Than softest lute could make,
Looking upon his weeping friends
With fervent love, he spake.

"Oh friends, beloved friends! weep not,
Nor be oppressed with wo;
'Tis of His will, who doeth right,
That I am called to go!

Fain would I tarry, but the cry
 Hath sounded in mine ear,
'Haste to depart, the Lord hath need
 Of thee no longer here!'

"Even like the master whom I serve,
 I pray ye not to grieve;
But as ye have believed in me,
 Also in Him believe!

"I go, but leave you not forlorn,
 As sheep without a guide;—
For Christ, the unfailing Comforter,
 Shall still with you abide!

"Oh weep not, friends; a better home
 Awaits me, and I go,
But to that home which is prepared
 For ye who love me so!
Farewell, farewell! Unto my God,
 And unto yours, I go!"

The Sabbath sun went down amid
 A golden, cloudless sky;
And the freed spirit, cleansed from sin,
 Arose to God on high.

Beneath the trees where he had died,
 They buried him, and there
Enwove the flowery boughs to form
 A quiet house of prayer.

Long time with them dwelt Marien,
  Until she was sent forth,
At the Lord's bidding, to perform
  New service on the earth.

Good speed to thee, thou blessed child,
  May angels guide thy bark,
'Mid slumbrous calm, 'mid tempests wild,
  And o'er the waters dark!

Good speed to thee, thou blessed child —
  The angel of the poor —
And win from sorrow and from sin
  The world from shore to shore!

OLD CHRISTMAS.

Now he who knows old Christmas,
He knows a carle of worth;
For he is as good a fellow,
As any upon the earth.

He comes warm cloaked and coated,
And buttoned up to the chin,
And soon as he comes a-nigh the door,
We open and let him in.

We know that he will not fail us,
So we sweep the hearth up clean;
We set him in the old armed chair,
And a cushion whereon to lean.

And with sprigs of holly and ivy
We make the house look gay,
Just out of an old regard to him, —
For it was his ancient way.

We broach the strong ale barrel,
And bring out wine and meat;
And thus have all things ready,
Our dear old friend to greet.

And soon the time wears round,
The good old carle we see,
Coming a-near; — for a creditor
Less punctual is than he!

He comes with a cordial voice
  That does one good to hear;
He shakes one heartily by the hand,
  As he hath done many a year.

And after the little children
  He asks in a cheerful tone,
Jack, Kate, and little Annie, —
  He remembers them every one!

What a fine old fellow he is,
  With his faculties all as clear,
And his heart as warm and light
  As a man in his fortieth year!

What a fine old fellow, in troth!
  Not one of your griping elves,
Who, with plenty of money to spare,
  Think only about themselves!

Not he! for he loveth the children;
  And holiday begs for all;
And comes, with his pockets full of gifts,
  For the great ones and the small!

With a present for every servant; —
  For in giving he doth not tire; —
From the red-faced, jovial butler,
  To the girl by the kitchen-fire.

And he tells us witty old stories,
  And singeth with might and main;
And we talk of the old man's visit
  Till the day that he comes again!

Oh he is a kind old fellow,
  For though that beef be dear,
He giveth the parish paupers
  A good dinner once a year!

And all the workhouse children
  He sets them down in a row,
And giveth them rare plum-pudding,
  And two pence a-piece also.

Oh, could you have seen those paupers,
  Have heard those children young,
You would wish with them that Christmas
  Came oft and tarried long!

He must be a rich old fellow,—
  What money he gives away!
There is not a lord in England
  Could equal him any day!

Good luck unto old Christmas,
  And long life, let us sing,
For he doth more good unto the poor
  Than many a crowned king!

THE TWELFTH HOUR

My friends, the spirit is at peace;
  Oh do not trouble me with tears;
Petition rather my release,
  Nor covet for me length of years,
Which are but weariness and wo;
Resign me, friends, before I go!

I know how strong are human ties;
  I know how strong is human fear!
But visions open to mine eyes,
  And words of power are in mine ear;
My friends, my friends, can ye not see,
Nor hear what voices speak to me?

"Thou human soul," they seem to say,
  "We are commissioned from above,
Through the dark portal to convey
  Thee to the paradise of love;
Thou needest not shrink, thou need'st not fear
We, thy sure help, are gathered near!

"Thy weakness on our strength confide;
  Thy doubt upon our steadfast trust;
And rise up, pure and glorified,
  From thine infirm and sinful dust,
Rise up, rise up! the eternal day
Begins to dawn — why wilt thou stay?

"Look forth — the day begins to dawn;
  The future openeth to thy view;
The veil of mystery is undrawn;
  The old things are becoming new;
The night of time is passing by:
  Poor trembler, do not fear to die!

"Come, come! the gates of pearl unfold
  The eternal glory shines on thee;
Body, relax thy lingering hold,
  And set the struggling spirit free!"
'Tis done, 'tis done! — before my sight
Opens the awful infinite:
I see, I hear, I live anew!
Oh friends, dear friends, — adieu, adieu!

THE BLIND BOY AND HIS SISTER.

"Oh brother," said fair Annie,
  To the blind boy at her side:
"Would thou could'st see the sunshine lie
On hill and valley, and the sky
Hung like a glorious canopy
  O'er all things far and wide!

"Would thou could'st see the waters
In many a distant glen;
The mountain flocks that graze around;
Nay, even this patch of stony ground,
These crags, with silver lichen crowned,
I would that thou could'st ken!

"Would thou could'st see my face, brother,
As well as I see thine;
For always what I cannot see
It is but half a joy to me.
Brother, I often weep for thee,
Yet thou dost ne'er repine!"

"And why should I repine, Annie?"
Said the blind boy with a smile;
"I ken the blue sky and the grey;
The sunny and the misty day:
The moorland valley stretched away
For man and many a mile!

I ken the night and day, Annie,
For all ye may believe;
And often in my spirit lies
A clear light as of mid-day skies;
And splendors on my vision rise,
Like gorgeous hues of eve.

"I sit upon the stone, Annie,
Beside our cottage door,
And people say, 'that boy is blind,'
And pity me, although I find
A world of beauty in my mind,
A never-ceasing store.

"I hear you talk of mountains,
  The beautiful, the grand;
Of splintered peaks so gray and tall;
Of lake, and glen, and waterfall;
Of flowers and trees; — I ken them all; —
  Their difference understand.

"The harebell and the gowan
  Are not alike to me,
Are different as the herd and flock,
The blasted pine-tree of the rock,
The waving birch, the broad, green oak,
  The river and the sea.

"And oh, the heavenly music,
  That as I sit alone,
Comes to mine inward sense as clear
As if the angel voices were
Singing to harp and dulcimer
  Before the mighty throne!

"It is not as of outward sound,
  Of breeze, or singing bird;
But wondrous melody refined;
A gift of God unto the blind;
An inward harmony of mind,
  By inward senses heard!

"And all the old-world stories
  That neighbors tell o'nights;
Of fairies on the fairy mound,
Of brownies dwelling under ground,
Of elves careering round and round,
  Of fays and water-sprites;

"All this to me is pleasantness, —
  Is all a merry show;
I see the antic people play, —
Brownie and kelpie, elf and fay,
In a sweet country far away,
  Yet where I seem to go.

"But better far than this, Annie,
  Is when thou read'st to me
Of the dear Saviour meek and kind,
And how he healed the lame and blind.
Am I not healed! — for in my mind
  His blessed form I see?

"Oh, love is not of sight, Annie,
  Is not of outward things;
For, in my inmost soul I know,
His pity for all mortal wo;
His words of love, spoke long ago,
  Unseal its deepest springs!

"Then do not mourn for me, Annie,
  Because that I am blind; —
The beauty of all outward sight;
The wondrous shows of day and night;
All love, all faith, and all delight,
  Are strong in heart and mind!"

EASTER HYMNS.

HYMN I.

THE TWO MARYS

Oh dark day of sorrow,
Amazement and pain;
When the promise was blighted,
The given was ta'en!

When the Master no longer
A refuge should prove;
And evil was stronger
Than mercy and love!

Oh dark day of sorrow,
Abasement and dread,
When the Master beloved
Was one with the dead!

We sate in our anguish
Afar off to see,
For we surely believed not
This sorrow could be!

But the trust of our spirits
Was all overthrown;

And we wept, in our anguish,
Astonished, alone!

At even they laid him
With aloes and myrrh,
In fine linen wound, in
A new sepulchre.

There, there will we seek him:
Will wash him with care;
Anoint him with spices:
And mourn for him there.

Oh strangest of sorrow!
Oh vision of fear!
New grief is around us —
The Lord is not here!

HYMN II.

THE ANGEL.

Women, why shrink ye
With wonder and dread? —
Seek not the living
Where slumbers the dead!

Weep not, nor tremble;
And be not dismayed;

The Lord hath arisen!
See where he was laid!

The grave-clothes, behold them ·
The spices; the bier;
The napkin that bound him;
But he is not here!

Death could not hold him;
The grave is a prison
That keeps not the living;
The Christ has arisen!

HYMN III.

THE LORD JESUS.

Why are ye troubled?
Why weep ye and grieve?
What the prophets have written,
Why slowly believe?

'Tis I, be not doubtful!
Why ponder ye so?
Behold in my body
The marks of my wo!

The willing have suffered;
The chosen been slain;

The end is accomplished!
Behold me again!

Death has been conquered —
The grave has been riven —
For sin a remission
Hath freely been given!

Fearless in spirit,
Yet meek as the dove,
Go preach to the nations
This gospel of love.

For the might of the mighty
Shall o'er you be cast;
And I will be with you,
My friends, to the last.

I go to the Father,
But I will prepare
Your mansions of glory,
And welcome you there.

There life never-ending;
There bliss that endures;
There love never-changing,
My friends, shall be yours!

But the hour is accomplished!
My children, we sever —
But be ye not troubled,
I am with you for ever!

HYMN IV.

THE ELEVEN.

The Lord is ascending! —
Rich welcomes to give him:
See, angels descending! —
The heavens receive him!

See, angels, archangels,
Bend down to adore! —
The Lord hath ascended,
We see him no more!

The Master is taken;
The friend hath departed;
Yet we are not forsaken,
Nor desolate-hearted!

The Master is taken;
The holy, the kind;
But the joy of his presence
Remaineth behind!

Our hearts burned within us
To hear but the word
Which he spake, ere our spirits
Acknowledged the Lord!

The Lord hath ascended!
Our hope is secure,

We trusted not lightly,—
The promise is sure;

The Lord hath ascended;
And we his true-hearted,
Go forth with rejoicing,
Though he hath departed!

THE POOR CHILD'S HYMN

We are poor and lowly born;
With the poor we bide;
Labor is our heritage,
Care and want beside.
What of this? our blessed Lord
Was of lowly birth,
And poor, toiling fishermen
Were his friends on earth!

We are ignorant and young;
Simple children all;
Gifted with but humble powers,
And of learning small.
What of this? our blessed Lord
Loved such as we;—
How he blessed the little ones
Sitting on his knee!

THE OLD FRIEND AND THE NEW

My old friend, he was a good old friend,
And I thought, like a fool, his face to mend;
I got another; but ah! to my cost
I found him unlike the one I had lost!
I and my friend, we were bred together:—
He had a smile like the summer weather;
A kind warm heart; and a hand as free:—
My friend, he was all the world to me!

I could sit with him and crack many a joke,
And talk of old times and the village folk;
He had been with us at the Christmas time;
He knew every tree we used to climb;
And where we played; and what befell,
My dear old friend remembered well.
It did me good but to see his face;
And I've put another friend in his place!
I wonder how such a thing could be,
For my old friend would not have slighted me!

Oh my fine new friend, he is smooth and bland,
With a jeweled ring or two on his hand;
He visits my lord and my lady fair;
He hums the last new opera air.
He takes not the children on his knee;
My faithful hound reproacheth me,
For he snarls when my new friend draweth near,
But my good old friend to the brute was dear!
I wonder how I such a thing could do,
As change the old friend for the new!

My rare old friend, he read the plays,
That were written in Master Shakspeare's days;
He found in them wit and moral good:—
My new friend thinks them coarse and rude:—
And many a pleasant song he sung,
Because they were made when we were young;
He was not too grand, not he, to know
The merry old songs made long ago.
He writ his name on the window-pane;—
It was cracked by my new friend's riding-cane!

My good old friend, "he tirled at the pin,"
He opened the door and entered in;
We were all glad to see his face,
As he took at the fire his 'customed place,
And the little children, loud in glee,
They welcomed him as they welcomed me
He knew our griefs, our joys he shared;
There cannot be friend with him compared,
We had tried him long, had found him true!
Why changed I the old friend for the new?

My new friend cometh in lordly state;
He peals a startling ring at the gate;
There's hurry and pomp, there's pride and din,
And my new friend bravely entereth in.
I bring out the noblest wines for cheer,
I make him a feast that costeth dear;
But he knows not what in my heart lies deep;—
He may laugh with me, but never shall weep,
For there is no bond between us twain;
And I sigh for my dear old friend again;
And thus, too late, I bitterly rue
That I changed the old friend for the new!

MABEL ON MIDSUMMER DAY.

A STORY OF THE OLDEN TIME.

PART I.

" Arise, my maiden, Mabel,"
The mother said, " arise,"
For the golden sun of Midsummer
Is shining in the skies.

" Arise, my little maiden,
For thou must speed away,
To wait upon thy grandmother
This livelong summer day.

" And thou must carry with thee
This wheaten cake so fine;
This new-made pat of butter;
This little flask of wine!

" And tell the dear old body,
This day I cannot come,
For the good man went out yester morn,
And he is not come home.

" And more than this, poor Amy
Upon my knee doth lie;
I fear me, with this fever-pain
That little child will die!

" And thou canst help thy grandmother;
  The table thou can'st spread;
Can'st feed the little dog and bird,
  And thou can'st make her bed.

" And thou can'st fetch the water,
  From the lady-well hard by;
And thou can'st gather from the wood
  The fagots brown and dry.

"Can'st go down to the lonesome glen,
  To milk the mother-ewe;
This is the work, my Mabel,
  That thou wilt have to do.

" But listen now, my Mabel,
  This is Midsummer day,
When all the fairy people
  From elf-land come away.

" And when thou art in lonesome glen,
  Keep by the running burn,
And do not pluck the strawberry-flower,
  Nor break the lady-fern.

" But think not of the fairy folk,
  Lest mischief should befall;
Think only of poor Amy,
  And how thou lov'st us all.

" Yet keep good heart, my Mabel,
  If thou the fairies see,
And give them kindly answer,
  If they should speak to thee.

"And when into the fir-wood
Thou go'st for fagots brown,
Do not, like idle children,
Go wandering up and down.

"But, fill thy little apron,
My child, with earnest speed;
And that thou break no living bough
Within the wood, take heed.

"For they are spiteful brownies
Who in the wood abide,
So be thou careful of this thing,
Lest evil should betide.

"But think not, little Mabel,
Whilst thou art in the wood,
Of dwarfish, willful brownies,
But of the Father good.

"And when thou goest to the spring
To fetch the water thence,
Do not disturb the little stream,
Lest this should give offence.

"For the queen of all the fairies
She loves that water bright;
I've seen her drinking there myself
On many a summer night.

"But she's a gracious lady,
And her thou need'st not fear;
Only disturb thou not the stream,
Nor spill the water clear!"

"Now all this will I heed, mother,
  Will no word disobey,
And wait upon the grandmother
  This livelong summer day!"

PART II.

AWAY tripped little Mabel,
  With the wheaten cake so fine;
With the new-made pat of butter,
  And the little flask of wine.

And long before the sun was hot,
  And morning mists had cleared,
Beside the good old grandmother
  The willing child appeared.

And all her mother's message
  She told with right good-will,
How that the father was away,
  And the little child was ill.

And then she swept the hearth up clean,
  And then the table spread;
And next she fed the dog and bird·
  And then she made the bed

"And go now," said the grandmother,
  "Ten paces down the dell,
And bring in water for the day;
  Thou know'st the lady-well!"

The first time that good Mabel went,
  Nothing at all saw she
Except a bird — a sky-blue bird —
  That sate upon a tree.

The next time that good Mabel went,
  There sate a lady bright
Beside the well, — a lady small,
  All clothed in green and white.

A curtsey low made Mabel,
  And then she stooped to fill
Her pitcher at the sparkling spring,
  But no drop did she spill.

"Thou art a handy maiden,
  The fairy lady said;
"Thou hast not spilled a drop, nor yet
  The fair spring troubled!

"And for this thing which thou hast done,
  Yet may'st not understand,
I give to thee a better gift
  Than houses or than land.

"Thou shalt do well, whate'er thou dost,
  As thou hast done this day;
Shalt have the will and power to please,
  And shalt be loved alway!"

Thus having said, she passed from sight,
  And naught could Mabel see,
But the little bird, the sky-blue bird
  Upon the leafy tree.

— "And now go," said the grandmother,
  "And fetch in fagots dry;
All in the neighboring fir-wood,
  Beneath the trees they lie."

Away went kind, good Mabel,
  Into the fir-wood near,
Where all the ground was dry and brown,
  And the grass grew thin and sere.

She did not wander up and down,
  Nor yet a live branch pull,
But steadily, of the fallen boughs
  She picked her apron full.

And when the wild-wood brownies
  Came sliding to her mind,
She drove them thence, as she was told,
  With home-thoughts sweet and kind.

But all that while the brownies
  Within the fir-wood still,
They watched her how she picked the wood,
  And strove to do no ill.

"And oh, but she is small and neat,"
  Said one, "'twere shame to spite
A creature so demure and meek,
  A creature harmless quite!"

"Look only," said another,
  "At her little gown of blue;
At her kerchief pinned about her head,
  And at her little shoe!"

"Oh, but she is a comely child,"
  Said a third, "and we will lay
A good-luck-penny in her path,
  A boon for her this day, —
Seeing she broke no living wood,
  No live thing did affray."

With that the smallest penny,
  Of the finest silver ore,
Upon the dry and slippery path,
  Lay Mabel's feet before.

With joy she picked the penny up,
  The fairy penny good;
And with her fagots dry and brown
  Went wondering from the wood.

"Now she has that," said the brownies,
  "Let flax be ever so dear,
Will buy her clothes of the very best,
  For many and many a year!"

— "And go, now," said the grandmother,
  Since falling is the dew,
Go down into the lonesome glen,
  And milk the mother-ewe!"

All down into the lonesome glen,
  Through copses thick and wild;

Through moist, rank grass, by trickling streams,
Went on the willing child.

And when she came to lonesome glen,
She kept beside the burn,
And neither plucked the strawberry-flower,
Nor broke the lady-fern.

And while she milked the mother-ewe
Within the lonesome glen,
She wished that little Amy
Were strong and well again.

And soon as she had thought this thought,
She heard a coming sound,
As if a thousand fairy folk
Were gathering all around.

And then she heard a little voice,
Shrill as the midge's wing,
That spake aloud, "A human child
Is here — yet mark this thing!

"The lady-fern is all unbroke,
The strawberry-flower unta'en!
What shall be done for her, who still
From mischief can refrain?"

"Give her a fairy-cake," said one,
"Grant her a wish," said three;
"The latest wish that she hath wished,"
Said all, "whate'er it be!"

— Kind Mabel heard the words they spake,
  And from the lonesome glen,
Unto the good old grandmother
  Went gladly back again.

Thus happened it to Mabel
  On that midsummer day,
And these three fairy blessings
  She took with her away.

— 'Tis good to make all duty sweet,
  To be alert and kind:
'Tis good, like little Mabel,
  To have a willing mind!

BIRDS AND FLOWERS

AND OTHER

COUNTRY THINGS.

THE STORMY PETEREL.

O STORMY, stormy Peterel,
Come rest thee, bird, awhile;
There is no storm, believe me,
Anigh this summer isle.

Come, rest thy waving pinions;
Alight thee down by me;
And tell me somewhat of the lore
Thou learnest on the sea!

Dost hear beneath the ocean
The gathering tempest form?
See'st thou afar the little cloud
That grows into the storm?

How is it in the billowy depths
Doth sea-weed heave and swell?
And is a sound of coming wo
Rung from each caverned shell?

Dost watch the stormy sunset
    In tempests of the west;
And see the old moon riding slow,
    With the new moon on her breast?

Dost mark the billows heaving
    Before the coming gale;
And scream for joy of every sound
    That turns the seaman pale?

Are gusty tempests mirth to thee?
    Lov'st thou the lightning's flash;
The booming of the mountain waves —
    The thunder's deafening crash?

O stormy, stormy Peterel,
    Thou art a bird of wo!
Yet would I thou could'st tell me half
    Of the misery thou dost know!

There was a ship went down last night, —
    A good ship and a fair;
A costly freight within her lay,
    And many a soul was there!

The night-black storm was over her,
    And 'neath the caverned wave,
In all her strength she perished,
    Nor skill of man could save.

The cry of her great agony
    Went upward to the sky;
She perished in her strength and pride,
    Nor human aid was nigh.

But thou, O stormy Peterel,
Went'st screaming o'er the foam; —
Are there no tidings from that ship
Which thou canst carry home?

Yes! He who raised the tempest up
Sustained each drooping one;
And God was present in the storm,
Though human aid was none!

THE POOR MAN'S GARDEN.

Ah yes, the poor man's garden!
It is great joy to me,
This little, precious piece of ground
Before his door to see!

The rich man has his gardeners, —
His gardeners young and old;
He never takes a spade in hand,
Nor worketh in the mould.

It is not with the poor man so,
Wealth, servants, he has none;
And all the work that's done for him,
Must by himself be done.

All day upon some weary task
    He toileth with good will;
And back he comes, at set of sun,
    His garden-plot to till.

The rich man in his garden walks,
    And 'neath his garden trees;
Wrapped in a dream of other things,
    He seems to take his ease.

One moment he beholds his flowers,
    The next they are forgot:
He eateth of his rarest fruits
    As though he ate them not.

It is not with the poor man so, —
    He knows each inch of ground,
And every single plant and flower
    That grows within its bound.

He knows where grow his wall-flowers,
    And when they will be out;
His moss-rose, and convolulus
    That twines his pales about.

He knows his red sweet-williams;
    And the stocks that cost him dear, —
That well-set row of crimson stocks,
    For he bought the seed last year.

And though unto the rich man
    The cost of flowers is naught,
A sixpence to a poor man
    Is toil, and care, and thought.

And here is his potatoe-bed,
All well-grown, strong, and green;
How could a rich man's heart leap up
At anything so mean!

But he, the poor man, sees his crop,
And a thankful man is he,
For he thinks all through the winter
How rich his board will be.

And how his merry little ones
Beside the fire will stand,
Each with a large potatoe
In a round and rosy hand.

The rich man has his wall-fruits,
And his delicious vines;
His fruit for every season!
His melons and his pines.

The poor man has his gooseberries;
His currants white and red;
His apple and his damson tree,
And a little strawberry-bed.

A happy man he thinks himself,
A man that's passing well, —
To have some fruit for the children,
And some besides to sell.

Around the rich man's trellised bower
Gay, costly creepers run;
The poor man has his scarlet-beans
To screen him from the sun.

And there before the little bench,
O'ershadowed by the bower,
Grow southern-wood and lemon-thyme,
Sweet-pea and gilliflower;

And pinks and clove-carnations,
Rich scented, side by side;
And at each end a hollyhock,
With an edge of London-pride.

And here comes the old grandmother,
When her day's work is done;
And here they bring the sickly babe,
To cheer it in the sun.

And here, on Sabbath mornings,
The good man comes to get
His Sunday nosegay, moss-rose bud,
White pink, and mignonette.

And here, on Sabbath evenings,
Until the stars are out,
With a little one in either hand,
He walketh all about.

For though his garden-plot is small,
Him doth it satisfy;
For there's no inch of all his ground
That does not fill his eye.

It is not with the rich man thus;
For though his grounds are wide,
He looks beyond, and yet beyond,
With soul unsatisfied.

Yes! in the poor man's garden grow
Far more than herbs and flowers;—
Kind thoughts, contentment, peace of mind,
And joy for weary hours.

THE OAK-TREE.

Sing for the Oak-Tree,
The monarch of the wood:
Sing for the Oak-Tree,
That groweth green and good;
That groweth broad and branching
Within the forest shade;
That groweth now, and yet shall grow
When we are lowly laid!

The Oak-Tree was an acorn once,
And fell upon the earth;
And sun and showers nourished it,
And gave the Oak-Tree birth.
The little sprouting Oak-Tree!
Two leaves it had at first,
Till sun and showers had nourished it,
Then out the branches burst.

The little sapling Oak-Tree!
Its root was like a thread

Till the kindly earth had nourished it,
Then out it freely spread:
On this side and on that side
It grappled with the ground;
And in the ancient, rifted rock
Its firmest footing found.

The winds came, and the rain fell;
The gusty tempests blew;
All, all were friends to the Oak-Tree,
And stronger yet it grew.
The boy that saw the acorn fall,
He feeble grew and gray;
But the Oak was still a thriving tree,
And strengthened every day!

Four centuries grows the Oak-Tree,
Nor doth its verdure fail;
Its heart is like the iron-wood,
Its bark like plated mail.
Now, cut us down the Oak-Tree,
The monarch of the wood;
And of its timbers stout and strong
We'll build a vessel good!

The Oak-Tree of the forest
Both east and west shall fly;
And the blessings of a thousand lands
Upon our ship shall lie!
For she shall not be a man-of-war,
Nor a pirate shall she be:—
But a noble, Christian merchant-ship
To sail upon the sea.

Then sing for the Oak-Tree,
    The monarch of the wood;
Sing for the Oak-Tree,
    That groweth green and good;
That groweth broad and branching,
    Within the forest-shade;
That groweth now, and yet shall grow,
    When we are lowly laid!

MORNING THOUGHTS.

The summer sun is shining
    Upon a world so bright!
The dew upon each grassy blade,
The golden light, the depth of shade,
All seem as they were only made
    To minister delight.

From giant trees, strong branched,
    And all their veined leaves;
From little birds that madly sing;
From insects fluttering on the wing;
Ay, from the very meanest thing
    My spirit joy recieves.

I think of angel voices,
    When the birds' songs I hear;
Of that celestial city, bright

With jacinth, gold, and chrysolite,
When, with its blazing pomp of light,
The morning doth appear!

I think of that great River
That from the Throne flows free;
Of weary pilgrims on its brink,
Who, thirsting, have come down to drink;
Of that unfailing Stream I think,
When earthly streams I see!

I think of pain and dying,
As that which is but naught,
When glorious morning, warm and bright,
With all its voices of delight,
From the chill darkness of the night,
Like a new life, is brought.

I think of human sorrow
But as of clouds that brood
Upon the bosom of the day,
And the next moment pass away;
And with a trusting heart I say
Thank God, *all things are good!*

THE USE OF FLOWERS.

God might have bade the earth bring forth
Enough for great and small,
The oak-tree and the cedar-tree,
Without a flower at all.

We might have had enough, enough
For every want of ours,
For luxury, medicine, and toil,
And yet have had no flowers.

The ore within the mountain mine
Requireth none to grow;
Nor doth it need the lotus-flower
To make the river flow.

The clouds might give abundant rain;
The nightly dews might fall,
And the herb that keepeth life in man
Might yet have drunk them all.

And wherefore, wherefore were they made,
All dyed with rainbow-light,
All fashioned with supremest grace,
Upspringing day and night;—

Springing in valleys green and low,
And on the mountains high,
And in the silent wilderness
Where no man passes by?

Our outward life requires them not —
    Then wherefore had they birth? —
To minister delight to man,
    To beautify the earth;

To comfort man — to whisper hope,
    Whene'er his faith is dim,
For who so careth for the flowers,
    Will much more care for him!

SUNSHINE.

I LOVE the sunshine everywhere, —
    In wood, and field, and glen;
I love it in the busy haunts
    Of town-imprisoned men.

I love it when it streameth in
    The humble cottage door
And casts the checkered casement shade
    Upon the red-brick floor.

I love it where the children lie
    Deep in the clovery grass,
To watch among the twining roots
    The gold-green beetles pass.

I love it on the breezy sea,
    To glance on sail and oar,
While the great waves, like molten glass,
    Come leaping to the shore.

I love it on the mountain-tops,
    Where lies the thawless snow,
And half a kingdom, bathed in light,
    Lies stretching out below.

And when it shines in forest-glades,
    Hidden, and green, and cool,
Through mossy boughs and veined leaves,
    How is it beautiful!

How beautiful on little stream,
    When sun and shade at play,
Make silvery meshes, while the brook
    Goes singing on its way.

How beautiful, where dragon-flies
    Are wondrous to behold,
With rainbow wings of gauzy pearl,
    And bodies blue and gold!

How beautiful, on harvest slopes,
    To see the sunshine lie!
Or on the paler reaped fields,
    Where yellow shocks stand high!

Oh, yes! I love the sunshine!
    Like kindness or like mirth
Upon a human countenance,
    Is sunshine on the earth!

Upon the earth; upon the sea;
And through the crystal air,
Or piled-up cloud; the gracious sun
Is glorious everywhere!

THE CHILD AND THE FLOWERS.

Put up thy work, dear mother;
Dear mother come with me,
For I've found within the garden,
The beautiful sweet-pea!

And rows of stately hollyhocks
Down by the garden-wall,
All yellow, white, and crimson,
So many-hued and tall!

And bending on their stalks, mother,
Are roses white and red;
And pale-stemmed balsams all a-blow,
On every garden-bed.

Put up thy work, I pray thee,
And come out, mother dear!
We used to buy these flowers,
But they are growing here!

Oh, mother! little Amy
Would have loved these flowers to see;—
Dost remember how we tried to get
For her a pink sweet-pea?

Dost remember how she loved
Those rose-leaves pale and sere?
I wish she had but lived to see
The lovely roses here!

Put up thy work, dear mother,
And wipe those tears away
And come into the garden
Before 'tis set of day!

CHILDHOOD.

Oh, when I was a little child,
My life was full of pleasure,
I had four-and-twenty living things,
And many another treasure.

But chiefest was my sister dear,
Oh, how I loved my sister!
I never played at all with joy,
If from my side I missed her.

I can remember many a time,
  Up in the morning early, —
Up in the morn by break of day,
  When summer dews hung pearly;

Out in the fields what joy it was,
  While the cowslip yet was bending,
To see the large round moon grow dim,
  And the early lark ascending!

I can remember, too, we rose
  When the winter stars shone brightly;
'Twas an easy thing to shake off sleep
  From spirits strong and sprightly.

How beautiful were those winter skies,
  All frosty-bright and unclouded,
And the garden-trees, like cypresses,
  Looked black, in the darkness shrouded!

Then the deep, deep snows were beautiful,
  That fell through the long night stilly,
When behold, at morn, like a silent plain,
  Lay the country wild and hilly!

And the fir-trees down by the garden side,
  In their blackness towered more stately;
And the lower trees were feathered with snow,
  That were bare and brown so lately.

And then, when the rare hoar-frost would come,
  'Twas all like a dream of wonder,
When over us grew the crystal trees,
  And the crystal plants grew under!

The garden all was enchanted land;
    All silent and without motion,
Like a sudden growth of the stalactite,
    Or the corallines of ocean!

'Twas all like a fairy forest then,
    Where the diamond cards were growing,
And within each branch the emerald green
    And the ruby red were glowing.

I remember many a day we spent
    In the bright hay-harvest meadow;
The glimmering heat of the noonday ground,
    And the hazy depth of shadow.

I can remember, as to-day
    The corn-field and the reaping,
The rustling of the harvest-sheaves,
    And the harvest-wain's upheaping:

I can feel this hour as if I lay
    Adown 'neath the hazel bushes,
And as if we wove, for pastime wild,
    Our grenadier-caps of rushes.

And every flower within that field
    To my memory's eye comes flitting,
The chiccory-flower, like a blue cockade,
    For a fairy-knight befitting.

The willow-herb by the water side,
    With its fruit-like scent so mellow;
The gentian blue on the marly hill,
    And the snap-dragon white and yellow.

I know where the hawthorn groweth red;
    Where pink grows the way-side yarrow;
I remember the wastes of woad and broom,
    And the shrubs of the red rest-harrow.

I know where the blue geranium grows,
    And the stork's-bill small and musky;
Where the rich osmunda groweth brown,
    And the wormwood white and dusky.

There was a forest anigh our home,—
    A forest so old and hoary;
How we loved in its ancient glooms to be,
    And remember its bygone story!

We sate in the shade of its mighty trees,
    When the summer noon was glowing
And heard in the depths of its undergroth
    The pebbly waters flowing.

We quenched our thirst at the forest-well;
    We ate of the forest berry;
And the time we spent in the good greenwood,
    Like the times of song, were merry.

We had no crosses then, no cares;
    We were children like yourselves then;
And we danced and sang, and made us mirth,
    Like the dancing moonlight elves then!

L'ENVOI.

Go, little book, and to the young and kind,
Speak thou of pleasant hours and lovely things,
Of fields and woods; of sunshine; dew and wind;
Of mountains, valleys, and of river-springs;
Speak thou of every little bird that sings;
Of every bright, sweet-scented flower that blows;
But chiefest speak of Him whose mercy flings
Beauty and love abroad, and who bestows
Light to the sun alike, with odor to the rose.

My little book, that hast been unto me
Even as a flower reared in a pleasant place,
This is the task that I impose on thee; —
Go forth; with serious style or playful grace,
Winning young, gentle hearts; and bid them trace
With thee, the spirit of Love through earth and air;
On beast and bird, and on our mortal race,
So, do thy gracious work; and onward fare,
Leaving, like angel-guest, a blessing everywhere!

SKETCHES OF NATURAL HISTORY.

THE COOT.

OH COOT! oh bold, adventurous Coot.
  I pray thee tell to me,
The perils of that stormy time,
  That bore thee to the sea!

I saw thee on the river fair,
  Within thy sedgy screen;
Around thee grew the bulrush tall,
  And reeds so strong and green.

The kingfisher came back again
  To view thy fairy place;
The stately swan sailed statelier by,
  As if thy home to grace.

But soon the mountain flood came down,
  And bowed the bulrush strong;
And far above those tall green reeds,
  The waters poured along.

"And where is she, the Water-Coot,"
  I cried, "that creature good?"
But then I saw thee in thine ark,
  Regardless of the flood.

Amid the foaming waves thou sat'st,
  And steered thy little boat;
Thy nest of rush and water-reed
  So bravely set afloat.

And on it went, and safely on
  That wild and stormy tide;
And there thou sat'st, a mother bird,
  Thy young ones at thy side.

Oh Coot! oh bold, adventurous Coot!
  I pray thee tell to me,
The perils of that stormy voyage
  That bore thee to the sea!

Hadst thou no fear, as night came down
  Upon thy watery way,
Of enemies, and dangers dire
  That round about thee lay?

Didst thou not see the falcon grim
  Swoop down as thou passed by?
And 'mong the waving water flags
  The lurking otter lie?

The eagle's scream came wildly near,
  Yet, caused it no alarm?
Nor man, who seeing thee, weak thing,
  Did strive to do thee harm?

And down the foaming waterfall,
  As thou was borne along,
Hadst thou no dread? Oh daring bird,
  Thou hadst a spirit strong!

Yes, thou hadst fear. But He who sees
  The sparrows when they fall,
He saw thee, bird, and gave thee strength
  To brave thy perils all.

He kept thy little bark afloat;
  He watched o'er thine and thee;
And safely through the foaming flood
  Hath brought thee to the sea.

THE EAGLE.

No, not in the meadow, and not on the shore,
And not on the wide heath with furze covered o'er,
Where the cry of the Plover, the hum of the bee,
Give a feeling of joyful security:
And not in the woods, where the nightingale's song,
From the chestnut and orange pours all the day long;
And not where the Martin has built in the eaves,
And the Redbreast e'er covered the children with leaves,
Shall ye find the proud Eagle! O no, come away!
I will show you his dwelling, and point out his prey
Away! let us go where the mountains are high,
With tall splintered peak towering into the sky;
Where old ruined castles are dreary and lone,
And seem as if built for a world that is gone;
There, up on the topmost tower, black as the night,
Sits the old monarch Eagle in full blaze of light:

He is king of these mountains: save him and his mate,
No Eagle dwells there; he is lonely and great!
Look, look how he sits! with his keen glancing eye,
And his proud head thrown back, looking into the sky;
And hark to the rush of his out-spreading wings,
Like the coming of tempest, as upward he springs,
And now how the echoing mountains are stirred,
For that was the cry of the Eagle you heard!
Now, see how he soars! like a speck in the height
Of the blue vaulted sky, and now lost in the light!
And now downward he wheels as a shaft from a bow
By a strong archer sent to the valleys below!
And that is the bleat of a lamb of the flock;—
One moment, and he re-ascends to the rock.—
Yes, see how the conqueror is winging his way,
And his terrible talons are holding their prey!
Great bird of the wilderness! lonely and proud,
With a spirit unbroken, a neck never bowed,
With an eye of defiance, august and severe,
Who scorn'st an inferior, and hatest a peer,
What is it that giveth thee beauty and worth?
Thou wast made for the desolate places of earth;
To mate with the tempest; to match with the sea;
And God showed his power in the Lion and thee!

THE GARDEN.

I HAD a Garden when a child;
  I kept it all in order;
'Twas full of flowers as it could be,
  And London-pride was its border.

And soon as came the pleasant Spring,
  The singing-birds built in it;
The Blackbird and the Thostle-cock,
  The Woodlark and the Linnet.

And all within my Garden ran
  A labyrinth-walk so mazy;
In the middle there grew a yellow Rose,
  At each end a Michaelmas Daisy.

I had a tree of Southern Wood,
  And two of bright Mezereon;
A Peony root, a snow-white Phlox,
  And a bunch of red Valerian;

A Lilac tree, and a Guelder-Rose;
  A Broom, and a Tiger-Lily;
And I walked a dozen miles to find
  The true wild Daffodilly.

I had Columbines, both pink and blue,
  And Thalictrum like a feather;
And the bright Goat's-beard, that shuts its leaves
  Before a change of weather.

I had Marigolds, and Gilliflowers,
And Pinks all Pinks exceeding;
I'd a noble root of Love-in-a-mist,
And plenty of Love-lies-bleeding.

I'd Jacob's Ladder, Aaron's Rod,
And the Peacock-Gentianella;
I had Asters more than I can tell,
And Lupins blue and yellow.

I set a grain of Indian Corn,
One day in an idle humor,
And the grain sprung up six feet or more!
My glory for a summer.

I found far off in the pleasant fields
More flowers than I can mention;
I found the English Asphodel,
And the spring and autumn Gentian.

I found the Orchis, fly and bee,
And the Cistus of the mountain;
And the Money-wort and the Adder's-tongue
Beside an old wood fountain.

I found within another wood,
The rare Pyrola blowing:
For wherever there was a curious flower,
I was sure to find it growing.

I set them in my garden beds,
Those beds I loved so dearly,
Where I labored after set of sun,
And in summer mornings early

O my pleasant garden-plot! —
  A shrubbery was beside it,
And an old and mossy Apple-tree,
  With a Woodbine wreathed to hide it.

There was a bower in my garden-plot,
  A Spiræa grew before it;
Behind it was a Laburnum-tree,
  And a wild Hop clambered o'er it.

Ofttimes I sat within my bower,
  Like a king in all his glory;
Ofttimes I read, and read for hours
  Some pleasant, wondrous story.

I read of gardens in old times,
  Old, stately Gardens, kingly,
Where people walked in gorgeous crowds,
  Or for silent musing, singly.

I raised up visions in my brain,
  The noblest and the fairest;
But still I loved my Garden best,
  And thought it far the rarest.

And all among my flowers I walked,
  Like a miser 'mid his treasure;
For that pleasant plot of Garden ground
  Was a world of endless pleasure.

THE SPIDER AND THE FLY.

AN APOLOGUE.

A NEW VERSION OF AN OLD STORY.

"Will you walk into my parlor?" said the Spider to the Fly,
"'Tis the prettiest little parlor that ever you did spy;
The way into my parlor is up a winding stair,
And I've many curious things to show when you are there."
"Oh no, no," said the little Fly, "to ask me is in vain,
For who goes up your winding stair can ne'er come down again."

"I'm sure you must be weary, dear, with soaring up so high;
Will you rest upon my little bed?" said the Spider to the Fly.
"There are pretty curtains drawn around; the sheets are fine and thin,
And if you like to rest awhile, I'll snugly tuck you in!"
"Oh no, no," said the little Fly, "for I've often heard it said,
They never, never wake again, who sleep upon your bed!"

Said the cunning Spider to the Fly, "Dear friend, what can I do,
To prove the warm affection I've always felt for you?

I have within my pantry good store of all that's nice;
I'm sure you're very welcome — will you please to take a slice?"
"Oh no, no," said the little Fly, "kind sir, that cannot be,
I've heard what's in your pantry, and I do not wish to see!"

"Sweet creature!" said the Spider, "you're witty and you're wise,
How handsome are your gauzy wings, how brilliant are your eyes!
I've a little looking-glass upon my parlor shelf,
If you'll step in one moment, dear, you shall behold yourself."
"I thank you, gentle sir," she said, "for what you're pleased to say,
And bidding you good morning now, I'll call another day."

The Spider turned him round about, and went into his den,
For well he knew the silly Fly would soon come back again:
So he wove a subtle web, in a little corner sly,
And set his table ready, to dine upon the Fly.
Then he came out to his door again, and merrily did sing,
"Come hither, hither, pretty Fly, with the pearl and silver wing;
Your robes are green and purple—there's a crest upon your head;
Your eyes are like the diamond bright, but mine are dull as lead!"

Alas, alas! how very soon this silly little Fly,
Hearing his wily, flattering words, came slowly flitting by;
With buzzing wings she hung aloft, then near and nearer drew,
Thinking only of her brilliant eyes, and green and purple hue—
Thinking only of her crested head—poor foolish thing! At last,
Up jumped the cunning Spider, and fiercely held her fast.
He dragged her up his winding stair, into his dismal den,
Within his little parlor—but she ne'er came out again!

And now, dear little chilldren, who may this story read,
To idle, silly, flattering words, I pray you ne'er give heed;
Unto an evil counsellor, close heart, and ear, and eye,
And take a lesson from this tale, of the Spider and the Fly.

TALES IN VERSE.

ANDREW LEE.

THE FISHER BOY.

Ah! Fisher Boy, I well know thee,
Brother thou art to Marion Lee!
What! didst thou think I knew thee not,
Couldst thou believe I had forgot?
For shame, for shame! what? I forget
The treasures of thy laden net!
And how we went one day together,
One day of showery summer weather,
Up the sea-shore, and for an hour
Stood sheltering from a pelting shower
Within an upturned, ancient boat,
That had not been for years afloat!
No, no, my boy! I liked too well
The old sea-stories thou didst tell;
I liked too well thy roguish eye—
Thy merry speech—thy laughter sly;
Thy old sea-jacket, to forget,—
And then the treasures of thy net!
Oh, Andrew! thou hast not forgot,
I'm very sure that thou hast not,
All that we talked about that day,
Of famous countries far away!

Of Crusoes in their islands lone,
That never were, nor will be known,
And yet this very moment stand
Upon some point of mountain land,
Looking out o'er the desert sea,
If chance some coming ship there be.
Thou know'st we talked of this — thou know'st
We talked about a ship-boy's ghost —
A wretched little orphan lad
Who served a master stern and bad,
And had no friend to take his part,
And perished of a broken heart;
Or by his master's blows, some said,
For in the boat they found him dead,
And the boat's side was stained and red!

And then we talked of many a heap
Of ancient treasure in the deep,
And the great serpent that some men
In far-off seas, meet now and then;
Of grand sea-palaces that shine
Through forests of old coralline;
And wondrous creatures that may dwell
In many a crimson Indian shell;
Till I shook hands with thee, to see
Thou wast a poet — Andrew Lee!
Though thou wast guiltless all the time
Of putting any thoughts in rhyme;
Ah, little fisher boy! since then,
Ladies I've seen and learned men,
All clever, and some great and wise,
Who study all things, earth and skies,
Who much have seen, and much have read,
And famous things have writ and said;

But Andrew, never have I heard
One who so much my spirit stirred,
As he who sate with me an hour,
Screened from the pelting thunder-shower –
Now laughing in his merry wit;
Now talking in a serious fit,
In speech that poured like water free;
And that was thou — Poor Andrew Lee

Then shame to think I knew thee not -
Thou hast not, nor have I forgot;
And long 'twill be ere I forget
How thou took'st up thy laden net,
And gave me all that it contained,
Because I too thy heart had gained!

THE WANDERER'S RETURN.

There was a girl of fair Provence,
  Fresh as a flower in May,
Who 'neath a spreading plane-tree sate,
  Upon a summer-day,
And thus unto a mourner young,
  In a low voice did say.

"And said I, I shall dance no more;
  For though but young in years,
I knew what makes men wise and sad,—
  Affection's ceaseless fears,
And that dull aching of the heart,
  Which is not eased by tears.

"But sorrow will not always last,
  Heaven keeps our griefs in view;
Mine is a simple tale, dear friend,
  Yet I will tell it you;
A simple tale of household grief
  And household gladness too.

"My father in the battle died,
  And left young children three;
My brother Marc, a noble lad,
  With spirit bold and free,
More kind than common brothers are;
  And Isabel and me.

"When Marc was sixteen summers old,
  A tall youth and a strong,
Said he, 'I am a worthless drone,
  I do my mother wrong —
I'll hence and win the bread I eat,
  I've burdened you too long!'

"Oh! many tears my mother shed;
  And earnestly did pray,
That he would still abide with us,
  And be the house's stay;
And be like morning to her eyes,
  As he had been alway.

"But Marc he had a steadfast will,
  A purpose fixed and good,
And calmly still and manfully
  Her prayers he long withstood;
Until at length she gave consent,
  Less willing than subdued.

"'Twas on a shining morn in June,
  He rose up to depart;
I dared not to my mother show
  The sadness of my heart;
We said farewell, and yet farewell,
  As if we could not part.

"There seemed a gloom within the house,
  Although the bright sun shone;
There was a want within our hearts —
  For he, the dearest one,
Had said farewell that morn of June,
  And from our sight was gone.

"At length most doleful tidings came,
Sad tidings of dismay;
The plague was in the distant town,
And hundreds died each day;
We thought, in truth, poor Marc would die,
'Mid strangers far away.

"Weeks passed, and months, and not a word
Came from him to dispel
The almost certainty of death
Which o'er our spirits fell;
My mother drooped from fear, which grew
Each day more terrible.

"At length she said, 'I'll see my son,
In life if yet he be,
Or else the turf that covers him!'
When sank she on her knee,
And clasped her hands in silent prayer,
And wept most piteously.

"She went into the distant town,
Still asking everywhere
For tidings of her long-lost son: —
In vain she made her prayer;
All were so full of wo themselves,
No pity had they to spare.

"To hear her tell that tale would move
The sternest heart to bleed;
She was a stranger in that place,
Yet none of her took heed;
And broken-hearted she came back,
A bowed and bruised reed.

"I marked her cheek yet paler grow,
  More sunken yet her eye;
And to my soul assurance came
  That she was near to die,
And hourly was my earnest prayer
  Put up for her on high.

"Oh, what a wo seemed then to us,
  The friendless orphan's fate!
I dared not picture to my mind,
  How drear, how desolate —
But, like a frightened thing, my heart
  Shrunk from a pang so great!

"We rarely left my mother's side,
  'Twas joy to touch her hand,
And with unwearying, patient love,
  Beside her couch to stand,
To wait on her, and every wish
  Unspoke to understand.

At length, oh joy beyond all joys!
  When we believed him dead,
One calm and sunny afternoon,
  As she lay on her bed
In quiet sleep, methought below
  I heard my brother's tread.

"I rose, and on the chamber stair,
  I met himself — no other —
More beautiful than ere before,
  My tall and manly brother!
I should have swooned, but for the thought
  Of my poor sleeping mother.

"I cannot tell you how we met;—
I could not speak for weeping;
Nor had I words enough for joy,—
My heart within seemed leaping,
I should have screamed, but for the thought
Of her who there lay sleeping!

"That Marc returned in joy to us,
My mother dreamed e'en then,
And that prepared her for the bliss
Of meeting him again;—
To tell how great that bliss, would need
The tongue of wisest men!

"His lightest tone, his very step,
More power had they to win
My drooping mother back to life,
Than every medicine;
She rose again, like one revived
From death where he had been!

"The story that my brother told
Was long, and full of joy;
Scarce to the city had he come,
A poor and friendless boy,
Than he chanced to meet a merchant good,
From whom he asked employ.

"The merchant was a childless man;
And in my brother's face
Something he saw that moved his heart
To such unusual grace;
'My son,' said he, 'is dead, wilt thou
Supply to me his place?'

"Even then, bound to the golden East,
  His ship before him lay;
And this new bond of love was formed
  There, standing on the quay;
My brother went on board with him,
  And sailed that very day!

"The letter that he wrote to us,
  It never reached our hand;
And while we drooped with anxious love,
  He gained the Indian strand,
And saw a thousand wondrous things,
  In that old, famous land.

And many rich and curious things,
  Bright bird and pearly shell,
He brought, as if to realize
  The tales he had to tell;
My mother smiled, and wept, and smiled,
  And listened, and grew well.

"The merchant loved him more and more,
  And did a father's part;
And blessed my brother for the love
  That healed his wounded heart;
He was a friend that heaven had sent
  Kind mercy to impart.

"So do not droop, my gentle friend,
  Though grief may burden sore;
Look up to God, for he hath love
  And comfort in great store,
And ofttimes moveth human hearts
  To bless us o'er and o'er"

ELLEN MORE.

"Sweet Ellen More," said I, "come forth
Beneath the sunny sky;
Why stand you musing all alone,
With such an anxious eye?
What is it, child, that aileth you?"
And thus she made reply:

"The fields are green, the skies are bright,
The leaves are on the tree,
And 'mong the sweet flowers of the thyme
Far flies the honey-bee;
And the lark hath sung since morning prime,
And merrily singeth he.

"Yet not for this shall I go forth
On the open hills to play,
There's not a bird that singeth now,
Would tempt me hence to stray; —
I would not leave our cottage door
For a thousand flowers to-day!

"And why?" said I, "what is there here
Beside your cottage door,
To make a merry girl like you
Thus idly stand to pore?
There is a mystery in this thing, —
Now tell me, Ellen More!"

The fair girl looked into my face,
  With her dark and serious eye;
Silently awhile she looked,
  Then heaved a quiet sigh;
And, with a half-reluctant will,
  Again she made reply.

"Three years ago, unknown to us,
  When nuts were on the tree,
Even in the pleasant harvest-time,
  My brother went to sea —
Unknown to us, to sea he went,
  And a woful house were we.

"That winter was a weary time,
  A long, dark time of wo,
For we knew not in what ship he sailed,
  And vainly sought to know;
And day and night the loud, wild winds
  Seemed evermore to blow.

"My mother lay upon her bed,
  Her spirit solely tossed
With dismal thoughts of storm and wreck
  Upon some savage coast;
But morn and eve we prayed to Heaven
  That he might not be lost.

"And when the pleasant spring came on,
  And fields again were green,
He sent a letter full of news,
  Of the wonders he had seen;
Praying us to think him dutiful
  As he afore had been

"The tidings that came next were from
A sailor old and gray,
Who saw his ship at anchor lie
In the harbor at Bombay;
But he said my brother pined for home,
And wished he were away.

"Again he wrote a letter long,
Without a word of gloom;
And soon, and very soon he said,
He should again come home;
I watched, as now, beside the door,
And yet he did not come.

"I watched and watched, but I knew not then
It would be all in vain;
For very sick he lay the while,
In a hospital in Spain. —
Ah, me! I fear my brother dear
Will ne'er come home again!

"And now I watch — for we have heard
That he is on his way,
And the letter said, in very truth,
He would be here to-day.
Oh! there's no bird that singeth now
Could tempt me hence away!"

— That self-same eve I wandered down
Unto the busy strand,
Just as a little boat came in
With people to the land;
And 'mongst them was a sailor-boy
Who leaped upon the sand.

I knew him by his dark blue eyes,
  And by his features fair;
And as he leaped ashore he sang
  A simple Scottish air,—
"There's nae place like our ain dear hame
  To be met wi' onywhere!"

A SWINGING SONG.

Merry it is on a summer's day,
All through the meadows to wend away;
To watch the brooks glide fast or slow,
And the little fish twinkle down below;
To hear the lark in the blue sky sing,
Oh, sure enough, 'tis a merry thing—
But 'tis merrier far to swing—to swing!

Merry it is on a winter's night,
To listen to tales of elf and sprite,
Of caves and castles so dim and old,—
The dismallest tales that ever were told;—
And then to laugh, and then to sing,
You may take my word is a merry thing,—
But 'tis merrier far to swing—to swing!

Down with the hoop upon the green,
Down with the ringing tamborine;—
Little heed we for this or for that;
Off with the bonnet, off with the hat!

Away we go like birds on the wing!
Higher yet! higher yet! "Now for the King!"
This is the way we swing — we swing!

Scarcely the bough bends, Claude is so light,
Mount up behind him — there, that is right!
Down bends the branch now; — swing him away;
Higher yet — higher yet — higher I say!
Oh, what a joy it is! Now let us sing
"A pear for the Queen—an apple for the King!"
And shake the old tree as we swing — we swing!

THE YOUNG MOURNER.

Leaving her sports, in pensive tone,
'Twas thus a fair young mourner said,
'How sad we are now we're alone, —
I wish my mother were not dead!

'I can remember she was fair;
And how she kindly looked and smiled,
When she would fondly stroke my hair,
And call me her beloved child.

"Before my mother went away,
You never sighed as now you do;
You used to join us at our play,
And be our merriest playmate too

"Father, I can remember when
  I first observed her sunken eye,
And her pale, hollow cheek; and then
  I told my brother she would die!

"And the next morn they did not speak,
  But led us to her silent bed;
They bade us kiss her icy cheek,
  And told us she indeed was dead!

"Oh, then I thought how she was kind,
  My own beloved and gentle mother!
And calling all I knew to mind,
  I thought there ne'er was such another!

"Poor little Charles, and I! that day
  We sate within our silent room;
But we could neither read nor play,—
  The very walls seemed full of gloom.

"I wish my mother had not died,
  We never have been glad since then!
They say, and is it true," she cried,
  "That she can never come again?"

The father checked his tears, and thus
  He spake, "My child, they do not err,
Who say she cannot come to us;
  But you and I may go to her.

"Remember your dear mother still,
  And the pure precepts she has given;
Like her, be humble, free from ill,
  And you shall see her face in heaven!"

THE SOLDIER'S STORY.

Heaven bless the boys!" the old man said,
"I hear their distant drumming, —
Young Arthur Bruce is at their head,
And down the street they're coming.

"And a very noble standard too
He carries in the van;
By the faith of an old soldier, he
Is born to make a man!"

A glow of pride passed o'er his cheek,
A tear came to his eye;
"Hurra, hurra! my gallant men!"
Cried he, as they came nigh.

"It seems to me but yesterday
Since I was one like ye,
And now my years are seventy-two,
Come here, and talk with me!"

They made a halt, those merry boys,
Before the aged man;
And "Tell us now some story wild
Young Arthur Bruce began;

"Of battle and of victory
Tell us some stirring thing!"
The old man raised his arm aloft,
And cried, "God save the King

"A soldier's is a life of fame,
  A life that hath its meed —
They write his wars in printed books,
  That every man may read.

"And if you'd hear a story wild,
  Of war and battle done,
I am the man to tell such tales,
  And you shall now have one.

"In every quarter of the globe
  I've fought — by sea, by land;
And scarce for five and fifty years
  Was the musket from my hand.

"But the bloodiest wars, and fiercest too,
  That were waged on any shore,
Were those in which my strength was spent,
  In the country of Mysore.

"And oh! what a fearful, deadly clime
  Is that of the Indian land,
Where the burning sun shines fiercely down
  On the hot and fiery sand!

"The life of man seems little worth,
  And his arm hath little power;
His very soul within him dies,
  As dies a broken flower.

"Yet spite of this, was India made
  As for a kingly throne;
There gold is plentiful as dust,
  As sand the diamond stone;

"And like a temple is each house,
  Silk-curtained from the sun;
And every man has twenty slaves,
  Who at his bidding run.

"He rides on the lordly elephant,
  In solemn pomp; — and there
They hunt the gold-striped tiger,
  As here they hunt the hare.

"Yet it is a dreadful clime! and we
  Up in the country far
Were sent,—we were two thousana men,
  In a disastrous war.

"The soldiers died in the companies
  As if the plague had been;
And soon in every twenty men,
  The dead were seventeen.

"We went to storm a fort of mud—
  And yet the place was strong—
Three thousand men were guarding it,
  And they had kept it long.

"We were in all three hundred souls,
  Feeble and worn and wan;
Like walking spectres of the tomb,
  Was every living man.

"Yet Arthur Bruce, now standing there,
  With the ensign of his band,
Reminds me of a gallant youth,
  Who fought at my right hand.

"Scarce five and twenty years of age,
And feeble as the rest,
Yet with the bearing of a king,
That noble soul expressed.

"But a silent grief was in his eye,
And oft his noble frame
Shook like a quivering aspen leaf,
And his color went and came.

"He marched by my side for seven days,
Most patient of our band;
And night and day he ever kept
Our standard in his hand.

"They fought with us like tigers,
Before that fort of mud;
And all around the burning sands
Were as a marsh with blood.

"We watched that young man,—he to us
Was as a kindling hope;
We saw him pressing on and on,
Bearing the standard up.

"At length it for a moment veered-
A ball had struck his hand,
But he seized the banner with his left,
Without a moment's stand.

"He mounted upward to the wall;
He waved the standard high,—
But then another smote him!—
And the captain standing by

"Said, 'Of this gallant youth take care,
He hath won for us the day!'
I and my comrades took him up,
And bore him thence away.

"There was no tree about the place,
So 'neath the fortress shade
We carried him, and carefully
Upon the red sand laid.

"I took the feather from my cap,
To fan his burning cheek;
I gave him water, drop by drop,
And prayed that he would speak.

"At length he said, 'Mine hour is come!
My soldier-name is bright;
But a pang there is within my soul,
That hath wrung me day and night;

"'I left my mother's home without
Her blessing;—she doth mourn,
Doth weep for me with bitter tears,—
I never can return!

"'This bowed my eagle-spirit down,
This robbed mine eye of rest;
I left her widowed and alone:—
Oh that I had been blessed!'

"No more he said,—he closed his eyes,
And yet he died not then;
He lived till the morrow morning came,
But he never spoke again."

This tale the veteran soldier told,
  Upon a summer's day; —
The boys came merrily down the street,
  But they all went sad away.

THE CHILD'S LAMENT.

I LIKE it not — this noisy street
  I never liked, nor can I now —
I love to feel the pleasant breeze
On the free hills, and see the trees,
  With birds upon the bough!

Oh, I remember long ago, —
  So long ago, 'tis like a dream —
My home was on a green hill-side,
By flowery meadows, still and wide,
  'Mong trees, and by a stream.

Three happy brothers I had then,
  My merry playmates every day —
I've looked and looked through street and square,
But never chanced I, anywhere,
  To see such boys as they.

We all had gardens of our own —
  Four little gardens in a row, —
And there we set our twining peas;
And rows of cress; and real trees
  And real flowers to grow.

My father I remember too,
  And even now his face can see;
And the gray horse he used to ride,
And the old dog that at his side
  Went barking joyfully!

He used to fly my brother's kites,
  And build them up a man of snow,
And sail their boats, and with them race,
And carry me from place to place,
  Just as I liked to go.

I'm sure he was a pleasant man,
  And people must have loved him well! —
Oh, I remember that sad day
When they bore him in a hearse away,
  And tolled his funeral bell!

Thy mother comes each night to kiss
  Thee, in thy little quiet bed —
So came my mother years ago;
And I loved her — oh! I loved her so,
  'Twas joy to hear her tread!

It must be many, many years
  Since then, and yet I can recall
Her very tone — her look — her dress,
Her pleasant smile and gentleness,
  That had kind words for all.

She told us tales, she sang us songs,
  And in our pastimes took delight,
And joined us in our summer glee,
And sat with us beneath the tree!

Nor wearied of our company,
   Whole days, from morn till night.

Alas! I know that she is dead,
   And in the cold, cold grave is hid;
I saw her in her coffin lie,
With the grim mourners standing by;
And silent people solemnly
   Closed down the coffin lid.

My brothers were not there — ah me!
   I know not where they went; some said
With a rich man beyond the sea
That they were dwelling pleasantly —
   And some that they were dead.

I cannot think that it is so,
   I never saw them pale and thin,
And the last time their voice I heard,
Merry were they as a summer-bird,
   Singing its bowers within.

I wish that I could see their faces,
   Or know at least that they were near;
Ah! gladly would I cross the sea,
So that with them I might but be,
For now my days pass wearily,
   And all are strangers here.

THE OLD MAN AND THE CARRION CROW.

THERE was a man and his name was Jack,
Crabbed and lean, and his looks were black —
His temper was sour, his thoughts were bad;
His heart was hard when he was a lad.
And now he followed a dismal trade,
Old horses he bought, and killed, and flayed;
Their flesh he sold for the dogs to eat:
You would not have liked this man to meet.
He lived in a low mud-house on a moor,
Without any garden before the door.
There was one little hovel behind, that stood,
Where he used to do his work of blood;
I never could bear to see the place,
It was stained and darkened with many a trace,
A trace of what I will not tell —
And then there was such an unchristian smell!

Now this old man did come and go,
Through the wood that grew in the dell below;
It was scant a mile from his own door-stone,
Darksome and dense, and overgrown;
And down in the drearest nook of the wood,
A tall and splintered fir-tree stood;
Half-way up, where the boughs outspread,
A carrion crow his nest had made,
Of sticks and reeds in the dark fir-tree,
Where lay his mate and his nestlings three;
And whenever he saw the man come by,
"Dead horse! dead horse!" he was sure to cry,

"Croak, croak!" if he went or came,
The cry of the crow was just the same;
Jack looked up as grim as could be,
And says, "What's my trade to the like of thee!"
"Dead horse! dead horse! croak, croak! croak, croak!"
As plain as words to his ear it spoke.
Old Jack stooped down and picked up a stone,
A stout, thick stick, and dry cow's bone,
And one and the other all three did throw,
So angry was he, at the carrion crow;
But none of the three reached him or his nest,
Where his three young ones lay warm at rest;
And "Croak, croak! dead horse! croak, croak!"
In his solemn way again he spoke;
Old Jack was angry as he could be,
And says he, "On the morrow, I'll fell thy tree,—
I'll teach thee, old fellow, to rail at me!"

As soon as 'twas light, if there you had been,
Old Jack at his work you might have seen;
I would you'd been there to see old Jack,
And to hear the strokes as they came "Thwack! thwack!"
And then you'd have seen how the croaking bird
Flew round as the axe's stroke he heard,
Flew round as he saw the shaking blow,
That came to his nest from the root below,
One after the other, stroke upon stroke;
"Thwack! thwack!" said the axe, said the crow "Croak! croak!"
Old Jack looked up with a leer in his eye,
And, "I'll hew it down!" says he, "by and by —
I'll teach thee to rail, my old fellow, at me!"
So he spit on his hands, and says, "Have at the tree!"

"Thwack!" says the axe, as the bark it clove;
"Thwack!" as into the wood it drove;
"Croak!" says the crow in a great dismay,
"Croak!" as he slowly flew away.
Flap, flap went his wings over hedge and ditch,
Till he came to a field of burning twitch;
The boy with a lighted lantern there,
As he stood on the furrow brown and bare,
He saw the old crow hop hither and thither,
Then fly with a burning sod somewhither.

Away flew the crow to the house on the moor,
A poor, old horse was tied to the door;
The burning sod on the roof he dropped,
Then upon the chimney-stone he hopped,
And down he peeped that he might see
How many there were in family —
There was a mother and children three.
"Croak! croak!" the old crow did say,
As from the roof he flew away,
As he flew away to the tree, to watch
The burning sod and the dry gray thatch;
He stayed not long till he saw it smoke,
Then he flapped his wings, and cried, "Croak, croak!"
Away to the wood again flew he,
And soon he espied the slanting tree,
And Jack, who stood laughing with all his might,
His axe in his hand — he laughed for spite;
In triumph he laughed, and took up a stone,
And hammered his axe-head faster on;
"Croak, croak!" came the carrion crow,
Flapping his wings with a motion slow;
"Thwack! thwack!" the spiteful man,
When he heard his cry, with his axe began·

"Thwack! thwack!" stroke upon stroke;
The crow flew by with a "Croak, croak!"
With a "Croak, croak!" again he came,
Just as the house burst into flame.
With a splitting crash, and a crackling sound,
Down came the tree unto the ground;
The old crow's nest afar was swung,
And the young ones here and there were flung;
And just at that moment came up a cry,
"Oh Jack, make haste, or else we die;
The house is on fire, consuming all,
Make haste, make haste, ere the roof-tree fall!"
The young crows every one were dead,
But the old crow croaked above his head;
And the mother-crow on Jack she springs,
And flaps in his face her great black wings;
And all the while he hears a wail,
That turns his cheek from red to pale —
'Twas wife and children standing there
Wringing their hands and tearing their hair!
"Oh wo, our house is burnt to cinder,
Bedding and clothes all turned to tinder;
Down to the very hearth-stone clean,
Such a dismal ruin ne'er was seen:
"What shall we do — where must we go?"
"Croak, croak!" says the carrion crow.

Now ye who read this story through,
Heed well the moral — 'tis for you; —
Strife brings forth strife; be meek and kind;
See all things with a loving mind;
Nor e'er by passion be misled, —
Jack by himself was punished.

MISCELLANEOUS PIECES.

THE SALE OF THE PET LAMB OF THE COTTAGE.

OH! poverty is a weary thing, 'tis full of grief and pain,
It boweth down the heart of man, and dulls his cunning brain,
It maketh even the little child with heavy sighs complain!

The children of the rich man have not their bread to win;
They hardly know how labor is the penalty of sin;
Even as the lilies of the field, they neither toil nor spin.

And year by year, as life wears on, no wants have they to bear;
In all the luxury of the earth they have abundant share;
They walk among life's pleasant ways, and never know a care

The children of the poor man — though they be
young, each one,
Early in the morning they rise up before the rising
sun,
And scarcely when the sun is set, their daily task is
done.

Few things have they to call their own, to fill their
hearts with pride, —
The sunshine of the summer's day, the flowers on the
highway side,
Or their own free companionship, on the heathy com-
mon wide.

Hunger, and cold, and weariness, these are a frightful
three;
But another curse there is beside, that darkens pov
erty: —
It may not have one thing to love, how small soe'er
it be.

A thousand flocks were on the hills — a thousand
flocks, and more, —
Feeding in sunshine pleasantly, — they were the rich
man's store;
There was the while, one little lamb, beside a cottage
door:

A little lamb that did lie down with the children 'neath
the tree;
That ate, meek creature, from their hands, and nestled
on their knee;
That had a place within their hearts, as one of the
family.

But want, even as an armed man, came down upon their shed,
The father labored all day long, that his children might be fed;
And, one by one, their household things were sold to buy them bread.

That father, with a downcast eye, upon his threshold stood,
Gaunt poverty each pleasant thought had in his heart subdued;
"What is the creature's life to us?" said he, "'twill buy us food!

"Ay, though the children weep all day, and with down-drooping head
Each does his small craft mournfully!—the hungry must be fed;
And that which has a price to bring, must go, to buy us bread!"

It went—oh! parting has a pang the hardest heart to wring,
But the tender soul of a little child with fervent love doth cling,
With love that hath no feignings false, unto each gentle thing!

Therefore most sorrowful it was those children small to see,
Most sorrowful to hear them plead for their pet so piteously;—
"Oh! mother dear, it loveth us; and what beside have we?

"Let's take him to the broad, green hills," in his impotent despair,
Said one strong boy, "let's take him off, the hills are wide and fair;
I know a little hiding-place, and we will keep him there!"

'Twas vain! — they took the little lamb, and straightway tied him down,
With a strong cord they tied him fast; — and o'er the common brown,
And o'er the hot and flinty roads, they took him to the town.

The little children through that day, and throughout all the morrow
From everything about the house a mournful thought did borrow;
The very bread they had to eat was food unto their sorrow! —

Oh! poverty is a weary thing, 'tis full of grief and pain —
It keepeth down the soul of man as with an iron chain;
It maketh even the little child with heavy sighs complain!

AMERICA.

A STORY OF THE INDIAN WAR.

THEY read of rapine, war, and wo,
  A party by an English fire,—
Of Indian warfare in the wood,
  Of stern and ruthless ire.

They read of torture worse than death—
  Of treachery dark—of natures base—
Of women savage as the beast—
  Of the red Indian race.

"Hold!" said the matron of the hearth,
  A woman beautiful in age;
"And let me of the Indian speak;
  Close, close that faithless page!

"My father was the youngest born
  In an old rural English hall;
The youngest out of five stout sons,
  With patrimony small.

"His boyhood was in greenwood spent;
  His youth was all a sylvan dream;
He tracked the game upon the hills;
  He angled in the stream.

"Quiet was he, and well content,
  With naught to fret, and none to chide;

For all that his young heart desired
  The woods and streams supplied.

"Small knowledge had a youth so trained,
  College or school ne'er knew his face;
And yet as he grew up, he grew
  Superior to his race.

"His brethren were of sordid sort,
  Men with coarse minds, and without range
He grew adventurous and bold,
  Inquisitive of change.

"And, as he grew, he took to books,
  And read whate'er the hall supplied;
Histories of admirals, voyages old,
  And travels far and wide.

"He read of settlers, who went forth
  To the far west, and pitched their tent
Within the woods, and grew, ere long,
  To a great prosperous settlement.

"He read of the bold lives they led,
  Full of adventure, hardy, free;
Of the wild creatures they pursued,
  Of game in every tree.

"And how the Indians, quaintly gay,
  Came down in wampum-belt and feather
To welcome them with courteous grace ·
How they and the free forest race
  Hunted and dwelt together.

"And how they and their chosen mates
 Led lives so sweet and primitive:
Oh! in such land, with one dear heart,
 What joy it were to live!

"So thought he, and such life it were
 As suited well his turn of mind;
For what within his father's house
 Was there to lure or bind?

"Four needy brothers, coarse and dull;
 A patrimony, quite outspent;
A mother, long since in her grave;
 A father, weak and indolent!

"At twenty he had ta'en a mate,
 A creature gentle, kind and fair;
Poor, like himself, but well content
 The forest-life to share.

"She left an old white-headed sire;
 A mother loving, thoughtful, good;
She left a home of love, to live
 For him, within the wood.

"And that old couple did provide,
 Out of their need, for many a want
Else unforseen; their daughter's dower
 In gifts of love, not scant.

"His father with cold scorn received
 So dowered a daughter, without name;
Nor could his purposed exile win
 Either assent or blame.

All was a chill of indifference;
And from his father's gate he went,
As from a place where none for him
Had kindred sentiment.

"And in the western world they dwelt;
Life, like a joyous summer morn,
Each hope fulfilled; and in the wild
To them were children born.

"All that his youth had dreamed he found
In that life's freshness; peril strange;
Adventure; freedom; sylvan wealth;
And ceaseless, blameless change.

"And there he, and his heart's true mate,
Essayed and found how sweet to live,
'Mid nature's store, with health and love,
That life so primitive!

"But that sweet life came to an end. —
As falls the golden-eared corn
Before the sickle, earthly bliss
In human hearts is shorn.

"Sickness — bereavement — widowhood —
Oh, these three awful words embrace
A weight of mortal wo that fell
Upon our sylvan dwelling-place!

"It matters not to tell of pangs,
Of the heart broken, the bereft;
I will pass over death and tears,
I will pass on to other years,
When only two were left!

"I and a sister; long had passed
 The anguish of that time, and we
Were living in a home of love,
 Though in a stranger's family.

Still in the wilderness we dwelt,
 And were grown up towards womanhood;
When our sweet life of peace was stirred
 By tales of civil feud.

"By rumors of approaching war,
 Of battle done, of armed bands;
Of horrid deeds of blood and fire,
 Achieved by Indian hands.

"We heard it first with disbelief:
 And long time after, when had spread
Wild war throughout the land, we dwelt
 All unassailed by dread.

"For they with whom our lot was cast,
 Were people of that Christian creed
Who will not fight, but trust in God
 For help in time of need.

"The forest round was like a camp,
 And men were armed day and night;
And every morning brought fresh news
 To heighten their affright.

"Though the green forest rose the smoke
 Of places burned the night before;
And from their victims, the red scalp
 The excited Indian tore.

"This was around us, yet we dwelt
In peace upon the forest bound;
Without defence, without annoy,
The Indian camped all round.

"The door was never barred by night,
The door was never closed by day;
And there the Indians came and went,
As they had done alway.

"For 'these of Onas are the sons,'
Said they, 'the upright peaceful men!'
Nor was harm done to those who held
The faith of William Penn.

"But I this while thought less of peace,
Than of the camp and battle stir;
For I had given my young heart's love
Unto a British officer.

"Near us, within the forest-fort,
He lay, leader of a band
Of fierce young spirits, sworn to sweep
The Indian from the land —

"The native Indian from his woods —
I deemed it cowardly and base;
And, with a righteous zeal I pled
For the free forest-race.

"But he, to whom I pled, preferred
Sweet pleading of another sort;
And we met ever 'neath the wood
Outside the forest-fort.

"The Indian passed us in the wood,
Or glared upon us from the brake;
But he, disguised, with me was safe,
For Father Onas' sake.

"At length the crisis of the war
Approached, and he, my soul's beloved,
With his hot band, impatient grown,
Yet further west removed.

"There he was taken by the foe,
Ambushed like tigers 'mid the trees:
You know what death severe and dread
The Indian to his foe decrees.

"A death of torture and of fire—
Protracted death; I knew too well,
Outraged and angered, as of late
Had been the Indian spirit, fell
Would be their vengeance, and, to him,
Their hate implacable.

"When first to me his fate was told,
I stood amazed, confounded, dumb;
Then wildly wept and wrung my hands,
By anguish overcome.

"'Wait, wait!' the peaceful people said;
'Be still and wait, the Lord is good!'
But when they bade me trust and wait,
I went forth in my anguish great,
To hide me in the wood.

"I had no fear; the Indian race
  To me were as my early kin:
And then the thought came to my brain,
To go forth, and from death and pain
  My best beloved to win.

"With me my fair young sister went,
  Long journeying on through wood and swamp:
Three long days' travel, ere we came
  To the great Indian camp.

"We saw the Indians as we went,
  Hid 'mong the grass with tiger ken;
But we were safe, they would not harm
  The daughters of the peaceful men.

"In thickets of the woods at length
  We came to a savannah green;
And there, beneath the open day,
  The Indian camp was seen.

"I turned me from that scene of war,
  And from the solemn council-talk,
Where stood the warriors, stern and cold,
War-crested, and with bearing bold,
Listening unto a sachem old,
  Who held aloft a tomahawk.

"I knew they were athirst for blood;
  That they had pity none to spare;—
Besides, bound to a tree, I saw
  An English captive there.

"I saw his war-plume, soiled and torn;
  I knew that he was doomed to die;
Pale, wounded, feeble, there he stood;
  The ground was crimsoned with his blood,
Yet stood he as a soldier should —
  Erect, with calm, determined eye.

"I would not he should see me then, —
  The sight his courage had betrayed;
Therefore unseen we stepped aside,
  Into the forest-glade.

"An Indian woman there was set,
  We knew her, and to her were known;
The wife of a great chief was she,
Decked in her Indian bravery;
  Yet there she sat alone.

"'Woman,' I said, the silence breaking,
  'Thou know'st us — know'st that we belong
To peaceful people, who have ne'er
  Done to thy nation wrong.

"'Thou know'st that ye have dwelt with us,
  As friend upon the hearth of friend; —
When have ye asked and been denied,
  That this good faith should end?'

"The Indian did not raise her head,
  As she replied in accents low,
'Why come ye hither unto me,
  When I am sitting in my wo?'

"'Woman,' I said, 'I ask for life —
For life, which in your hands doth lie;
Go bid thy tribe release the bands
Of him now doomed to die!

"'Go, Indian woman, and do this,
For thou art mighty with thy race!'
The Indian made me no reply,
But looked into my face.

"'Mighty! said'st thou?' at length she spoke,
'Mighty! — to one no longer wife!
The hatchet and the tomahawk
Lie by me on the forest-walk;
The great chief in my hut lies low,
The ruthless pale-face struck the blow —
And yet thou com'st to me for life!'

"'By that chief's memory,' I cried,
'Whom ne'er the peaceful men gainsaid;
To whom the peaceful men were dear;
Rise, though thou stricken be, and aid!

"'Crave not REVENGE,' and with my words
My tears flowed fast, though hers were dry;
'But look upon this pictured face,
And say if such a one shall die!'

'Long looked she on the pictured face,
Which from my neck I took and gave;
Long looked she ere a word was spoke,
And then she slowly silence broke,
'The hatchet is not buried yet;
The tomahawk with blood is wet;
And the great chief is in his grave!

"'Yet for the father Onas' sake —
For their sakes who no blood have shed,
We will not by his sons be blamed
For taking life which they have claimed; —
The red man can avenge his dead!'

"So saying, with her broken heart —
She went forth to the council-stone;
And when the captive was brought out,
'Mid savage war-cry, taunt, and shout,
The stepped into the fierce array,
As the bereaved Indian may,
And claimed the victim for her own.

"He was restored. What need of more
To tell the joy that thence ensued!
But sickness followed long and sore,
And he for a twelvemonth or more,
With our good, peaceful friends abode.

"But we, two plighted hearts, were wed;
A merry marriage ye may wis; —
And guess ye me a happy life —
In England here, an honored wife, —
Sweet friends, ye have not guessed amiss!

"But never more let it be said,
The red man is of nature base;
Nor let the crimes that have been taught,
Be by the crafty teachers brought
As blame against the Indian race!"

MOURNING ON EARTH.

She lay down in her poverty,
  Toil-stricken, though so young;
And the words of human sorrow
  Fell trembling from her tongue.

There were palace-houses round her,
  And pomp and pride swept by
The walls of that poor chamber,
  Where she lay down to die.

Two were abiding with her,
  The lowly of the earth, —
Her feeble, weeping sister,
  And she who gave her birth.

She lay down in her poverty,
  Toil-stricken, though so young;
And the words of human sorrow
  Fell from her trembling tongue.

"Oh Lord, thick clouds of darkness
  About my soul are spread,
And the waters of affliction
  Have gathered o'er my head!

"Yet what is life? A desert,
  Whose cheering springs are dry,
A weary, barren wilderness! —
  Still it is hard to die!

"For love, the clinging, deathless,
  Is with my life entwined;
And the yearning spirit doth rebel
  To leave the weak behind!

"Oh Saviour, who didst drain the dregs
  Of human wo and pain,
In this, the fiercest trial-hour,
  My doubting soul sustain!

"I sink, I sink! support me;
  Deep waters round me roll;
I fear! I faint! O Saviour,
  Sustain my sinking soul!"

REJOICING IN HEAVEN.

"Oh spirit, freed from bondage,
  Rejoice, thy work is done!
The weary world is 'neath thy feet,
  Thou brighter than the sun!

"Arise, put on the garments
  Which the redeemed wore!
Now sorrow hath no part in thee,
  Thou sanctified from sin!

"Awake and breathe the living air
  Of our celestial clime!

Awake to love which knows no change,
Thou, who hast done with time!

"Awake, lift up thy joyful eyes,
See, all heaven's host appears;
And be thou glad exceedingly,
Thou, who hast done with tears!

"Awake! ascend Thou art not now
With those of mortal birth,—
The living God hath touched thy lips,
Thou who hast done with earth!"

THE

POETICAL WORKS

OF

ELIZA COOK.

A NEW EDITION.

BOSTON:
PHILLIPS, SAMPSON, & CO.,
110 WASHINGTON STREET.
1853.

MELAIA, AND OTHER POEMS.

MELAIA.

'Twas in the age when Arts and Peace
Revived once more in mighty Greece—
When Fame forsook the camp and blade,
And turned from purple fields to wreathe
Her meeds again for those who bade
The canvass glow, the marble breathe,
'Twas in this age Melonian stood
The highest in his sculpture art;
Known as the great, loved as the good;
With hand but rivalled by his heart.
His was the power to wake the gaze,
Yielding the spirit's speechless praise—
His was the spell that flings control
Over the eye, breast, brain, and soul;
Chaining our senses to the stone
Till we become
As fixed and dumb
As the cold form we look upon.

Melonian was about to leave
His idol toil one summer eve.

When at his door a stranger guest
Appeared, in venerable guise,
Whose weight of years had dimmed his eyes,
And meekly lowered his "haught crest."
His garb was of a shape and sort
That plainly augured little wealth;
But his frank smile gave good report
Of rich content and placid health.
No stern and frowning gloom was seen
To curl his lip or shade his mien;
His bending limbs, and silvered head,
Stricken with patriarchal age,
Gave ample sign that he had read
Life's volume to its closing page.
Melonian rose; the stranger bowed: —

"Artist," cried he "I've come to scan
Thy blazoned works, — is it allowed?
Though great, perhaps thou'rt not too proud
To please an old and curious man.
The restless wings of Rumor waft
Fair tidings of thy works and craft!
Crowds speak of thee with lauding joy.
I like thy name, and would employ
Thy hand. Say, Artist what may be
The sum that forms thy common fee?"

The Sculptor smiled. "Friend!" he exclaimed,
"My charge may startle when 'tis named.
Excuse me, Stranger, if I say
I deem 'tis more than thou canst pay.
Two thousand byzantines I ask
For simplest form or briefest task."

"Two thousand! 'tis indeed fair store
Of gold, but *he* deserved much more.
Have what thou wilt, 'tis ne'er too much;
  Double the sum, it shall be thine;
But will thy chisel deign to touch
  A form nor human nor divine?
I see thou hast a goodly band
  Of gods and heroes scattered round;
But I invoke thy master hand
  To carve me but a simple hound."

"A hound! a dog!" Melonian cried:
How's this, old man, would'st thou deride
My noble art? I blush with shame.
Say, dost thou mock my skill and fame?
I, first in Greece, think'st thou 'twould suit
Such hand to carve a cur! — a brute?"

"Hold!" said the Guest. "I must not hear
Such light words thrown to one so dear.
Long as I've trod the world, I've found
Naught half so worthy as my hound;
And thou, Melonian, wouldst not spurn
His claims and merit, didst thou learn
The strange and strong, nay, holy tie
That linked so firm and tenderly.
Of all the boons that men possess,
To aid, to cheer, instruct, and bless,
The dog, — bold, fond, and beauteous beast —
Is far from either last or least.
His love lives on through change of lot;
  His faith will chain him on our grave,
To howl and starve; but thou mayst not
  Have proved their love and faith: I have.

"Thy guerdon's sure: look on this ring,
A precious, though a bauble, thing;
The meanest jewel would suffice
To render safe thy utmost price.
But do my bidding, and the stone
Of richest lustre is thine own.
Behold and judge!" — The Sculptor gazed
Upon the slender hand upraised,
And saw a finger thin and white,
  Encircled with a hoop of gold,
Imbedding diamonds of light,
  Nor loosely worn nor cheaply sold.—
"Speak," cried the Stranger; "dost thou choose
  To carve my dog? decide and tell....
Enough: I see thou dost refuse
  The favor craved. Artist, farewell."

Melonian seized his hand: "Nay, nay,
  Thy parting is not thus with me;
Thy speech, thy bearing all betray
  Thou art not what thou seem'st to be;
There's more than meets the eye and ear
  In thee. Say who, and what thou art!
I'm honest, and thou need'st not fear
  A gossip tongue nor traitor heart.
May I beseech thee to relate
Thy secret pilgrimage and fate?
You start — aye, 'tis a bold request;
But you have stirred within my breast
That quick and sudden interest
Which is not easily suppressed.
The warmth you've kindled doth defy
The rules of gentle courtesy;

And prompts, perchance, to ruder word
And freer tone than should be heard.
Your pardon, if I give offence;
  But, trust me, mine's no wily soul —
  This fervor, bursting all control,
Is not the seeming of pretence."

The Stranger spoke not for a while,
  But strove to check a rising sigh,
  And fixed his calm and searching eye
Upon the Sculptor's brow. The smile
Which erst illumed his mouth had fled,
And with it every trace of red
From cheek and lips; a change had spread
O'er his fair mien, as though some deep
Keen pangs had woke from memory's sleep.
Where is the one who hath not had
  Some anguish trial, long gone by,
Steal, spectre-like, all dark and sad
  On busy thought, till the full eye
And aching breast betrayed too well
The past still held undying spell?
Some pensive vision of this kind
Seemed shadowing the Stranger's mind.

"My fate," said he, "hath been to see
  And bear mortality's extremes.
My days have run 'twixt cloud and sun,
  But oh! with more of dark than beams.
What I was once has been concealed
  Right cautiously from other ears;
My tongue has never yet revealed
  The state that marked my earlier years;

But *thou* shalt hear it. I will trust
 The earnest radiance in thy face;
 'Tis spirit-lit, and I can trace
The breathing of a soul all just.
Listen, Melonian; but I claim
Thy sacred vow, that words or name
Pass not thy lips, till death has laid
This breaking form in peace and shade.
Say, Sculptor, dost thou yield thine oath?"

"Ay!" cried Melonian; "but the troth
Of simple promise is, with me,
As strong a bond as there can be.
My oath! Ay, take it if thou wilt;
 Yet is that bosom base and cold,
 And little worth, that does not hold
A broken word as meanest guilt.
But stay, my friend, here's rich rare wine,
Of years, I ween, outnumbering thine;
I know its vintage to be good;
Pour, fill, and drink — 'twill warm thy blood;
Come, pledge me deep, thy cheek is pale;
First brace thy heart, then tell thy tale."

The cup was drained, and Friendship's power
Had grown so great in one short hour,
'Twere difficult for host or guest
To say which liked the other best

"Now," cried the Stranger, "hear me tell
My simple tale; and mark me well,
Though my plain style may sound uncouth,
It yields naught else than bitter truth.

My long and checkered course began
Far hence, in sultry Hindostan.
Perchance I was a monarch's heir;
  My toys, the sceptre and the crown;
Shown like an idol to the stare
Of a vast nation; taught to wear
A princely port, and proudly share
A power I should one day bear,
  All kingly — all my own.

"I know full well ye cannot see
A trace of what there once might be;
My sand is almost out, and now
Ye find but furrows on my brow.
I know no records linger there,
Save those endorsed by age and care;
Heaven gives no stamp; Misfortune's tide
Brings prince and peasant side by side;
And who can tell the monarch when
He ranks and herds with other men?

"Ye smile, as though it were a thing
  Absurd, a jest to rouse your mirth,
To say my sire might be a king,
And hold dominion o'er the earth.
Yet such he was, and such was I.
  Nay, start not! — 'Tis but empty sound;
Strip off the robes of purple dye,
Throw all the peacock trappings by,
  And nothing more than man is found;
And often *less* — some scorpion worm,
That crawls and stings in human form;

Some upright brute, whose ruthless might,
In covert of a regal den,
Lays waste all mercy, sense, and right,
Defies a God, and tramples men.
But who expects the sapling tree
To flourish, nursed in royalty,
Amid the worst the world can lend
To choke and tangle, warp and rend,
'Mid all to blast the goodly shoot,
And turn fair bloom to bitter fruit?
The monarch's glance hath little chance
To scan a page in Nature's book.
The lessons there are sealed with care;
He must not, dare not, cannot look.
Lulled by the songs that courtiers sing,
No harsher music suffered near,
If Truth should whisper, she would ring
A strange alarum in his ear.
Could ye but see what I have seen,
And know as much as I have known,
Ye would not wonder there have been
Such graceless tyrants on a throne.

"I had an empire at my nod,
And ruled it like a demigod;
I was caressed as one divine;
Wealth, might — scarce limited — were mine.
My word could free the veriest slave,
Or doom the guiltless to a grave.
I was a feared and homaged one;
Perched on Ambition's utmost height,
And thought, as other fools have done,
Ne'er to be lower or less bright.

But I was taught a mighty change,
  In spirit, feeling, place, and word;
I've brooked the trials, wild and strange,
  Which some might question if they heard.

"I've proved how hard it is to cope
With traitors' blows and blasted hope;
I've drunk the cup of dark despair,
  E'en to the dregs; I've brunted all
Of searing pain and withering care
  That Heaven can send to goad and gall;
Yet have I stood the trying test,
And found at last my hour of rest.

"Old age is garrulous, they say,
  And this choice wine has wrought so well,
That my tongue gains a swifter play,
  And my lax heartstrings warmly swell.
But come, I'll speed my tale, and pray
  None else may have such tale to tell.

"'Twas on the nightfall of a day,
  When slaughter's red and fierce career
Had lasted from the breaking ray,
Leaving, as twilight died away,
  Some thousands on one common bier.

"The night came on, the work was done,
The glory ours, the battle won;
My hand was tired of the sword,
And gladly to its sheath restored
The dripping blade; for though my life
Hath oft been risked in human strife,

Elate and proud to have my name
Grow dreaded for its soldier fame;
Though I have stumbled o'er the slain,
'Mid splintered bone and scattered brain;
Though I have seen the streaming blood
Drench the green sod and tinge the flood;
Still, when the raging hour had sped,
  I sighed to think such things had been;
And though I helped to strew the dead,
  I sickened at the carnage scene.
My soul was reckless in the crash
Of ringing shield and striking clash.
Then I had all the tiger's will,
And all the lion's strength, to kill;
But when I trod the dead-strewn plain,
With mercy at her post again,
I felt a shuddering horror lurk,
To think I'd mingled in such work.

"'Twas on the night of such a day,
  Exhausted and o'erspent,
I flung my heavy mail away,
  And hied me to my tent.
There, close beside my couch, I found
A young and almost lifeless hound;
Some random sword or falling spear
Had deeply gashed his neck and ear:
He panted fast, he freely bled,
  His eyeballs had a glazy beam;
He moaned with anguish as his head
  Fell weltering in his own life-stream.
I asked who owned him—all were mute,—
  Not one stood forth to make a claim.

Who brought him there ?—None knew the brute,
  Nor how, nor whence, nor when he came.
Poor wretch! I could not let him lie
Unheeded, there to bleed and die:
The girdle from my waist I tore,
To bind the wound and staunch the gore.

" 'Twas done; I marked enough to see
  He was a dog of noble breed,
A whelp that promised fair to be
  The first in beauty, strength, and speed.
I liked the beast, and turned to give
Command that I would have him live
It was enough; he found repose,
Secure from further wounds and foes.

" Full soon he won my right good-will;
    I liked him well,
    As ye may tell,
By how he claims my homage still.
His fleetness held the longest chase;
He never knew the second place;
The prey once seized, he'd ne'er resign
His hold for any voice but mine;
The bribe was vain, the threat defied,
I was his lord, and none beside.

"*He* did not serve me for my throne,
  Yet was he grateful, fond, and brave,
He loved me for myself alone.
He was that good and gracious thing,
That rare appendage to a king,
  A friend that never played the slave.

"There was one other tie to hold
  My heart; I never loved but two;
That other — must the name be told!
Yes, yes, — it was my queenly bride,
My worshipped star, my joy, my pride:
  But *she* was false; — my *dog* was true.

"I saw her in a lowly grade,
Too bright a blossom for the shade;
I wooed, but with an honest love;
I spread no snares to catch the dove;
The bar of rank was trampled down,
I stooped, and raised her to my crown,

"Oh, how I doted on her smile,—
That sunbeam o'er a gulf of guile;
How I adored her orbs of blue,
Clear, full, and lustrous in their hue;
Rich as the deep cerulean light
Of autumn's melting moonlit night!

"I've met their tender glance, half hid
Beneath the thick-fringed falling lid;
I've seen the pearly drops of grief
Swim like the dew on violet's leaf;
I've watched their pleasure-kindled ray
Flash out like summer lightning's play;
And thought, had old Prometheus caught
  The gleaming spark from eyes like those,
He would have found the fire he sought
  On earth — nor made the gods his foes.

"Her golden hair, with glossy sheen,
  Fell round her temples rich and free,
With all the graceful beauties seen
  In flowers of the laburnum tree.
Her soft cheeks made the maple fade,
  Such tint, such bloom, was theirs alone;
The sculptor's art could ne'er impart
  Her stately bearing to the stone.

"Oh, why does Heaven bequeath such gifts,
  To fascinate all eyes that mark,
With magnet charm, till something lifts
  The mask, and shows how foully dark
The dazzling reptile is within,
Beneath its painted harlot skin?
If it were so, the outward part
Bore witness of the mind and heart,
How many a one must shun the light,
Or show a leper to the sight!

"I know I carried much of taint,
  That gave offence to Heaven and man,
But if ye seek a sage or saint,
  Search courts, and find him if ye can.

"I was corrupt, and did much wrong,
  But never breathed of harm to her;
Mine was that passion, warm and strong,
Which keeps its radiance pure and long,
  However else the soul may err.
I loved her with a zeal intense,
That thralled each colder, wiser sense;
I drank the nectar from her lip,
As bees the honeyed poison sip;

I trusted her, my tongue revealed
All — much that should have been concealed;
She labored, not in vain, to wrest
Some potent secret from my breast;
And then she leagued with traitor band;
A toil was spread, foul work was planned,
A rueful deed was to be done,
And I the victim, — she the one —
Oh, mercy! have I speech and breath!
She, she to weave the mesh of death!

"What's this upon my cheek? a tear!
Weak drop, what business hast thou here?
I fondly hoped the shattered string
Had been by now a tuneless thing;
But touch it lightly as I will,
It gives a mournful echo still.
Oh! when the heart has once been riven,
   The wound will firmly close no more;
Let Memory's searching probe be driven,
   It bleeds and quivers, freshly sore.

"This must not be; — more wine, I say;
Your nectar juice shall sweep away
The phantom pang. Fill up — I'll drain
This bowl, and to my tale again.

"She leagued with traitors! 'Twas no dream
I'd proof of all the hellish scheme;
I'd noticed much of late to make
The drowsiest suspicion wake.
Strange glances interchanged by those
I guessed were less of friends than foes;

And more than once I'd plainly heard
A whispered treasonable word.
But these I brooked, and thought to quell
All petty brawls that might betide;
Till I beheld the Hecate spell
Was conjured by my trusted bride.

"Chance gave a paper to my sight,
Meant for another eye to meet.
It stated that the coming night
Would render treachery complete.
It told, what fiends would scarce proclaim,
Of treason, murder! — and the same
Bore impress of her seal and name. —
Mute with dismay, I still read on;
And oh! the direst that could be,
I found her very honor gone —
She loved another, and not me.

"I stood with fire in every vein;
My pulses beat with frenzied stroke;
I breathed with that short heaving strain
Which teaches what it is to choke.
A moment, and there came a chill,
A stagnant, icy chill, as though
The blood recoiled, afraid to fill
A heart made weak with such a blow.

"The jarring chaos could not last;
Such struggling state is quickly past;
Such conflict is too close and strong
For mortal strength to bear with long.
When we have learned the very worst,
The spirit soon must yield, or burst.

"I was betrayed, ay, e'en to life;
Sedition round, and death in view.
And they who see the assassin's knife
Must aptly think and promptly do.
My love was wrecked, my faith decieved;
The strokes that ever madden most.
Without these, all had been retrieved;
With them I cared not what was lost.

"My kingship flitted o'er my brain,
My pompous sway, my courtier train;
I laughed, and rent the ermine vest,
That only mocked my abject state;
I dashed the jewels from my breast,
And sought my palace gate.

"I trod all soft and stealthily;
The path was clear I meant to fly.
Ne'er call me coward, till ye bear
The test by which I then was tried;
Remember, had I tarried there,
The stroke was sure — I'd meanly died.

"I knew some minions round me then
Were more of demons than of men.
Their aim was sure, if life the mark;
Once set on blood, they'd keep the track,
And would not scruple in the dark
To sheathe their dagger in my back.

"With fearful haste, I saddled straight
An Arab courser, newly broke,
Whose strength and grace were fit to mate
With those that form Apollo's yoke.

'Twas no meet moment to restrain
His mettled zeal. Away he sped,
With tossing mane
And flinging rein,
Upon the way he chose to tread.
The die was cast — flight, instant flight,
Alone could lend me hope to live.
The monarch-born, the gem bedight,
The flattered god, the ever right,
Was now a friendless fugitive.

"Away! away! the clattering hoof
Reëchoed from the palace roof.
I fled, unrivalled by the wind,
Nor threw a single glance behind.
Crown, sceptre, throne—such dreams were o'er;
Melaia was a king no more.

"I fled; but soon the deep-toned bay
Of bloodhound followed on my way;
And even now there's a rebound
Of joyous throb, a glow that steals
Swift through my frame, to tell I found
My gallant dog upon my heels.

"How welcome are the words that tell
The culprit, doomed to death and pain,
That he may quit his chains and cell,
And rove the world all free again!
How precious is the ray of light
That breaks upon the blind one's eye,
Unfolding to his wondering sight
The glorious scenes of earth and sky!

But never to despairing ear,
Or hopeless orb, was aught so dear
  As he to me appeared to be
In that dark hour of flight and fear.

" I checked my steed, and lost some time,
To let that dumb retainer climb,
With whimpering joy, and fondly greet
The hand he ever sprung to meet.
I stooped above his glossy head,
And many a streaming tear I shed,
Ay, like a child ; — but recollect,
In perils we must not reject
The meanest aid. The straw or plank
Will lure us then to snatch and thank.

" I lingered, but, ere long, my ear
Had warnings of pursuers near.
My rowels touched my Arab's side ;
Away he leaped like rushing tide,
That rolls to fling its sweeping waste
With furious all-defying haste.

" On, on, we went, I took no heed
  How such a strange career would end.
I urged my barb to meteor speed,
  But cared not where that speed might tend.
He sprung, he flew, as though he knew
  A frenzied wretch was on his back ;
And kept his pace for goodly space,
  Upon his own free chosen track.
He bore me on for many an hour,
  With headlong sweep, and bounding power

At last he faltered on his path;
I goaded, but the goad was vain.
Where was I? with the sun's full wrath
Around me on the desert plain.

"What an unthought-of goal I'd won!
Mercy! what wildering race I'd run!
'Twould soon be o'er, my failing horse
Was strangely wheeling on his course
His strength was out, his spirit flagged,
His fire was spent, he faintly lagged;
His dripping flanks and reeking neck,
Were white with rifts of foaming fleck.
His labored breath was quick and short,
His nostrils heaved with gasping snort;
He tottered on, — his will was good, —
His work had not belied his blood.

"Another mile, and then he fell.
His part was o'er — he played it well.
With snapping girth, and reeling head,
He groaned, and sunk, — my steed was dead.

"Above me one vast conclave spread,
No dappled clouds, no mellow blue;
Hot, darting rays, like torches, shed
A light of most unearthly hue.

"Below was one smooth glittering sheet,
That crisped and cracked beneath my feet;
No springing herb, no daisied sod, —
All barren, joyless, and untrod.
My dog was fawning at my side,
Untired with my rapid ride;

But I rebuked the sportive bound,
That scattered choking dust around.

" My breath was faint, my skin was dry,
The little moisture in my eye
Served but to scald; the striking beams
Fell on my form like sulphur streams.
What hideous change! I, who had known
The sickening splendor of a throne,
I, humbled wretch, was craving now
A moment's shadow for my brow.

"Thus to be left on such a spot,
Appeared the climax of my lot.
Death hovered there in such gaunt shape,
That Hope scarce whispered of escape;
But I was not in fitting state
To weigh the chances of my fate.

"I wended on with hasty stride,
'Twixt torrid earth and brazen sky,
Reckless of all that might betide,
To meet the worst, to live or die.
But some conjecture, quick and wild,
Flashed sudden o'er me, and beguiled
To flattering Hope. I vaguely guessed
That nigh the desert, in the west,
A city stood. That thought inspired
And held me on a while untired.

"I doubted if my wasting strength
Could last the unknown burning length.
It might; yet, oh! 'twas fearful risk,
To toil between the blazing disk

Of eastern sun and shining sand,
With lips unmoistened, cheek unfanned.
'Twas frightful ordeal, but yet
Dire evils pass if boldly met.

"I will not tire thy patient ear
  With tedious detail of my wo;
But bring my rambling speech to bear
  On that I wish thee most to know.

'Hour after hour brought on the night,
With something less of heat and light.
You may believe I was outworn;
And trembling, famished, and forlorn,
I flung me on the dewless ground,
  And fast and bitter tears I wept,
Till pillowed on my faithful hound,
  Like a tired child, I sobbed, and slept.

"Slumber like mine wrought little good,
I started as the sun uprose,
And fancied that my boiling blood
  Had gathered torture from repose.
I felt my temples glow, and beat
With faster pulse and fiercer heat.
I would have wept again, but now
My very tears refused to flow.

"I woke — I lived, to meet, to bear
With famine, thirst, and blank despair:
I cast my eager straining eye
From sky to sand, from sand to sky;
No, no relief! my hound and I
Were all that broke the vacancy.

"The whirling blast, the breaker's dash,
The snapping ropes, the parting crash,
The sweeping waves that boil and lash,
The stunning peal, the hissing flash,
The hasty prayer, the hopeless groan,
The stripling sea-boy's gurgling tone,
Shrieking amid the flood and foam,
The names of mother, love, and home;
The jarring clash that wakes the land,
When, blade to blade, and hand to hand,
Unnumbered voices burst and swell,
In one unceasing war-whoop yell;
The trump of discord ringing out,
The clamor strife, the victor shout: —
Oh! these are noises any ear
Will dread to meet and quail to hear!
But let the earth or waters pour
The loudest din or wildest roar;
Let Anarchy's broad thunders roll,
  And Tumult do its worst to thrill,
There is a *silence* to the soul
  More awful, and more startling still

"To hear our very breath intrude
Upon the boundless solitude,
Where mortal tidings never come,
With busy feet or human hum;
All hushed above, beneath, around —
No stirring form, no whispered sound; —
This is a loneliness that falls
Upon the spirit, and appals
More than the mingled rude alarms
Arising from a world in arms.

"This is a silence bids us shrink,
As from a precipice's brink;
But ye will rarely meet it, save
In the hot desert, or cold grave.
Cut off from life and fellow men,
This silence was around me then.
'Twas horrible, but once again
I dragged along the scorching plain,
Till the consuming orb of day
Shot down the close meridian ray.

"Exhausted nature now had done
Its utmost 'neath a desert sun,
And moments of delirium came;
A staggering weakness seized my frame;
My feet refused their task, when, lo!
My gaze met
Many a minaret.
A city rose; 'twas nigh; but, oh!
The beacon star now shone in vain;
Though short the space, I ne'er could gain
That other league. My limbs, my heart,
All failed; I felt my sinews start
With the last shudder of despair;
And Hope expired — my grave was there.

"'Twas thirst, 'twas maddening thirst alone,
That wrung my spirit's inmost groan.
Hunger is bitter, but the worst
Of human pangs, the most accursed
Of Want's fell scorpions, is thirst.

"I looked upon this precious ring,
That few besides a king could buy

What was its value, would it bring
A cup of water? No! its gleam,
That flashed back to the brazen beam,
  But taunted with its brilliancy.

"My strange distempered fancy wrought
The doom of Tantalus; for naught
Broke on my frantic waking dream
But the deep well and limpid stream:
Distorted vision conjured near
All that is cool, fresh, moist, and clear.
I saw the crystal fountain play
In leaping sheets of snowy spray;
I heard the undulating wave
Of the swift river gush and lave;
I saw the dew on grass and flower;
I heard the gentle summer shower,
  With its soft pattering bubbles drip;
I heard the dashing waterfall —
Oh! it was cruel mockery all.
  I laughed, and then my shrunken lip
Oozed thickened gore; with upraised hand,
I sunk upon the shining sand,
A Maker's mercy to implore.
  I fervently invoked a name
  Which, I confess with much of shame,
I'd rarely called upon before.

"Mid pleasure, plenty, and success,
  Freely we take from Him who lends;
We boast the blessings we possess,
  Yet scarcely thank the One who sends.
But let Affliction pour its smart,
  How soon we quail beneath the rod!

With shattered pride, and prostrate heart,
  We seek the long-forgotten God.
Let Him but smite us, soon we bleed,
And tremble like a fragile reed;
Then do we learn, and own, and feel
The Power that wounds alone can heal.
'Twas thus with me; the desert taught
  Lessons with bitter truth replete.
They chastened sorely, but they brought
  My spirit to its Maker's feet.

"My glance was for a moment thrown
  Towards the Heaven I addressed;
But the fierce rays came rushing down
      Upon my brow
      With furnace glow,
      Dense, lurid, red,
      Till my smote head
    Fell faint and stricken on my breast.

"Thus while I knelt my hound looked up —
  Fate was about to give the last,
The o'erflowing drop to Misery's cup —
  He started, fled, and bounded fast.

"Oh! what a moment! all the past
Was blended in that little space.
He fled me at his utmost pace;
Like arrow from the string he flew
Right on — he lessened to my view.
'Twas o'er; he vanished from my sight;
I breathed his name, and groaned outright.
      I was alone;
      My dog had gone —

He that I deemed the firmly true —
In the last hour *he* left me too.

"I saw no more; I snatched my breath
Like those who meet a drowning death;
One cry of hopeless agony
Escaped my lips, while earth and sky
Grew dark, and reeled before mine eye.
A whirling pang shot through my brain,
Of mingled madness, fire, and pain.
'Twas rending, but it was the last.
Thank God, it came like lightning flame,
And desolated as it past.

"No more of this; I only know,
I felt strange pressure on my brow;
The world was not; I can but tell,
That senseless, lone, and blind, I fell,

"The next that memory can mark
Is of a clear and shrill-toned bark.
Sense tardily came back; I woke
Beneath a gentle pawing stroke.
I gazed with wild and doubting stare —
My dog! my noble dog was there —
It was my Murkim that I saw,
With blood, wet blood, upon his jaw.
What sight for eyes like mine to meet!
I shrieked, I started to my feet.
Judge of my joy; beside him lay
A small and lifeless beast of prey.
I seized it; I was in no mood
To play the epicure in food;

I waited not to think on what
That prey might be, or whence 'twas got.
Had you but seen me clutch and fall,
Like famished wolf or cannibal,
Upon that mangled, raw repast,
My hands, my teeth, all tearing fast;
Had you beheld my dry lips drain
The current from each reeking vein!
  No nectar half so sweet or fresh;
  Oh, it was rare delicious fare;
I never quaffed such lucious draught,
  Nor tasted viand like that flesh.
It soothed my brain, it cooled my eye,
  It quenched the fire upon my brow;
It gave me breath, strength, energy;
And, looking to the city nigh,
  I felt that I could reach it now.
Could I do less than kneel and bless
My Saviour in the wilderness?
But what will all of speech avail?
The choicest eloquence would fail;
The feeling that absorbed my heart
  Was of that deep entrancing kind
  Which doth defy the lips to find
A fitting language to impart
Its glowing zeal and passionate start.
My lips would falter to discuss
  The sense he kindled in my breast·
My dog had snatched from death, and thus —
  I leave thee to suppose the rest.

" Again I took my onward way,
  Once more I tracked the desert ground;

Again I knelt to thank, to pray,
Nor deem me impious, if I say
  That next to God I held my hound.

"I reached the city; many a year
    Has rolled away,
    Since that long day,
But yet, behold this truant tear
Proclaims that trying day is set
Among the few we ne'er forget.

"Methinks I'm getting sad — and see,
The sun's behind yon orange tree:
'Tis well my tale holds little more;
It wearies, and I wish it o'er.
Some time, perchance, when thou'rt inclined,
  I'll yield thee more of what befell
The throne and bride I left behind:
  But now I do not care to dwell
    On what, to me,
    Will ever be
A most ungrateful theme to tell.

"I walked the world unmarked, unknown,
Remote from man, but not alone;
I kept one friend, the closely bound,
The dear, the changeless, in my hound,
He had become my spirit's part,
  And rarely did he leave my side;
He shared my board, my couch, my heart,
  Till, pressed by time, he drooped, and died
Of sheer old age. Why, Murkim, why
Did not Melaia too then die!

I miss thee still, I mourn thee yet.
But lo! again my cheek is wet.
Fool that I am — this will not do —
Artist, this suits nor me nor you:
My words have just worn down the sun,
One question, friend, and I have done.

"I've told thee how he bore and braved
The darkest checker in my lot;
You know his worth; he served and saved.
Now, wilt thou carve my dog, or not?"

Pillars have mouldered, ages waned,
Since this plain tale beguiled an hour;
And Time and War had both profaned
The glory-seat of arts and power;
Famed Greece, the beautiful and great,
Was but a wrecked and fallen state;
She was but as a funeral urn,
Holding the ashes worlds revere,
O'er which the coldest heart will mourn,
And strangers hang to shed the tear:
Each monument was laid in dust,
By some ungodly savage hand;
Her palace gates had gathered rust,
Her picture scrolls had fed the brand:
When, mid the relics scattered round
One of surpassing skill was found;
The work was rare,
The marble fair,
The form, a bold and couchant hound.

The old and wise, with judgment stern,
In curious search were seen to turn
With careless glance from all the rest,
And own that image first and best:
The artist boy was seen to pause,
Ecstatic in his rapt applause.
No idle wanderer passed it by,
But marked with brighter, closer eye.
They lingered there to ask and trace
  The legend such a form might lend;
But naught was known save what its base
  Told, in the words, "Melaia's Friend."

A ROMAUNT.

TRACY DE VORE AND HUBERT GREY.

A TALE.

Know ye not the stripling child
  That strolls from the castle wall,
To play with the mate he likes the best,
  By the mountain waterfall?

With delicate hand, and polished skin,
  Like Parian marble fair;
Know ye him not? 'Tis Tracy de Vore,
  The Baron's beautiful heir.

'Tis Tracy de Vore, the castle's pride,
  The rich, the nobly born,
Pacing along the sun-lit sod
  With the step of a playful fawn.

The waving plume in his velvet cap
  Is bound with a golden band;
His rich and broidered suit exhales
  The breath of Arabia's land.

His light and fragile form is graced
  With a girdle of silvered blue;

And of matchless azure the belt would seem,
  Were it not for his eyes' own hue.

Look on those eyes, and thou wilt find
  A sadness in their beam,
Like the pensive shade that willows cast
  On the sky-reflecting stream.

Soft-flowing curls of an auburn shade
  Are falling around his brow!
There's a mantling blush that dwells on his cheek,
  Like a rose-leaf thrown on the snow.

There's a halcyon smile spread o'er his face,
Shedding a calm and radiant grace;
There's a sweetness of sound in his talking tones,
Betraying the gentle spirit he owns.

And scarcely an accent meets his ear
  But the voices of praise and love;
Caressed and caressing, he lives in the world
  Like a petted and beautiful dove.

He is born to bear the high command
Of the richest domain in Switzerland;
And the vassals pray that fame and health
May bless the child of rank and wealth!
Oh! truly does every lip declare
What a cherub-like boy is Lord Tracy's heir!

And now on the green and sedgy bank
  Another stripling form is seen:

His garb is rough, his halloo loud;
  He is no baron's heir, I ween.

Know ye him not? 'tis the mountain child,
Born and reared 'mid the vast and the wild;
And a brighter being ne'er woke to the day
Than the herdsman's son, young Hubert Grey.

There's a restless flashing in his eye,
  That lights up every glance;
And now he tracks the wheeling bird;
And now he scans the distant herd;
And now he turns from earth and sky,
  To watch where the waters dance.

A ruddy tinge of glowing bronze
  Upon his face is set;
Closely round his temples cling
  Thick locks of shaggy jet.

Mark him well! there's a daring mien
In Hubert Grey that is rarely seen;
And suiting that mien is the life he leads,
Where the eagle soars, and the chamois feeds.

He loves to climb the steepest crag,
  Or plunge in the rapid stream;
He dares to look on the thunder cloud,
  And laugh at the lightning's gleam.

The snow may drift, the rain may fall,
  But what does Hubert care?
As he playfully wrings, with his hardy hand
  His drenched and dripping hair.

He can tread through the forest, or over the rocks,
In the darkest and dreariest night,
With as sure a step, and as gay a song,
As he can in the noonday's light.

The precipice, jutting in ether air,
Has naught of terror for him;
He can pace the edge of the loftiest peak
Without trembling of heart or limb.

He heeds not the blast of the winter storm,
Howling on o'er the pine-covered steep;
In the day he will whistle to mimic its voice,
In the night it lulls him to sleep.

And now he has brought, from his mountain home,
(With feet and forehead bare,)
A tiny boat, and lance-wood bow,
The work of his young hand I trow,
To please the Baron's heir;
And now, at the waterfall, side by side,
Stand the herdsman's son and the castle's pride!

Tracy de Vore hath high born mates
Invited to share his play;
But none are half so dear to him
As lowly Hubert Grey.

He hath a spaniel taught to mark,
And wait his word with a joyous bark;
He hath a falcon taught to fly
When he looses its silver chain;

To range, at his bidding, round the sky,
  Then seek his hand again.

His ear is used to the softest song;
  To the lute and gay guitar;
But the native strain of the herdsman's son
  Is sweeter to him by far!

He hath toys and trinkets, bought with gold;
  And a palfrey in the stall;
But Hubert's bow, and Hubert's boat, —
  Oh, they are worth them all!

And Hubert Grey hath learnt to love
  The smile of Tracy de Vore;
He delights in leading the timid boy
  Where he never trod before.

He teaches him how to note the hours,
  By where the sunbeams rest;
He wades for him where the virgin flowers
Gracefully bend 'neath the cascade's showers,
  To pluck the whitest and best.
He tells him the curious legends of old,
  Known by each mountaineer;
He tells him the story of ghost and fay;
  Waking his wonder and fear.

Never so joyful is Hubert's shout
As when his eagle-eyes look out,
And spy afar, in the plain below,
Young Tracy's cap with its plume of snow.

Never so glad is Tracy de Vore
  As when he can steal away
From his father's watchful doting care,
  To rove with Hubert Grey.

And now, at the waterfall, side by side,
Stand the Herdsman's son and the Baron's pride!
The summer beams are falling there
On the mountain boy and the noble heir!

Time flies on, a year has sped,
  And summer comes again:
The sun is shining warm and bright,
  O'er forest, hill, and plain!

But never again will Tracy de Vore
  Stroll from the castle wall,
To play with the one he loves the best,
  By the mountain waterfall.

There's silence in the mansion now;
  Loud mirth is turned to sighing;
The Baron weeps, the vassals mourn,
  For the noble heir is dying!

Look on the lip that so sweetly smiled,
  The cheek that was freshly fair;
Oh, cruelly sad is the tale they tell!
  Consumption revels there.

With panting breath, and wasting frame,
  The languid boy lives on,

With just enough of life to show
  That life will soon be gone!

Pallid and weak, he is slowly led,
Like an infant, from his downy bed;
He turns his dimmed and sunken eye
To look once more upon the sky;
But, ah! he cannot bear the rays
Of a glowing sun to meet his gaze.

He breathes a sigh, and once again
Looks out upon the grassy plain;
He sees his milk-white palfrey there,
His own pet steed, so sleek and fair;
But there's no silken rein to deck
The beauty of his glossy neck;
No saddle-cloth is seen to shine
  Upon its sides — the steed doth lack
A coaxing hand, and seems to pine,
  To miss the one that graced its back.

Young Tracy stands, his azure eye
  Dwells fondly on the favorite brute;
The struggling tear-drop gathers fast,
  But still his lip is mute.

He looks once more in the castle court,
The scene of many a festive sport;
He sees his spaniel dull and lone,
He hears its plaintive whining tone;
He looks beyond the castle wall,
Where he used to play by the waterfall;
He thinks on the days of health and joy,
When he roved abroad with the mountain boy

And the gushing tears start down his cheek,
His eyelids fall — he cannot speak —
He turns away — a damask couch
  Receives his fainting form:
Exhausted, trembling, pale, he sinks,
  Like a lily from the storm!

The mother sits beside the couch,
  Her arm around him thrown,
And bitterly she grieves above
  Her beautiful, her own!

He is dying fast — he murmurs forth
  The name of Hubert Grey,—
"Where — where is he I love so well?
  Why comes he not to-day?

"Oh! bring him to me ere I die" —
  Enough — away! away!
With eager speed dash man and steed,
  To summon Hubert Grey!

And where is he? the herdsman's son,
The bold, the bright, the dauntless one!
The dew is off the shadiest spot,
The noon is nigh — why comes he not?

Long since, the mountain boy was brought
  Within the castle gate;
For none could soothe the pining heir,
  Like his old and lowly mate.

And, true as sunrise, with the dawn
Hath Hubert bent his steps at morn

Over the crags where torrents roar,
To tarry till night with Tracy de Vore!
But where is he now? the sun is hot,
The noon is past — why comes he not?

The vassal Oswald wends his way:
  To Hubert's home he hies;
To the herdsman's hut that stands alone,
Where cataract streams dash wildly on,
  Where giant mountains rise.

He calls aloud: "Hist, Hubert Grey!
Quick! back with me on the gallant bay!
  Why have ye kept so long away?
The darling heir is dying fast;
This day, this hour may be his last! —
  Come, haste thee, quick, I say!"

The door flings back — the herdsman's wife
  Comes forth with wondering look;
"'Tis strange!" she cries, "three hours ago
He started, with his staff and bow,
  And the castle way he took!

"He talked of gathering for the heir
A bunch of wild-flowers, sweet and rare —
He talked of climbing Morna's height,
  Where the large blue-bells grow;
They overhang — yes, yes — oh Heaven! —
  That dark ravine below!

"Hubert! my child! where art thou gone?
  Thy mother calls to thee!"
No answer! — "To the rock!" she cries —
  "On, Oswald! on with me!"

Together, up the craggy path,
  Speed Oswald and the herdsman's wife:
She calls and listens — calls again —
  Her heart with fear is rife.

And Oswald gives the well-known sign;
  He whistles shrill and clear;
He winds his horn, and blows the blast
  That Hubert loved to hear.

But ah! the whistle and the horn
  Are only echoed back;
No Hubert comes — and now they reach
  The highest mountain track.

The foot of Oswald presses on
  Right cautiously and slow;
For few would dare, like Hubert Grey,
  Near Morna's edge to go!

The dark gulf breaks with frightful yawn,
  Terrific to the gaze;
A murky horror shades the spot,
  Beneath meridian rays.

But hush! — that sound — a hollow moan —
Again, a stifled, gurgling groan!
The mother stands, nor speaks, nor moves,
  Transfixed with mute dismay!
The vassal fears, his footsteps shrink,
He trembles as he gains the brink;
He shudders, looks with straining eyes
Adown the abyss — "Oh God!" he cries,
  "'Tis he — 'tis Hubert Grey!"

Yes, yes, 'tis he! — the herdsman's son —
The bold, the bright, the dauntless one!
He hath bent him o'er to reach the flowers
  That spring along the dreaded steep;
His brain grows dizzy — yet again —
He snatches, totters, shrieks, in vain —
  He falls ten fathoms deep!

The groan that met his mother's ear
  Gave forth his latest breath;
The mountain boy is sleeping fast
  The dreamless sleep of death!

Thrown wildly back, his clotted hair
Leaves his gashed forehead red and bare.
Look on his cheek — his dauntless brow —
Oh God, there's blood upon them now!
His hand is clenched with stiffened clasp,
The wild-flowers still within its grasp:

The vulture perched upon the crag,
  Seems waiting for its prey;
The vulture that, at morning's light,
  His halloo scared away.

Stretched like a lion-cub he lies;
As wild he lived, as lonely dies;
The mountain-born, the free, the brave,
Too soon hath found a mountain-grave.
And many an eye shall weep his fate,
  And many a heart shall rue the day;
For a brighter being ne'er had life
  Than the herdsman's son, young Hubert Grey

And Tracy de Vore, the Baron's heir,
The meek, the cherub-like, the fair,
He is sinking to eternal rest,
Soft pillowed on his mother's breast;
He knows not that his lowly mate
Hath met so horrible a fate.

No dark convulsion shakes his frame;
  No change comes o'er his face;
The icy hand hath touched his heart,
  But left no scathing trace.

One murmuring sigh escapes his lip;
  The sweetest toned, the last;
Like the faint echo harp-strings give
  Of thrilling music past.

The signet seal of other worlds
  Falls softly on his brow;
He seemed but sleeping when it came,
  He seems but sleeping now.

For death steals softly and smilingly
  To close his earthly day;
Like the autumn breeze that gently wafts
  The summer leaf away.

The Baron weeps; his look declares
  All hope, all joy has fled;
His soul's adored, his house's pride,
  His only born, is dead.
The castle is dark — no sound is heard
  But the wailing of deep despair;

The lord and the vassal are mourning aloud
  For the well loved, noble heir!
Oh, truly does every heart deplore
  The young and beautiful Tracy de Vore!

And sorrow hath found a dwelling-place
  In the herdsman's lowly hut;
The door is fast against the sun,
  The casement is closely shut.

Death gave no warning *there*, but struck
  With a fierce and cruel blow;
Like the barb that sinks from hand unseen
  In the heart of the bounding roe.

The mother laments with a maniac's grief;
  Her sobbing is bitterly loud;
Her eye is fixed on her mangled boy,
  As he lies in his winding shroud.

The herdsman's voice hath lost its tone;
  His brow is shaded o'er;
There's a hopeless anguish in his breast,
  That he never felt before.

There's a tear on his cheek when the sun gets up;
  He sighs at the close of day;
His mates would offer the cheering cup,
  But he turns his lip away:
He mourns for the one that promised well
To walk his land like another Tell!

The doleful tidings speed swiftly on
Of the promising spirits forever gone;
And the words fall sadly on the ear
Of every listening mountaineer.

They grieve for their own, their free-born child,
Nestled and reared mid the vast and wild;
For there trod not the hills a dearer one
To the hearts of all than the herdsman's son.

They sigh to look on the turrets below,
And think 'tis the lordly abode of wo;
They sigh to miss from the waterfall's side,
The mountain boy and the Baron's pride!

And many a tongue shall tell the tale,
  And many a heart shall rue the day,
When the hut and castle lost their hopes
  In Tracy de Vore and Hubert Grey!

MISCELLANEOUS POEMS.

THE OLD ARM-CHAIR.

I LOVE it, I love it; and who shall dare
To chide me for loving that old arm-chair?
I've treasured it long as a sainted prize,
I've bedewed it with tears, and embalmed it with sighs;
'Tis bound by a thousand bands to my heart:
Not a tie will break, not a link will start.
Would ye learn the spell? a mother sat there,
And a sacred thing is that old arm-chair.

In childhood's hour I lingered near
The hallowed seat with listening ear;
And gentle words that mother would give,
To fit me to die and teach me to live.
She told me shame would never betide,
With truth for my creed and God for my guide;
She taught me to lisp my earliest prayer,
As I knelt beside that old arm-chair.

I sat and watched her many a day,
When her eye grew dim, and her locks were gray;
And I almost worshipped her when she smiled
And turned from her Bible to bless her child.

Years rolled on, but the last one sped —
My idol was shattered, my earth-star fled;
I learnt how much the heart can bear,
When I saw her die in that old arm-chair.

'Tis past! 'tis past! but I gaze on it now
With quivering breath and throbbing brow:
'Twas there she nursed me, 'twas there she died;
And memory flows with lava tide.
Say it is folly, and deem me weak,
While the scalding drops start down my cheek
But I love it, I love it, and cannot tear
My soul from a mother's old arm-chair.

SONG OF THE RUSHLIGHT.

Oh, scorn me not as a fameless thing,
Nor turn with contempt from the song I sing.
'Tis true I am not suffered to be
On the ringing board of wassail glee;
My pallid gleam must never fall
In the gay saloon or lordly hall;
But many a tale does the rushlight know
Of secret sorrow and lonely wo.

I am found in the closely-curtained room,
Where a stillness reigns that breathes of the tomb.
Where the breaking heart and heavy eye
Are waiting to see a loved one die —

Where the doting child with noiseless tread
Steals warily to the mother's bed,
To mark if the faint and struggling breath
Is fluttering still in the grasp of death.

The panting has ceased, the cheek is still,
And the ear of the child bends closer still.
It rests on the lips, but listens in vain,
For those lips have done with life and pain;
I am wildly snatched, and held above
The precious wreck of hope and love.
The work is sealed, for my glimmering ray
Shows a glazing eye and stiff'ning clay.

I am the light that quivering flits
In the joyless home where the fond wife sits,
Waiting the one that flies his hearth,
For the gambler's dice and drunkard's mirth.
Long hath she kept her wearying watch,
Now bitterly weeping, now breathless to catch
The welcome sound of a footstep near,
Till she weeps again as it dies on her ear.

Her restless gaze, as the night wears late,
Is anxiously thrown on the dial plate;
And a sob responds to the echoing sound
That tells the hand hath gone its round:
She mournfully trims my slender wick,
As she sees me fading and wasting quick;
And many a time has my spark expired,
And left her still the weeping and tired.

I am the light that dimly shines
Where the friendless child of genius pines —

Where the godlike mind is trampled down
By the callous sneer and freezing frown —
Where Want is playing a demon part,
And sends its iron to the heart,—
Where the soul burns on in the bosom that mourns
Like the incense fire in funeral urns.

I see the hectic fingers fling
The thoughts intense that flashingly spring,
And my flickering beam illumes the page
That may live in the fame of a future age;
I see the pale brow droop and mope,
Till the breast turns sick with blasted hope —
Till the harsh cold world has done its worst,
And the goaded spirit has groaned and burst.

I am the light that's doomed to share
The meanest lot that man can bear;
I see the scanty portion spread,
Where children struggle for scraps of bread —
Where squalid forms and faces seem
Like phantoms in a hideous dream —
Where the soul may look, with startled awe,
On the work of Poverty's vulture claw.

Many a lesson the bosom learns
Of hapless grief while the rushlight burns;
Many a scene unfolds to me
That the heart of Mercy would bleed to see:
Then scorn me not as a fameless thing,
Nor turn with contempt from the song I sing;
But smile as ye will, or scorn as ye may,
There's naught but truth to be found in my lay.

THE MOTHER WHO HAS A CHILD AT SEA.

There's an eye that looks on the swelling cloud,
Folding the moon in a funeral shroud,
That watches the stars dying one by one,
Till the whole of heaven's calm light hath gone,
There's an ear that lists to the hissing surge,
As the mourner turns to the anthem dirge:
That eye! that ear! oh, whose can they be,
But a mother's who hath a child at sea?

There's a cheek that is getting ashy white,
As the tokens of storm come on with night;
There's a form that's fixed at the lattice pane,
To mark how the gloom gathers over the main,
While the yeasty billows lash the shore
With loftier sweep and hoarser roar:
That cheek! that form! oh, whose can they be,
But a mother's who hath a child at sea?

The rushing whistle chills her blood,
As the north wind hurries to scourge the flood;
And the icy shiver spreads to her heart,
As the first red lines of lightning start.
The ocean boils! All mute she stands,
With parted lips and tight-clasped hands:
Oh, marvel not at her fear, for she
Is a mother who hath a child at sea.

She conjures up the fearful scene
Of yawning waves, where the ship between,

With striking keel and splintered mast,
Is plunging hard and foundering fast.
She sees her boy, with lank drenched hair,
Clinging on to the wreck with a cry of despair
Oh, the vision is madd'ning! No grief can be
Like a mother's who hath a child at sea.

She presses her brow — she sinks and kneels,
Whilst the blast howls on and the thunder peals:
She breathes not a word, for her passionate prayer
Is too fervent and deep for the lips to bear;
It is poured in the long convulsive sigh,
In the straining glance of an upturned eye,
And a holier offering cannot be
Than the mother's prayer for her child at sea.

Oh! I love the winds when they spurn control,
For they suit my own bond-hating soul;
I like to hear them sweeping past,
Like the eagle's pinions, free and fast;
But a pang will rise, with sad alloy,
To soften my spirit and sink my joy,
When I think how dismal their voices must be
To a mother who hath a child at sea!

OH! DEAR TO MEMORY ARE THOSE HOURS.

Oh! dear to memory are those hours
When every pathway led to flowers;
When sticks of peppermint possessed
A sceptre's power o'er the breast,
And heaven was round us while we fed
On rich ambrosial gingerbread.
I bless the days of infancy,
When, stealing from a mother's eye,
Elysian happiness was found
On that celestial field, the ground;
When we were busied, hands and hearts,
In those important things, dirt tarts.
Don't smile, for sapient, full-grown man,
Oft cogitates some mighty plan;
And, spell-bound by the bubble dream,
He labors till he proves the scheme
About as useful and as wise
As manufacturing dirt pies:
There's many a change on Folly's bells
Quite equals mud and oyster shells.

Then shone the meteor rays of youth,
Eclipsing quite the lamp of truth;
And precious those bright sunbeams were
That dried all tears, dispersed all care;
That shed a stream of golden joy,
Without one atom of alloy.
Oh! ne'er in mercy strive to chase
Such dazzling phantoms from their place!

However trifling, mean, or wild,
The deeds may seem of youth or child,
While they still leave untarnished soul,
The iron rod of stern control
Should be but gentle in its sway,
Nor rend the magic veil away.

I doubt if it be kind or wise
To quench the light in opening eyes,
By preaching fallacy and wo
As all that we can meet below.
I ne'er respect the ready tongue
That augurs sorrow to the young;
That aptly plays a sybil's part,
To promise nightshade to the heart.
Let them exult! their laugh and song
Are rarely known to last too long.
Why should we strive with cynic frown
To knock their fairy castles down?
We know that much of pain and strife
Must be the common lot of life:
We know the world *is* dark and rough,
But time betrays that soon enough!

SPRING.

WELCOME, all hail to thee!
Welcome, young Spring!
Thy sun-ray is bright
On the butterfly's wing.
Beauty shines forth
In the blossom-robed trees;
Perfume floats by
On the soft southern breeze.

Music, sweet music,
Sounds over the earth;
One glad choral song
Greets the primrose's birth;
The lark soars above,
With its shrill matin strain;
The shepherd boy tunes
His reed pipe on the plain.

Music, sweet music,
Cheers meadow and lea;—
In the song of the blackbird,
The hum of the bee;
The loud happy laughter
Of children at play
Proclaim how they worship
Spring's beautiful day,

The eye of the hale one,
With joy in its gleam,

Looks up in the noontide,
And steals from the beam;
But the cheek of the pale one
Is marked with despair,
To feel itself fading,
When all is so fair.

The hedges, luxuriant
With flowers and balm,
Are purple with violets,
And shaded with palm;
The zephyr-kissed grass
Is beginning to wave;
Fresh verdure is decking
The garden and grave.

Welcome! all hail to thee,
Heart-stirring May!
Thou hast won from my wild harp
A rapturous lay.
And the last dying murmur
That sleeps on the string
Is welcome. All hail to thee
Welcome, young Spring!

SAILING SONG.

We have left the still earth for the billows and breeze
'Neath the brightest of moons on the bluest of seas;
We have music — hark! hark! there's a tone o'er the deep
Like the murmuring breath of a lion asleep.
There's enough of bold dash in the rich foam that laves
Just to whisper the slumber-wrapt might of the waves;
But yet there's a sweetness about the full swell
Like the sound of the mermaid — the chords of the shell.

We have jewels. Oh! what is your casket of gems
To the pearls hanging thick on the red coral stems?
Are there homes of more light than the one where we are,
For it nestles the dolphin and mirrors the star?
We may creep, we may scud, we may rest, we may fly;
There's no check to our speed, there's no dust for our eye;
Oh! well may our spirits grow wild as the breeze,
'Neath the brightest of moons on the bluest of seas!

THE GIPSY'S TENT.

Our fire on the turf, and our tent 'neath a tree –
Carousing by moonlight, how merry are we!
Let the lord boast his castle, the baron his hall,
But the house of the gipsy is widest of all.
We may shout o'er our cups, and laugh loud as we will,
Till echo rings back from wood, welkin, and hill;
No joys seem to us like the joys that are lent
To the wanderer's life and the gipsy's tent.

Some crime and much folly may fall to our lot;
We have sins, but pray where is the one who has not?
We are rogues, arrant rogues:—yet remember! 'tis rare
We take but from those who can very well spare.
You may tell us of deeds justly branded with shame,
But if great ones heard truth you could tell them the same:
And there's many a king would have less to repent,
If his throne were as pure as the gipsy's tent.

Pant ye for beauty? Oh, where would ye seek
Such bloom as is found on the tawny one's cheek?
Our limbs, that go bounding in freedom and health,
Are worth all your pale faces and coffers of wealth.
There are none to control us; we rest or we roam;
Our will is our law, and the world is our home:
E'en Jove would repine at *his* lot if he spent
A night of wild glee in the gipsy's tent.

THE FREE.

The wild streams leap with headlong sweep
In their curbless course o'er the mountain steep
All fresh and strong they foam along,
Waking the rocks with their cataract song.
My eye bears a glance like the beam on a lance,
While I watch the waters dash and dance;
I burn with glee, for I love to see
The path of any thing that's free.

The skylark springs with dew on his wings,
And up in the arch of heaven he sings
Trill-la, trill-la — oh, sweeter far
Than the notes that come through a golden bar.
The joyous bay of a hound at play,
The caw of the rook on its homeward way —
Oh! these shall be the music for me,
For I love the voices of the free.

The deer starts by with his antlers high,
Proudly tossing his head to the sky;
The barb runs the plain unbroke by the rein,
With streaming nostrils and flying mane;
The clouds are stirred by the eaglet bird,
As the flap of its swooping pinion is heard.
Oh! these shall be the creatures for me,
For my soul was formed to love the free.

The mariner brave, in his bark on the wave,
May laugh at the walls round a kingly slave;
And the one whose lot is the desert spot
Has no dread of an envious foe in his cot.
The thrall and state at the palace gate
Are what my spirit has learnt to hate:
Oh! the hills shall be a home for me,
For I'd leave a throne for the hut of the free.

WINTER.

We know 'tis good that old Winter should come,
Roving a while from his Lapland home;
'Tis fitting that we should hear the sound
Of his reindeer sledge on the slippery ground:

For his wide and glittering cloak of snow
Protects the seeds of life below;
Beneath his mantle are nurtured and born
The roots of the flowers, the germs of the corn.

The whistling tone of his pure strong breath
Rides purging the vapors of pestilent death.
I love him, I say, and avow it again,
For God's wisdom and might show well in his train.

But the naked — the poor! I know they quail
With crouching limbs from the biting gale;

They pine and starve by the fireless hearth,
And weep as they gaze on the frost-bound earth.

Stand nobly forth, ye rich of the land,
With kindly heart and bounteous hand
Remember 'tis now their season of need,
And a prayer for help is a call ye must heed.

A few of thy blessings, a tithe of thy gold,
Will save the young, and cherish the old.
'Tis a glorious task to work such good —
Do it, ye great ones! Ye can, and ye should.

He is not worthy to hold from heaven
The trust reposed, the talents given,
Who will not add to the portion that's scant,
In the pinching hours of cold and want.

Oh! listen in mercy, ye sons of wealth,
Basking in comfort and glowing with health;
Give whate'er ye can spare, and be ye sure
He serveth his Maker who aideth the poor

SNOW.

BRAVE Winter and I shall ever agree,
Though a stern and frowning gaffer is he.
I like to hear him, with hail and rain,
Come tapping against the window pane;
I joy to see him come marching forth
Begirt with the icicle gems of the north;
But I like him best when he comes bedight
In his velvet robes of stainless white.

A cheer for the snow — the drifting snow!
Smoother and purer than beauty's brow!
The creature of thought scarce likes to tread
On the delicate carpet so richly spread.
With feathery wreaths the forest is bound,
And the hills are with glittering diadems crowned
'Tis the fairest scene we can have below.
Sing, welcome, then, to the drifting snow!

The urchins gaze with eloquent eye
To see the flakes go dancing by.
In the thick of the storm how happy are they
To welcome the first deep snowy day!
Shouting and pelting — what bliss to fall
Half-smothered beneath the well-aimed ball!
Men of four-score, did ye ever know
Such sport as ye had in the drifting snow?

I'm true to my theme, for I loved it well.
When the gossiping nurse would sit and tell

The tale of the geese — though hardly believed —
I doubted and questioned the words that deceived.
I rejoice in it still, and love to see
The ermine mantle on tower and tree.
'Tis the fairest scene we can have below.
Hurrah! then, hurrah! for the drifting snow!

THE GIPSY CHILD.

He sprung to life in a crazy tent,
Where the cold wind whistled through many a rent;
Rude was the voice, and rough were the hands
That soothed his wailings and swathed his bands.
No tissue of gold, no lawn was there,
No snowy robe for the new-born heir;
But the mother wept, and the father smiled
With heartfelt joy o'er their gipsy child.

He grows like the young oak, healthy and broad,
With no home but the forest, no bed but the sward
Half naked, he wades in the limpid stream,
Or dances about in the scorching beam.
The dazzling glare of the banquet sheen
Hath never fallen on him, I ween;
But fragments are spread and the wood-fire piled,
And sweet is the meal of the gipsy child.

He wanders at large, while maidens admire
His raven hair and his eyes of fire;
They mark his cheek's rich tawny hue,
With the deep carnation flushing through:
He laughs aloud, and they covet his teeth,
All pure and white as their own pearl wreath;
And the courtly dame and damsel mild
Will turn to gaze on the gipsy child.

Up with the sun, he is roving along,
Whistling to mimic the blackbird's song;
He wanders at nightfall to startle the owl,
And is baying again to the watch-dog's howl.
His limbs are unshackled, his spirit is bold,
He is free from the evils of fashion and gold
His dower is scant and his life is wild,
But kings might envy the gipsy child.

THE QUIET EYE.

THE orb I like is not the one
 That dazzles with its lightning gleam,
That dares to look upon the sun
 As though it challenged brighter beam.
That orb may sparkle, flash, and roll;
 Its fire may blaze, its shaft may fly;
But not for me: I prize the soul
 That slumbers in a quiet eye.

There's something in its placid shade
  That tells of calm unworldly thought;
Hope may be crowned, or joy delayed —
  No dimness steals, no ray is caught:
Its pensive language seems to say,
  "I know that I must close and die;
And death itself, come when it may,
  Can hardly change the quiet eye.

There's meaning in its steady glance,
  Of gentle blame or praising love,
That makes me tremble to advance
  A word that meaning might reprove.
The haughty threat, the fiery look,
  My spirit proudly can defy;
But never yet could meet and brook
  The upbraiding of a quiet eye.

There's firmness in its even light,
  That augurs of a breast sincere:
And, oh! take watch how ye excite
  That firmness till it yield a tear.
Some bosoms give an easy sigh,
  Some drops of grief will freely start;
But that which sears the quiet eye
  Hath its deep fountain in the heart.

OLD DOBBIN.

HERE'S a song for old Dobbin, whose temper and worth
Are too rare to be spurned on the score of his birth.
He's a creature of trust, and what more should we heed?
'Tis deeds and not blood make the man and the steed.

He was bred in the forest, and turned on the plain,
Where the thistle-burs clung to his fetlocks and mane.
All ugly and rough, not a soul could espy
The spark of good-humor that dwelt in his eye.

The summer had waned, and the autumn months rolled
Into those of stern winter, all dreary and cold;
But the north wind might whistle, the snow-flake might
dance,
The colt of the common was left to his chance.

Half starved and half frozen, the hail-storm would pelt,
Till his shivering limbs told the pangs that he felt;
But we pitied the brute, and, though laughed at by all,
We filled him a manger and gave him a stall.

He was fond as a spaniel, and soon he became
The pride of the herd-boy, the pet of the dame.
You may judge of his fame, when his price was a
crown;
But we christened him Dobbin, and called him our own.

He grew out of colthood, and, lo! what a change!
The knowing ones said it was mortally strange;

For the foal of the forest, the colt of the waste,
Attracted the notice of jockeys of taste.

The line of his symmetry was not exact;
But his paces were clever, his mould was compact:
And his shaggy thick coat now appeared with a gloss,
Shining out like the gold that's been purged of its
dross.

We broke him for service, and tamely he wore
Girth and rein, seeming proud of the thraldom he bore;
Every farm has a steed for all work and all hours,
And Dobbin, the sturdy bay pony, was ours.

He carried the master to barter his grain,
And ever returned with him safely again:
There was merit in that, for deny it who may,
When the master could *not*, Dobbin *could* find his way.

The dairy-maid ventured her eggs on his back:
'Twas him, and him only, she'd trust with the pack.
The team horses jolted, the roadster played pranks,
So Dobbin alone had her faith and her thanks.

We fun-loving urchins would group by his side;
We might fearlessly mount him, and daringly ride;
We might creep through his legs, we might plait his
long tail;
But his temper and patience were ne'er known to fail.

We would brush his bright hide till 'twas free from a
speck;
We kissed his brown muzzle, and hugged his thick
neck;

Oh! we prized him like life, and a heart-breaking sob
Ever burst when they threatened to sell our dear Dob.

He stood to the collar, and tugged up the hill,
With the pigs to the market, the grist to the mill;
With saddle or halter, in shaft or in trace,
He was staunch to his work, and content with his place.

When the hot sun was crowning the toil of the year,
He was sent to the reapers with ale and good cheer;
And none in the corn-field more welcome was seen
Than Dob and his well-laden panniers, I ween.

Oh! those days of pure bliss shall I ever forget,
When we decked out his head with the azure rosette;
All frantic with joy to be off to the fair,
With Dobbin, good Dobbin, to carry us there?

He was dear to us all, ay, for many long years;
But, mercy! how's this? my eye's filling with tears.
Oh! how cruelly sweet are the echoes that start
When Memory plays an old tune on the heart!

There are drops on my cheek, there's a throb in my breast,
But my song shall not cease, nor my pen take its rest,
Till I tell that old Dobbin still lives to be seen,
With his oats in the stable, his tares on the green.

His best years have gone by, and the master who gave
The stern yoke to his youth has enfranchised the slave.
So browse on, my old Dobbin, nor dream of the knife,
For the wealth of a king should not purchase thy life.

THE OLD FARM-GATE.

WHERE, where is the gate that once served to divide
The elm-shaded lane from the dusty road-side?
I like not this barrier gaily bedight,
With its glittering latch and its trellis of white.
It is seemly, I own—yet, oh! dearer by far
Was the red-rusted hinge and the weather-warped bar.
Here are fashion and form of a modernized date,
But I'd rather have looked on the old farm-gate.

'Twas here where the urchins would gather to play
In the shadows of twilight or sunny mid-day;
For the stream running nigh, and the hillocks of sand,
Were temptations no dirt-loving rogue could withstand.
But to swing on the gate-rails, to clamber and ride,
Was the utmost of pleasure, of glory, and pride;
And the car of the victor or carriage of state
Never carried such hearts as the old farm-gate.

'Twas here where the miller's son paced to and fro,
When the moon was above and the glow-worms below;
Now pensively leaning, now twirling his stick,
While the moments grew long and his heart-throbs
grew quick.
Why, why did he linger so restlessly there,
With church-going vestment and sprucely combed
hair?
He loved, oh! he loved, and had promised to wait
For the one he adored, at the old farm-gate.

'Twas here where the gray-headed gossips would meet;
And the falling of markets, or goodness of wheat —
This field lying farrow — that heifer just bought —
Were favorite themes for discussion and thought.
The merits and faults of a neighbor just dead —
The hopes of a couple about to be wed —
The Parliament doings — the bill and debate —
Were all canvassed and weighed at the old farm-gate.

'Twas over that gate I taught Pincher to bound
With the strength of a steed and the grace of a hound.
The beagle might hunt, and the spaniel might swim,
But none could leap over that postern like him.
Wnen Dobbin was saddled for mirth-making trip,
And the quickly-pulled willow-branch served for a whip,
Spite of lugging and tugging he'd stand for his freight,
While I climbed on his back from the old farm-gate.

'Tis well to pass portals where pleasure and fame
May come winging our moments and gilding our name;
But give me the joy and the freshness of mind,
When, away on some sport — the old gate slammed behind —
I've listened to music, but none that could speak
In such tones to my heart as the teeth-setting creak
That broke on my ear when the night had worn late,
And the dear ones came home through the old farm-gate.

Oh! fair is the barrier taking its place,
But it darkens a picture my soul longed to trace.
I sigh to behold the rough staple and hasp,
And the rails that my growing hand scarcely could clasp.

Oh! how strangely the warm spirit grudges to part
With the commonest relic once linked to the heart!
And the brightest of fortune — the kindliest fate —
Would not banish my love for the old farm-gate.

BUTTERCUPS AND DAISIES.

I NEVER see a young hand hold
The starry bunch of white and gold,
But something warm and fresh will start
About the region of my heart.
My smile expires into a sigh;
I feel a struggling in the eye,
'Twixt humid drop and sparkling ray,
Till rolling tears have won their way;
For soul and brain will travel back
  Through memory's checkered mazes,
To days when I but trod life's track
  For buttercups and daisies.

Tell me, ye men of wisdom rare,
Of sober speech and silver hair,
Who carry counsel, wise and sage,
With all the gravity of age;
Oh! say, do ye not like to hear
The accents ringing in your ear,
When sportive urchins laugh and shout,
Tossing those precious flowers about

Springing with bold and gleesome bound,
  Proclaiming joy that crazes,
And chorusing the magic sound
  Of buttercups and daisies?

Are there, I ask, beneath the sky
Blossoms that knit so strong a tie
With childhood's love? Can any please
Or light the infant eye like these?
No, no; there's not a bud on earth,
Of richest tint or warmest birth,
Can ever fling such zeal and zest
Into the tiny hand and breast.
Who does not recollect the hours
  When burning words and praises
Were lavished on those shining flowers,
  Buttercups and daisies?

There seems a bright and fairy spell
About their very names to dwell;
And though old Time has marked my brow
With care and thought, I love them now.
Smile, if ye will, but some heart-strings
Are closest linked to simplest things;
And these wild flowers will hold mine fast,
Till love, and life, and all be past;
And then the only wish I have
  Is that the one who raises
The turf-sod o'er me plant my grave
  With buttercups and daisies.

THE IDIOT BORN.

"Out, thou silly moon-struck elf;
Back, poor fool, and hide thyself!"
This is what the wise ones say,
Should the idiot cross their way,
But if we would closely mark,
We should see him not *all* dark;
We should find we must not scorn
The teaching of the idiot-born.

He will screen the newt and frog;
He will cheer the famished dog;
He will seek to share his bread
With the orphan, parish fed;
He will offer up his seat
To the stranger's wearied feet.
Selfish tyrants, do not scorn
The teaching of the idiot-born.

Use him fairly, he will prove
How the simple breast can love;
He will spring with infant glee
To the form he likes to see.
Gentle speech or kindness done
Truly binds the witless one.
Heartless traitors, do not scorn
The teaching of the idiot-born.

He will point with vacant stare
At the robes proud churchmen wear

But he'll pluck the rose, and tell
God hath painted it right well.
He will kneel before his food.
Softly saying, "God is good."
Haughty prelates, do not scorn
The teaching of the idiot-born.

Art thou great as man can be?—
The same hand moulded him and thee.
Hast thou talent?—Taunt and jeer
Must not fall upon his ear.
Spurn him not; the blemished part
Had better be the head than heart.
Thou wilt be the fool to scorn
The teaching of the idiot-born.

THE POET.

Look on the sky, all broad and fair;
Sons of the earth, what see ye there?
The rolling clouds to feast thine eye
With golden burnish and Tyrian dye;
The rainbow's arch, the sun of noon,
The stars of eve, the midnight moon:
These, these to the coldest gaze are bright
They are marked by all for their glory and light;
But tbeir color and rays shed a richer beam
As they shine to illumine the poet's dream.

Children of pleasure, how ye dote
On the dulcet harp and tuneful note —
Holding your breath to drink the strain,
Till throbbing joy dissolves in pain.
There's not a spell aught else can fling
Like the warbling voice and the silver string;
But a music to other ears unknown,
Of deeper thrill and sweeter tone,
Comes in the wild and gurgling stream
To the poet rapt in his blissful dream.

The earth may have its buried stores
Of lustrous jewels and coveted ores;
Ye may gather hence the marble stone
To house a monarch or wall a throne;
Its gold may fill the grasping hand,
Its gems may flash in the sceptre wand;
Bnt purer treasures and dearer things
Than the coins of misers or trappings of kings —
Gifts and hoards of a choicer kind
Are garnered up in the poet's mind.

The mother so loves that the world holds none
To match with her own fair lisping one;
The wedded youth will nurture his bride
With all the fervor of passion and pride;
Hands will press and beings blend
Till the kindliest ties knit friend to friend.
Oh! the hearts of the many can truly burn,
They can fondly cherish and closely yearn;
But the flame of love is more vivid and strong
That kindles within a child of song.

Life hath much of grief and pain
To sicken the breast and tire the brain;
All brows are shaded by sorrow's cloud,
All eyes are dimmed, all spirits bowed;
Sighs will break from the care-worn breast,
Till death is asked as a pillow of rest;
But the gifted one, oh! who can tell
How his pulses beat and his heart's strings swell?
His secret pangs, *his* throbbing wo
None but himself and his God can know.

Crowds may join in the festive crew,
Their hours may be glad and their pleasures true
They may gaily carouse and fondly believe
There's no greater bliss for the soul to receive.
But ask the poet if he will give
His exquisite moments like them to live;
And the scornful smile on his lips will play,
His eye will flash with exulting ray—
For he knows and feels that to him is given
The joys that yield a glimpse of heaven.

Oh! there's something holy about each spot
Where the weary sleep and strife comes not;
And the good and great ones passed away
Have worshippers still o'er their soulless clay;
But the dust of the bard is most hallowed and dear;
'Tis moistened and blest by the warmest tear.
The prayers of the worthiest breathe his name,
Mourning his loss and guarding his fame;
And the truest homage the dead can have
Is rendered up at the poet's grave

THE SONG OF MARION.

Not yet, not yet. I thought I saw
  The foldings of his plaid.
Alas! 'twas but the mountain pine,
  That cast a fitful shade.
The moon is o'er the highest crag,
  It gilds each tower and tree,
But Wallace comes not back to bless
  The hearts in Ellerslie.

Not yet, not yet. Is that his plume
  I see beneath the hill?
Ah, no! 'tis but the waving fern:
  The heath is lonely still.
Dear Wallace, day-star of my soul,
  Thy Marion weeps for thee;
She fears lest evil should betide
  The guard of Ellerslie.

Not yet, not yet. I heard a sound,
  A distant crashing din;
'Tis but the night-breeze bearing on
  The roar of Corie Lin.
The gray-haired harper cannot rest,
  He keeps his watch with me;
He kneels — he prays that God may shield
  The laird of Ellerslie.

Not yet, not yet. My heart will break:
  Where can the brave one stay?

I know 'tis not his own free will
 That keeps him thus away.
The lion may forsake his lair,
 The dove its nest may flee,
But Wallace loves too well, to leave
 His bride and Ellerslie.

Not yet, not yet. The moon goes down,
 And Wallace is not here;
And still his sleuth-hound howls, and still
 I shed the burning tear.
Oh, come, my Wallace, quickly come,
 As ever, safe and free:
Come, or thy Marion soon will find
 A grave in Ellerslie!

THE SEXTON.

"Mine is the fame most blazoned of all
 Mine is the goodliest trade;
Never was banner so wide as the pall,
 Nor sceptre so feared as the spade."

This is the lay of the sexton gray—
 King of the churchyard he—
While the mournful knell of the tolling bell
 Chimes in with his burden of glee.

He dons a doublet of sober brown,
And a hat of slouching felt;
The mattock is over his shoulder thrown,
The heavy keys clank at his belt.

The dark damp vault now echoes his tread,
While his song rings merrily out;
With a cobweb canopy over his head,
And coffins falling about.

His foot may crush the full-fed worms,
His hand may grasp a shroud,
His gaze may rest on skeleton forms,
Yet his tones are light and loud.

He digs the grave, and his chant will break
As he gains a fathom deep —
"Whoever lies in the bed I make,
I warrant will soundly sleep."

He piles the sod, he raises the stone,
He clips the cypress tree;
But whate'er his task, 'tis plied alone —
No fellowship holds he.

For the sexton gray is a scaring loon —
His name is linked with death.
The children at play, should he cross their way,
Will pause with fluttering breath.

They herd together, a frightened host,
And whisper with lips all white, —
"See, see, 'tis he, that sends the ghost
To walk the world at night."

The old men mark him, with fear in their eye,
At his labor mid skulls and dust;
They hear him chant, "The young *may* die,
But we know the aged *must*."

The rich will frown, as his ditty goes on —
"Though broad your lands may be,
Six narrow feet to the beggar I mete,
And the same shall serve for ye."

The ear of the strong will turn from his song,
And Beauty's cheek will pale;
"Out, out," cry they, "what creature would stay,
To list thy croaking tale!"

Oh! the sexton gray is a mortal of dread;
None like to see him come near;
The orphan thinks on a father dead,
The widow wipes a tear.

All shudder to hear his bright axe chink,
Upturning the hollow bone;
No mate will share his toil or his fare,
He works, he carouses alone,

By night, or by day, this, this is his lay:
"Mine is the goodliest trade;
Never was banner so wide as the pall,
Nor sceptre so feared as the spade."

NATURE'S GENTLEMAN.

Whom do we dub as gentlemen ? The knave, the fool, the brute —
If they but own full tithe of gold and wear a courtly suit !
The parchment scroll of titled line, the riband at the knee,
Can still suffice to ratify and grant such high degree :
But nature, with a matchless hand, sends forth *her* nobly born,
And laughs the paltry attributes of wealth and rank to scorn ;
She moulds with care a spirit rare, half human, half divine,
And cries exulting, "Who can make a gentleman like mine ? "

She may not spend her common skill about the outward part,
But showers beauty, grace, and light, upon the brain and heart ?
She may not choose ancestral fame his pathway to illume —
The sun that sheds the brightest day may rise from mist and gloom.
Should fortune pour her welcome store, and useful gold abound,
He shares it with a bounteous hand and scatters blessings round.

The treasure sent is rightly spent, and serves the end
designed,
When held by nature's gentleman, the good, the just,
the kind.

He turns not from the cheerless home, where sorrow's
offsprings dwell;
He'll greet the peasant in his hut — the culprit in his
cell.
He stays to hear the widow's plaint of deep and mourn-
ing love,
He seeks to aid her lot below, and prompt her faith
above.
The orphan child, the friendless one, the luckless, or
the poor,
Will never meet his spurning frown, or leave his bolted
door;
His kindred circles all mankind, his country all the
globe —
An honest name his jewelled star, and truth his ermine
robe.

He wisely yields his passions up to reason's firm con-
trol —
His pleasures are of crimeless kind, and never taint the
soul.
He may be thrown among the gay and reckless sons of
life,
But will not love the revel scene, or head the brawling
strife.
He wounds no breast with jeer or jest, yet bears no
honeyed tongue!
He's social with the gray-haired one and merry with
the young;

He gravely shares the council-speech or joins the rustic game,
And shines as nature's gentleman, in every place the same.

No haughty gesture marks his gait, no pompous tone his word,
No studied attitude is seen, no palling nonsense heard;
He'll suit his bearing to the hour — laugh, listen, learn, or teach,
With joyous freedom in his mirth, and candor in his speech.
He worships God with inward zeal, and serves him in each deed;
He would not blame another's faith nor have one martyr bleed;
Justice and mercy form his code; he puts his trust in Heaven;
His prayer is, "If the heart mean well, may all else be forgiven!"

Though few of such may gem the earth, yet such rare gems there are,
Each shining in his hallowed sphere as virtue's polar star.
Though human hearts too oft are found all gross, corrupt, and dark,
Yet, yet some bosoms breathe and burn; lit by Promethean spark,
There are some spirits nobly just, unwarped by pelf or pride.
Great in the calm, but greater still when dashed by adverse tide,—

They hold the rank no king can give, no station can disgrace,
Nature puts forth *her* gentleman, and monarchs must give place.

THE SABBATH BELL.

PEAL on, peal on, I love to hear
The old church ding-dong soft and clear!
The welcome sounds are doubly blest
With future hope and earthly rest.
Yet were no calling changes found
To spread their cheering echoes round,
There's not a place where man may dwell,
But he can hear a Sabbath bell.

Go to the woods, when Winter's song
Howls like a famished wolf along;
Or when the south winds scarcely turn
The light leaves of the trembling fern,
Although no cloister chimes ring there,
The heart is called to faith and prayer;
For all Creation's voices tell
The tidings of the Sabbath bell.

Go to the billows, let them pour
In gentle calm or headlong roar;
Let the vast ocean be thy home,
Thou'lt find a God upon the foam;

In rippling swell or stormy roll,
The crystal waves shall wake thy soul;
And thou shalt feel the hallowed spell
Of the wide water's Sabbath bell.

The lark upon his skyward way.
The robin on the hedge-row spray,
The bee within the wild thyme's bloom,
The owl amid the cypress gloom,
All sing in every varied tone
A vesper to the Great Unknown.
Above — below — one chorus swells
Of God's unnumbered Sabbath bells.

HANG UP HIS HARP; HE'LL WAKE NO MORE!

His young bride stood beside his bed,
  Her weeping watch to keep;
Hush! hush! he stirred not — was he dead,
  Or did he only sleep?

His brow was calm, no change was there
  No sigh had filled his breath;
Oh! did he wear that smile so fair
  In slumber or in death?

"Reach down his harp," she wildly cried
  "And if one spark remain,

Let him but hear 'Loch Erroch's side;'
He'll kindle at the strain.

"That tune e'er held his soul in thrall;
It never breathed in vain;
He'll waken as its echoes fall,
Or never wake again."

The strings were swept. 'Twas sad to hear
Sweet music floating there;
For every note called forth a tear
Of anguish and despair.

"See! see!" she cried, "the tune is o'er,
No opening eye, no breath;
Hang up his harp; he'll wake no more;
He sleeps the sleep of death."

TO A FAVORITE PONY.

Come, hie thee on, my gentle Gyp;
Thy rider bears nor spur nor whip,
But smooths thy jetty, shining mane,
And loosely flings the bridle-rein.

The sun is down behind the hill,
The noise is hushed about the mill,
The gabbling geese and ducks forsake
Their sports upon the glassy lake,

The herd-boy folds his bleating charge,
The watch-dog, chainless, roves at large,
The bees are gathered in the hive,
The evening flowers their perfumes give
On, on, my gentle Gyp! but stay;
Say, whither shall we bend our way?
Down to the school-house, where the boys
Greet us with rude caressing noise?
Where urchins leave their balls and bats,
To stroke thy neck with fondling pats;
Where laughing girls bring oats and hay,
And coax thy ears; well knowing they
Can sport right fearlessly and free
With such a gentle brute as thee?
Or shall we take the sandy road
Towards the wealthy squire's abode?
Where the lodge gate, so wide and high,
Swings nobly back for you and I;
I'll warrant me, that gate thou'dst find,
Though reinless, riderless, and blind.

Thou'rt restless, Gyp; come, start and go:—
You take the hill; well, be it so —
The squire's abode, I plainly see,
Has equal charms for you and me.
'Tis there thou art allowed to pick
The corners of the clover rick;
'Tis there, by lady's hand thou'rt fed
On pulpy fruit, and finest bread.
The squire himself declares thou art
The prettiest pony round the part:
Nor black, nor chestnut, roan, nor gray,
Can match with thy rich glossy bay

He says, thy neck's proud curving line
The artist's pencil might define;
With blood and spirit, yet so mild,—
A fitting plaything for a child;
So meekly docile, thou'rt indeed
More like a pet lamb than a steed;
That when thou'rt gone, St. Leonard's plain
Will never see thy like again!
He says all this! No wonder, then,
I think the squire the best of men:
For they who praise thy form and paces
Are sure to get in my good graces.

The squire tells truth; to say the least,
Thou really art a clever beast;
A better one, take altogether,
Ne'er looked from out a hempen tether:
And oft, I hope, thou'lt ne'er be having
The plague of glander, gall, or spavin.
Full many a mile thou'st borne me, Gyp,
Without a stumble, shy, or slip;
Excepting, when that deep morass,
All overgrown with weeds and grass,
Betrayed us to a headlong tumble,
And made me feel a little humble;
But on we went, though well bespattered,
Thy knees uncut, *my* bones unshattered!

My gentle Gyp! I've seen thee prove
How fast a twelve hand brute can move;
I've seen thee keep the foremost place
And win the hard contested race;
I've seen thee lift as light a leg
As Tam O'Shanter's famous Meg,

Who galloped on right helter-skelter,
With goblins in her rear to pelt her;
And, closely pressed by evil kind,
Left her unhappy tail behind.
Stop, fair and softly, gentle Gyp—
I've jingled thus far in our trip;
But now we're nigh the well-known gate;
So steady — stand at ease — and wait —
While I restore to hiding-place
My paper and my pencil-case;
Stand steady — and another time
I'll sing thy praise in better rhyme.

A B C.

Oh, thou Alpha Beta row,
Fun and freedom's earliest foe,
Shall I e'er forget the primer,
Thumbed beside some Mrs. Trimmer,—
While mighty problem held me fast,
To know if Z was first or last?
And all Pandora had for me
Was emptied forth in A B C.

Teasing things of toil and trouble,
Fount of many a rolling bubble,
How I strived, with pouting pain,
To get thee quartered on my brain;

But when the giant feat was done,
How nobly wide the field I'd won!
Wit, reason, wisdom, all might be
Enjoyed throngh simple A B C.

Steps that lead to topmost height
Of wordly fame and human might,
Ye win the orator's renown,
The poet's bays, the scholar's gown;
Philosophers must bend and say
'Twas ye who oped their glorious way.
Sage, statesman, critic, where is he
Who's not obliged to A B C?

Ye really ought to be exempt
From slighting taunt and cool contempt;
But drinking deep from learning's cup,
We scorn the hand that filled it up.
Be courteous, pedants — stay and thank
Your servants of the Roman rank,
For F. R. S. and LL. D.
Can only spring from A B C.

A LOVE SONG.

Dear Kate, I do not swear and rave,
  Or sigh sweet things as many can;
But though my lip ne'er plays the slave
  My *heart* will not disgrace the *man*.

I prize thee — ay, my bonnie Kate,
  So firmly fond this breast can be,
That I would brook the sternest fate
  If it but left me health and thee.

I do not promise that our life
  Shall know no shade on heart or brow;
For human lot and mortal strife
  Would mock the falsehood of such vow.
But when the clouds of pain and care
  Shall teach us we are not divine,
My deepest sorrows thou shalt share,
  And I will strive to lighten thine.

We love each other, yet perchance
  The murmurs of dissent may rise;
Fierce words may chase the tender glance,
  And angry flashes light our eyes.
But we must learn to check the frown,
  To reason rather than to blame;
The wisest have their faults to own,
  And you and I, girl, have the same.

You must not like me less, my Kate,
  For such an honest strain as this;
I love *thee* dearly, but I hate
  The puling rhymes of "kiss" and "bliss."
There's truth in all I've said or sung;
  I woo thee as a man *should* woo;
And though I lack a honeyed tongue,
  Thou'lt never find a breast more true.

CUPID'S ARROW.

Young Cupid went storming to Vulcan one day,
And besought him to look at his arrow.
" 'Tis useless," he cried; "you must mend it, I say;
'Tisn't fit to let fly at a sparrow.
There's something that's wrong in the shaft or the dart,
For it flutters quite false to my aim;
'Tis an age since it fairly went home to the heart,
And the world really jests at my name.

"I have straightened, I've bent, I've tried all, I declare,
I've perfumed it with sweetest of sighs;
'Tis feathered with ringlets my mother might wear,
And the barb gleams with light from young eyes;
But it falls without touching — I'll break it, I vow,
For there's Hymen beginning to pout;
He's complaining his torch burns so dull and so low
That Zephyr might puff it right out."

Little Cupid went on with his pitiful tale,
Till Vulcan the weapon restored.
"There, take it, young sir; try it now — if it fail,
I will ask neither fee nor reward."
The urchin shot out, and rare havoc he made;
The wounded and dead were untold;
But no wonder the rogue had such slaughtering trade,
For the arrow was laden with *gold.*

NIGHT.

THE God of day is speeding his way
Through the golden gates of the west;
The rosebud sleeps in the parting ray,
The bird is seeking its nest.

I love the light — yet welcome, Night
For, beneath thy darkling fall
The troubled breast is soothed in rest,
And the slave forgets his thrall.

The peasant child, all strong and wild,
Is growing quiet and meek;
All fire is hid 'neath his heavy lid,
The lashes yearn to the cheek.

He roves no more in gamesome glee,
But hangs his weary head,
And loiters beside the mother's knee
To ask his lowly bed.

The butterflies fold their wings of gold,
The dew falls chill in the bower,
The cattle wait at the kineyard gate,
The bee hath forsaken the flower;

The roar of the city is dying fast,
Its tongues no longer thrill;
The hurrying tread is faint at last,
The artizan's hammer is still.

Night steals apace. She rules supreme;
  A hallowed calm is shed:
No footstep breaks, no whisper wakes —
  'Tis the silence of the dead.

The hollow bay of a distant dog
  Bids drowsy Echo start;
The chiming hour from an old church tower
  Strikes fearfully on the heart.

All spirits are bound in slumber sound,
  Save those o'er a death-bed weeping;
Or the soldier one that paces alone,
  His guard by the watch-fire keeping.

With ebon wand and sable robe,
  How beautiful, Night, art thou!
Serenely set on a throne of jet,
  With stars about thy brow!

Thou com'st to dry the mourner's eye,
  That, wakeful, is ever dim;
To hush for awhile the grieving sigh,
  And give strength to the wearied limb.

Hail to thy sceptre, Ethiop queen!
  Fair mercy marks thy reign;
For the care-worn breast may take its rest,
  And the slave forget his chain.

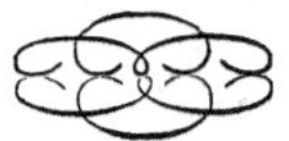

AWAY FROM THE REVEL.

Away from the revel! the night-star is up;
Away, come away, there is strife in the cup!
There is shouting of song, there is wine in the bowl;
But listen and drink, they will madden thy soul!

The foam of the goblet is sparkling and bright,
Rising like gems in the torches' red light;
But the glance of thine eye, if it lingers there,
Will change its mild beam for the maniac's glare.

The pearl-studded chalice, displaying in pride,
May challenge thy lip to the purple draught's tide;
But the pearl of the dew-drop, the voice of the breeze,
Are dearer, and calmer, more blessed than these.

Oh! come, it is twilight; the night-star is up;
Its ray is more bright than the silver-rimmed cup;
The boat gently dances, the snowy sail fills,
We'll glide o'er the waters, or rove on the hills.

We'll kneel on the mountain, beneath the dark pine;
Our hearts' prayer the incense, and nature the shrine;
Back on the festal we'll look from the wave,
As the eye of the free on the chains of the slave!

Oh! come, it is twilight; the moon is awake;
The breath of the vesper-chime rides o'er the lake;
There is peace all around us, and health in the breeze,
And what can be dearer, more blessed than these?

I MISS THEE, MY MOTHER.

I MISS thee, my Mother! Thy image is still
The deepest impressed on my heart,
And the tablet so faithful in death must be chill
Ere a line of that image depart.
Thou wert torn from my side when I treasured thee most —
When my reason could measure thy worth;
When I knew but too well that the idol I'd lost
Could be never replaced upon earth.

I miss thee, my Mother, in circles of joy,
Where I've mingled with rapturous zest;
For how slight is the touch that will serve to destroy
All the fairy web spun in my breast!
Some melody sweet may be floating around —
'Tis a ballad I learnt at thy knee;
Some strain may be played, and I shrink from the sound,
For my fingers oft woke it for thee.

I miss thee, my Mother; when young health has fled,
And I sink in the languor of pain,
Where, where is the arm that once pillowed my head
And the ear that once heard me complain?
Other hands may support, gentle accents may fall —
For the fond and the true are yet mine:
I've a blessing for each; I am grateful to all —
But whose care *can* be soothing as thine?

I miss thee, my Mother, in summer's fair day.
  When I rest in the ivy-wreathed bower,
When I hang thy pet linnet's cage high on the spray,
  Or gaze on thy favorite flower.
There's the bright gravel-path where I played by thy side
  When time had scarce wrinkled thy brow,
Where I carefully led thee with worshipping pride
  When thy scanty locks gathered the snow.

I miss thee, my Mother, in winter's long night:
  I remember the tales thou wouldst tell —
The romance of wild fancy, the legend of fright —
  Oh! who could e'er tell them so well?
Thy corner is vacant: thy chair is removed:
  It was kind to take *that* from my eye:
Yet relics are round me — the sacred and loved
  To call up the pure sorrow-fed sigh.

I miss thee, my Mother! Oh, when do I not?
  Though I know 'twas the wisdom of Heaven
That the deepest shade fell on my sunniest spot,
  And such tie of devotion was riven;
For when thou wert with me my soul was below,
  I was chained to the world I then trod;
My affections, my thoughts, were all earth-bound; but now
  They have followed thy spirit to God!

THERE'S A STAR IN THE WEST.

THERE's a star in the west that shall never go down
  Till the records of valor decay;
We must worship its light, though it is not our own,
  For liberty burst in its ray.
Shall the name of a Washington ever be heard
  By a freeman, and thrill not his breast?
Is there one out of bondage that hails not the word
  As the Bethlehem star of the west?

"War, war to the knife! be enthralled or ye die,"
  Was the echo that woke in his land;
But it was not *his* voice that promoted the cry,
  Nor *his* madness that kindled the brand.
He raised not his arm, he defied not his foes,
  While a leaf of the olive remained;
Till goaded with insult, his spirit arose
  Like a long-baited lion unchained.

He struck with firm courage the blow of the brave,
  But sighed o'er the carnage that spread:
He indignantly trampled the yoke of the slave,
  But wept for the thousands that bled.
Though he threw back the fetters and headed the strife,
  Till man's charter was fairly restored;
Yet he prayed for the moment when freedom and life
  Would no longer be pressed by the sword.

Oh! his laurels were pure; and his patriot name
  In the page of the future shall dwell,

And be seen in all annals, the foremost in fame,
  By the side of a Hofer and Tell.
Revile not my song, for the wise and the good
  Among Britons have nobly confessed
That his was the glory and ours was the blood
  Of the deeply-stained field of the west.

THE LOVED ONE WAS NOT THERE.

We gathered round the festive board,
  The crackling faggot blazed,
But few would taste the wine that poured,
  Or join the song we raised.
For there was now a glass unfilled —
  A favored place to spare;
All eyes were dull, all hearts were chilled —
  The loved one was not there.

No happy laugh was heard to ring,
  No form would lead the dance;
A smothered sorrow seemed to fling
  A gloom in every glance.
The grave had closed upon a brow,
  The honest, bright, and fair;
We missed our mate, we mourned the blow —
  The loved one was not there.

THE MOURNERS.

King Death sped forth in his dreaded power
To make the most of his tyrant hour;
And the first he took was a white-robed girl,
With the orange bloom twined in each glossy curl.
Her fond betrothed hung over the bier,
Bathing her shroud with the gushing tear:
He madly raved, he shrieked his pain,
With frantic speech and burning brain.
"There's no joy," cried he, "now my dearest is gone.
Take, take me, Death; for I cannot live on!"

The sire was robbed of his eldest-born,
And he bitterly bled while the branch was torn
Other scions were round as good and fair,
But none seemed so bright as the breathless heir.
"My hopes are crushed," was the father's cry;
"Since my darling is lost, I, too, would die."
The valued friend was snatched away,
Bound to another from childhood's day;
And the one that was left exclaimed in despair,
"Oh! he sleeps in the tomb—let me follow him there!"

A mother was taken, whose constant love
Had nestled her child like a fair young dove;
And the heart of that child to the mother had grown,
Like the ivy to oak, or the moss to the stone:
Nor loud nor wild was the burst of wo,
But the tide of anguish ran strong below;

And the reft one turned from all that was light,
From the flowers of day and the stars of night;
Breathing where none might hear or see —
" Where thou art, my mother, thy child would be."

Death smiled as he heard each earnest word:
"Nay, nay," said he, "be this work deferred;
I'll see thee again in a fleeting year,
And, if grief and devotion live on sincere,
I promise then thou shalt share the rest
Of the being now plucked from thy doating breast;
Then, if thou cravest the coffin and pall
As thou dost this moment, my spear shall fall."
And Death fled till Time on his rapid wing
Gave the hour that brought back the skeleton king.

But the lover was ardently wooing again,
Kneeling in serfdom, and proud of his chain;
He had found an idol to adore,
Rarer than that he had worshipped before:
His step was gay, his laugh was loud,
As he led the way for the bridal crowd;
And his eyes still kept their joyous ray,
Though he went by the grave where his first love lay.
"Ha! ha!" shouted Death, "'tis passing clear
That I am a guest not wanted here!"

The father was seen in his children's games,
Kissing their flushed brows and blessing their names!
And his eye grew bright as he marked the charms
Of the boy at his knee and the girl in his arms:
His voice rung out in the merry noise,
He was first in all their hopes and joys;

He ruled their sports in the setting sun,
Nor gave a thought to the missing one.
"Are ye ready?" cried Death, as he raised his dart.
"Nay! nay!" shrieked the father; "in mercy depart!"

The friend again was quaffing the bowl,
Warmly pledging his faith and soul;
His bosom cherished with glowing pride
A stranger form that sat by his side;
His hand the hand of that stranger pressed;
He praised his song, he echoed his jest;
And the mirth and wit of that new-found mate
Made a blank of the name so prized of late.
"See! see!" cried Death, as he hurried past,
"How bravely the bonds of friendship last!"

But the orphan child! Oh, where was she?
With clasping hands and bended knee,
All alone on the church-yard's sod,
Mingling the names of mother and God.
Her dark and sunken eye was hid,
Fast weeping beneath the swollen lid;
Her sigh was heavy, her forehead was chill,
Betraying the wound was unhealed still;
And her smothered prayer was yet heard to crave
A speedy home in the self-same grave.

Hers was the love all holy and strong;
Hers was the sorrow fervent and long;
Hers was the spirit whose light was shed
As an incense fire above the dead.
Death lingered there, and paused awhile;
But she beckoned him on with a welcoming smile.

"There's a solace," cried she, "for all others to find,
But a mother leaves no equal behind."
And the kindest blow Death ever gave
Laid the mourning child in the parent's grave.

THE KING OF THE WIND.

He burst through the ice-pillared gates of the north,
And away on his hurricane wings he rushed forth;
He exulted all free in his might and his speed,
He mocked at the lion and taunted the steed;
He whistled along, through each cranny and creek;
He whirled o'er the mountains with hollow-toned shriek;
The arrow and eagle were laggard behind,
And alone in his flight sped the King of the Wind.

He swept o'er the earth — the tall battlements fell,
And he laughed, as they crumbled, with maniac yell;
The broad oak of the wood dared to wrestle again,
Till, wild in his fury, he hurled it in twain;
He grappled with pyramids, works of an age,
And dire records were left of his havoc and rage.
No power could brave him, no fetters could bind;
Supreme in his sway was the King of the Wind.

He careered o'er the waters with death and despair,
He wrecked the proud ship and his triumph was there
The cheeks that had blanched not at foeman or blade
At the sound of his breathing turned pale and afraid;

He rocked the stanch lighthouse, he shivered the mast,
He howled— the strong life-boat in fragments was cast;
And he roared in his glory, " Where, where will ye find
A despot so great as the King of the Wind! "

THE WREATHS.

Whom do we crown with the laurel leaf?
The hero god, the soldier chief,
But we dream of the crushing cannon-wheel,
Of the flying shot and the reeking steel,
Of the crimson plain where warm blood smokes,
Where clangor deafens and sulphur chokes:
Oh, who can love the laurel wreath,
Plucked from the gory field of death?

Whom do we crown with summer flowers?
The young and fair in their happiest hours.
But the buds will only live in the light
Of a festive day or a glittering night;
We know the vermil tints will fade —
That pleasure dies with the bloomy braid:
And who can prize the coronal
That's formed to dazzle, wither, and fall?

Who wears the cypress, dark and drear?
The one who is shedding the mourner's tear:
The gloomy branch for ever twines
Round foreheads graved with sorrow's lines.

'Tis the type of a sad and lonely heart,
That hath seen its dearest hopes depart.
Oh, who can like the chaplet band
That is wove by Melancholy's hand?

Where is the ivy circlet found?
On the one whose brain and lips are drowned
In the purple stream — who drinks and laughs
Till his cheeks outflush the wine he quaffs.
Oh, glossy and rich is the ivy crown,
With its gems of grape-juice trickling down;
But, bright as it seems o'er the glass and bowl
It has stain for the heart and shade for the soul.

But there's a green and fragrant leaf
Betokens nor revelry, blood, nor grief:
'Tis the purest amaranth springing below,
And rests on the calmest, noblest brow:
It is not the right of the monarch or lord,
Nor purchased by gold, nor won by the sword;
For the lowliest temples gather a ray
Of quenchless light from the palm of bay.

Oh, beautiful bay! I worship thee —
I homage thy wreath — I cherish thy tree;
And of all the chaplets Fame may deal,
'Tis only to this one I would kneel;
For as Indians fly to the banian branch,
When tempests lower and thunders launch,
So the spirit may turn from crowds and strife,
And seek from the bay-wreath joy and life.

OLD PINCHER.

WHEN I gave to old Dobbin his song and his due
Apollo I feared would look scornfully blue;
I thought he might spurn the low station and blood,
And turn such a Pegasus out of his stud.

But another "four-footed" comes boldly to claim
His place beside Dobbin in merits and fame;
He shall have it, — for why should I be over nice,
Since Homer immortalized Ilion — and mice?

I frolicked a youngling, wild, rosy, and fat,
When Pincher was brought in the butcher-boy's hat;
And the long-promised puppy was hailed with a joy
That ne'er was inspired by a gold-purchased toy.

"What a darling!" cried I; while my sire, with a
frown,
Exclaimed, "Hang the brute! though 'tis easy to
drown:"
But I wept at the word, till my sorrowful wail
Won his total reprieve from the rope or the pail.

Regarding his beauty, I'm silent: forsooth,
I've a little old-fashioned respect for the truth;
And the praise of his color or shape to advance
Would be that part of history known as romance.

There were some who most rudely denounced him a
"cur."
How I hated that name, though I dared not demur

I thought him all fair; yet I'll answer for this,
That the fate of Narcissus could ne'er have been his.

Now Dobbin, the pony, belonged to us all,
Was at every one's service, and every one's call;
But Pincher, rare treasure, possession divine,
Was held undisputed as whole and sole mine.

Together we rambled, together we grew.
Many plagues had the household, but we were the two
Who were branded the deepest; all doings reviled
Were sure to be wrought by "that dog and that child."

Unkenneled and chainless, yet truly he served;
No serfdom was known, yet his faith never swerved:
A dog has a heart, — secure that, and you'll find
That *love* even in brutes is the safest to bind.

If my own kin or kind had demolished my ball,
The transgression were marked with a scuffle and squall;
But with perfect consent he might mouth it about,
Till the very last atom of sawdust was out.

When halfpence were doled for the holiday treat,
How I longed for the comfits, so lusciously sweet:
But cakes *must* be purchased, for how could I bear
To feast on a luxury Pinch could not share?

I fondled, I fed him, I coaxed or I cuffed, —
I drove or I led him, I soothed or I huffed:
He had beatings in anger, and huggings in love,
But which were most cruel, 'twere a puzzle to prove.

If he dared to rebel, I might battle and wage
The fierce war of a tyrant with petulant rage:
I might ply him with kicks, or belabor with blows,
But Pincher was never once known to oppose.

Did a mother appear the loud quarrel to learn,
If 'twere only with him it gave little concern:
No ill-usage could rouse him, no insult could chafe;
While Pinch was the playmate her darling was safe.

If the geese on the common gave signal of fear,
And screams most unmusical startled the ear,
The cause was soon guessed; for my foremost delight
Was in seeing Pinch put the old gander to flight.

Had the pantry been rifled of remnant of beef,
Shrewd suspicions were formed of receiver and thief,
For I paused not at crime, and I blushed not at fibs
That assisted to nurture his well-covered ribs.

The warren was sacred, yet he and I dared
To career through its heath till the rabbits were scared;
The gamekeeper threatened me Pinch should be shot;
But the threat was by both of us always forgot.

The linen, half bleached, must be rinsed o'er again;
And our footsteps in mud were "remarkably" plain.
The tulips were crushed, to the gardener's dismay,
And when last we were seen we were bending that way.

When brought to the bar for the evil we'd done,
Some atrocious spoilation I chose to call "fun:"

Though Pinch was Tiberius, those who might try
Knew well that the active Sejanus was I.

But we weathered all gales, and the years sped away,
Till his "bonnie black" hide was fast turning to gray
When accents were heard most alarmingly sad,
Proclaiming that Pincher, my Pincher, was mad.

It was true: his fixed doom was no longer a joke;
He that moment must die: my young heart was nigh broke.
I saw the sure fowling-piece moved from its rest,
And the sob of keen anguish burst forth unsuppressed.

A shot, — a faint howl, — and old Pincher was dead.
How I wept while the gardener prepared his last bed!
Something fell on his spade too, wet, sparkling, and clear;
Though *he* said 'twas a dew-drop, *I* know 'twas a tear.

Our winter-night circle was now incomplete;
We missed the fond brute that had snoozed at our feet:
All his virtues were praised, all his mischief forgot,
We lauded his merits, and sighed o'er his lot.

Poodle, spaniel, and grayhound, were brought for my care,
Of beauty and breed reckoned preciously rare;
But the playmate of infancy, friend of my youth,
Was linked with a lasting affection and truth.

He was never supplanted; nay, mention him now,
And a something of shadow will steal from my brow,

"Poor fellow!" will burst in such tone of regret,
That whispers my heart is his lurking-place yet.

No wonder; for memory brings back with him
The thoughts that will render the lightest eye dim;
He is mingled with all that I idolized most,
The brightest, the purest, the loved, and the lost.

The smile of a parent, the dearest, the best,
The joys of my forest home spring to my breast,
And those days re-appear with a halo divine,
When old Pincher, a mother, and childhood were mine.

SONG OF THE BLIND ONE.

They talk of rainbows in the sky, and blossoms on the earth,
They sing the beauty of the stars in songs of love and mirth;
They say the mountain sod is fair — they tell of dew-drops bright,
They praise the sun that warms the day, and moon that cheers the night.
I do not sigh to watch the sky, I do not care to see
The lustre drop on green-hill top, or fruit upon the tree:
I've prayed to have my lids unsealed, but 'twas not to behold
The pearly dawn of misty morn, or evening cloud of gold.

No, no, my Mary, I would turn from flower, star, and sun,
For well I know thou'rt fairer still, my own, my gentle one.

I hear the music others deem most eloquent and sweet,
The merry lark above my head — the cricket at my feet;
The laughing tones of childhood's glee that gladden while they ring,
The robin in the winter-time — the cuckoo in the spring;
But never do I think those tones so beautiful as thine,
When kind words from a kinder heart confirm that heart is mine.
There is no melody of sound that bids my soul rejoice,
As when I hear my simple name breathed by thy happy voice;
And, Mary, I will ne'er believe that flower, star, or sun
Can ever be so bright as thou mv true, my gentle one.

THE OLD WATER-MILL.

And is this the old mill-stream that ten years ago
Was so fast in its current, so pure in its flow;
Whose musical waters would ripple and shine
With the glory and dash of a miniature Rhine?

Can this be its bed? I remember it well
When it sparkled like silver through meadow and dell;
When the pet-lamb reposed on its emerald side,
And the minnow and perch darted swift through its
tide.

And here was the miller's house, peaceful abode!
Where the flower-twined porch drew all eyes from the
road;
Where roses and jasmine embowered the door
That never was closed to the wayworn or poor.

Where the miller, God bless him! oft gave us "a
dance,"
And led off the ball with his soul in his glance;
Who, forgetting gray hairs, was as loud in his mirth
As the veriest youngsters that circled his hearth.

Blind Ralph was the only musician we had,
But his tunes — oh! such tunes — would make any
heart glad;
"The Roast Beef of Old England," and "Green grow
the Rushes,"
Woke our eyes' brightest beams and our cheeks' warm-
est flushes.

No lustre resplendent its brilliancy shed,
But the wood fire blazed high, and the board was well
spread;
Our seats were undamasked, our partners were rough.
Yet, yet we were happy, and that was enough!

And here was the mill where we idled away
Our holiday hours on a clear summer day

Where Roger, the miller's boy, lolled on a sack,
And chorused his song to the merry click-clack.

But, lo! what rude sacrilege here hath been done?
The streamlet no longer purls on in the sun;
Its course has been turned, and the desolate edge
Is now mournfully covered with duck-weed and sedge.

The mill is in ruins. — No welcoming sound
In the mastiff's quick bark and the wheels dashing round;
The house, too, untenanted — left to decay —
And the miller, long dead: all I loved passed away!

This play-place of childhood was graved on my heart,
In rare Paradise colors that now must depart;
The old water-mill's gone, the fair vision is fled,
And I weep o'er its wreck as I do for the dead.

ROVER'S SONG.

I'm afloat! I'm afloat on the fierce rolling tide;
The ocean's my home! and my bark is my bride!
Up — up with my flag! let it wave o'er the sea;
I'm afloat! I'm afloat, and the rover is free!

I fear not a monarch — I heed not the law;
I've a compass to steer by, a dagger to draw;

And ne'er as a coward or slave will I kneel,
While my guns carry shot, or my belt bears a steel!

Quick — quick — trim her sails; let her sheets kiss the wind;
And I warrant we'll soon leave the sea-gull behind;
Up — up with my flag! let it wave o'er the sea!
I'm afloat! I'm afloat! and the rover is free;

The night gathers o'er us; the thunder is heard;
What matter? our vessel skims on like a bird;
What to her is the dash of the storm-ridden main?
She has braved it before, and will brave it again!

The fire-gleaming flashes around us may fall;
They may strike; they may cleave; but they cannot appal.
With lightnings above us, and darkness below,
Through the wild waste of waters right onward we go!

Hurrah! my brave crew! ye may drink; ye may sleep;
The storm-fiend is hushed; we're alone on the deep;
Our flag of defiance still waves o'er the sea;
Hurrah, boys! hurrah, boys! the rover is free!

KINGS.

Oh, covet not the throne and crown,
  Sigh not for rule and state;
The wise would fling the sceptre down,
  And shun the palace gate.

Let wild ambition wing its flight;
  Glory is free to all:
But they who soar a regal height
  Will risk a deadly fall.

Take any high imperial name,
  The great among the great;
What was the guerdon of his fame,
  And what his closing fate?

The hero of immortal Greece,
  Unhappy, fled to wine,
And died in Saturnalian peace,
  As drunkard, fool, and swine.

The first in arms, Rome's victor son,
  Fell by a traitor's aim,
And drew the purple robes he'd won
  To hide his blood and shame.

Bold Richard, England's lion heart,
  Escaped the burning fray,
To sink beneath a peasant's dart,
  And groan his life away.

Gaul's eagle, he whose upraised hand
  Swayed legions of the brave,
Died in a prison, "barred and banned,"
  An exile and a slave.

Scores may be found whose tyrant-time
  Knew not one hour of rest;
Their lives one course of senseless crime,
  Their every deed unblest.

Ye blazing stars of gems and gold,
  What aching hearts ye mock!
Strong marble walls, do ye not hold
  Sword, poison, axe, and block?

Many have cursed the crown they've worn,
  When, hurled from place and rank,
They met a people's groaning scorn,
  And trod the scaffold plank.

"Uneasy lies the monarch's head,"
  Despite his dazzling wreath;
The hireling by his dying bed
  May aid the work of death.

His cringing horde may bow the neck,
  Though bid to lick the dust:
He may have serf to wait his beck,
  But not one friend to trust.

Ye lowly born, oh! covet not,
  One right the sceptre brings;
The honest name and peaceful lot
  Outweigh the pomp of kings

TO FANCY.

Spirit of ethereal birth!
Aërial visitant of earth!
Flashing vivid through the soul,
Warm as the spark Prometheus stole
Hither, Fancy, hither come;
'Neath thine iris wings I'll roam.

Take me to the crystal caves,
Glassy chambers of the waves;
Where the dolphin's golden back
Splashes gems around its track,
Cleaving through the rocky cells,
Green with weeds, and rich with shells;
Where the Nereids keep their court,
Where the mermaids hold their sport;
Where the syren sings to sleep
All the tenants of the deep;
Take me through the proud blue sea,
Show its beauties all to me!

Waft me where the stars appear,
Where the other worlds career;
Let me scan the dazzling scroll
God's hand only can unroll!
Let me hear the saints rejoice,
Giving praise with harp and voice;
Let me tread the welkin round,
Lulled in soft Elysian sound;

Let me rove the the fields of light,
Give their glories to my sight.

Take me where the fairies spring
Round about their moon-lit ring
Where the dancing elfin sprites
Consecrate their mystic rites;
Lead where Hippocrene's bright fount
Gushes down the flowery mount;
Where Apollo's hand bestows
Fadeless wreaths on poets' brows.
Hither, Fancy, hither come;
'Neath thine iris wings I'll roam!

THE SACRILEGIOUS GAMESTERS.

A STRANGER journeyed through the town,
One dark and wintry night;
And, as he passed the ivied church,
He marked a flitting light.

It shed a restless waving gleam
Through the Gothic window pane;
And now it vanished for a space,
And now it came again.

He stood, and thought it wondrous strange
That such a scene should be;
He stood, and now the pale red beam
Shone strong and steadily.

He looked around; all else was dark,
  Not e'en a star was left;
The townsmen slumbered, and he thought
  Of sacrilege and theft.

He roused two sleepers from their beds,
  And told what he had seen;
And they, like him, were curious
  To know what it should mean.

They hied together to the church,
  And heard strange sounds within
Of undistinguishable words,
  And laughter's noisy din!

The window's high; a ladder, quick,
  Is placed with stealthy care,
And one ascends — he looks below;
  Oh! what a sight is there!

The white communion-cloth is spread
  With cards, and dice, and wine;
The flaming wax-lights glare around,
  The gilded sconces shine.

And three of earthly form have made
  The altar-rail their seat,
With the Bible and the books of prayer
  As footstools for their feet.

Three men, with flashing bloodshot eyes
  And burning fevered brows,
Have met within those holy walls
  To gambol and carouse.

But the darkest work is not yet told:
Another guest is there,
With the earth-worm trailing o'er his cheek
To hide in his matted hair!

He lifted not the foaming cup,
He moved not in his place;
There was slime upon his livid lips,
And dust upon his face.

The foldings of a winding-sheet
His body wrapped around,
And many a stain the vestment bore
Of the clay from the charnel ground.

A rent appeared, where his withered hands
Fell out on the sacred board;
And between those hands a goblet stood,
In which bright wine was poured.

Oh! he was not like the other three,
But ghastly, foul, and cold;
He was seated there a stiffened corpse
All horrid to behold.

He had been their mate for many a year,
Their partner many a game;
He had shared alike their ill-got gold
And their deeply tarnished fame.

He had died in the midst of his career,
As the sinful ever die,
Without one prayer from a good man's heart,
One tear from a good man's eye!

He had died a guilty one, unblessed,
  Unwept, unmourned by all;
And scarce a footstep ever bent
  To his grave by the old church wall.

The other three had met that night,
  And revelled in drunken glee,
And talked of him who a month ago
  Formed one of their company.

They quaffed another brimming glass,
  And a bitter oath they swore
That he who had joined their game so oft
  Should join their game once more.

And away they strode to the old church wall,
  Treading o'er skull and tomb,
And dragged him out triumphantly,
  In the midnight murky gloom.

They carry him down the chancel porch,
  And through the fretted aisle,
And many a heartless, fiendish laugh
  Is heard to ring the while.

They place him at the hallowed shrine,
  They call upon his name,
They bid him wake to life again,
  And play his olden game.

They deal the cards :— the ribald jest
  And pealing laugh ring on.
A stroke — a start — the echoing clock
  Proclaims the hour of one!

And two of the three laugh louder still,
  But the third stares wildly round:
He drops the cards, as if his hand
  Were palsied at the sound!

His cheeks have lost their deepened flush,
  His lips are of paler hue,
And fear hath fallen on the heart
  Of the youngest of that crew!

His soul is not yet firmly bound
  In the fetters of reckless sin!
Depravity hath not yet wrought
  Its *total* work within!

The strong potation of the night
  Drowned all that might remain
Of feeling; and his hand shrunk not
  While madness fired his brain!

But now the charm hath lost its spell,
  The heated fumes have passed;
And banished reason to her throne,
  Usurped, advances fast.

He rises — staggers — looks again
  Upon the shrouded dead!
A shudder steals upon his frame:
  His vaunted strength is fled!

He doubts — he dreams — can, can it be?
  A mist is o'er his eyes;
He stands aghast. — "Oh! what is this?
  Where? where?" — he wildly cries.

"Where am I? — see the altar-piece —
The holy Bible: say —
Is this the place where I was brought
A tiny boy to pray?

"The church — the church-yard too — I know
I have been *there* to-night;
For what? Ha! mercy! see that corpse!
Oh, hide me from the light!

"I have been deemed a profligate,
A gamester, and a knave,
But ne'er was known to scoff at God
Or violate the grave!

"I've long been what man should not be,
But not what I am now.
Oh help me! help! My tongue is parched!
There's fire upon my brow!

"Oh save me! hide me from myself!
I feel my pulses start:
The horror of this drunken crime
Hath fixed upon my heart!

"Again! I feel the rushing blood!
I die! — the unforgiven!
Again, it comes; all — all is dark —
I choke — Oh! mercy, Heaven!"

One struggling groan — he reels — he falls —
On the altar-steps he lies;
And the others gasp with fear, for now
Two corpses meet their eyes!

But, hark! swift footsteps echo round:
  Encircled now they stand:
Surprised, detected, they are seized
  By many a grappling hand.

And soon the dreadful tale is spread,
  And many a finger raised
To point them out; while the listening one
  Looks fearfully amazed.

They are shunned by all; the son, the sire,
  The heedless and the gay;
Their old associates leave their side,
  And turn another way.

Hate, shame, and scorn, have set a mark
  Upon them. One by one,
Of all they knew, forsakes their path,
  Till they are left alone.

And they have sought another land,
  And breathe another clime;
Where men may deem them fellow-men,
  Nor hear their blasting crime!

And gossips, in their native town,
  Even now are heard to tell
Of the sacrilegious crew that turned
  The old church to a hell.

WINTER.

WINTER is coming! who cares? who cares?
Not the wealthy and proud, I trow;
"Let it come," they cry, "what matters to us
How chilly the blast may blow?

"We'll feast and carouse in our lordly halls,
The goblet of wine we'll drain;
We'll mock at the wind with shouts of mirth,
And music's echoing strain.

"Little care we for the biting frost,
While the fire gives forth its blaze;
What to us is the dreary night,
While we dance in the waxlight's rays?"

'Tis thus the rich of the land will talk;
But think! oh, ye pompous great,
That the harrowing storm *ye* laugh at within
Falls bleak on the *poor at your gate!*

They have blood in their veins, aye, pure as thine
But naught to quicken its flow; —
They have limbs that feel the whistling gale,
And shrink from the driving snow.

Winter is coming — oh! think, ye great,
On the roofless, naked, and old;
Deal with them kindly, as man with man,
And spare them a tithe of your gold!

THOSE WE LOVE.

We leave our own — our father-land,
To lead the wanderer's fearful life —
On stormy seas or desert sand,
In pilgrim peace or busy strife;
But there's a hope to save and cheer
Through all of danger, toil, and pain;
It shines to dry the starting tear,
And lights the pathway back again
To those we love.

Let others give us gems and gold,
With gems and gold we'd lightly part —
We take them, but we do not hold
The treasures sacred in the heart.
Such costly boons may have the power
To win our thanks and wake our pride;
But dearer is the withered flower
That has been worn and thrown aside
By those we love.

We pine beneath the regal dome,
We prize not all that's rich and fair;
We cannot rest in princely home,
If those we cherish dwell not there.
But let the spirit choose its lot,
We'd rather take the rover's tent,
Or gladly share the peasant's cot,
And bless the flying moments spent
With those we love.

And when at last the hand of death
  Has dimmed the glance and chilled the breast,
When trembling word and fleeting breath
  Dwell on the name we like the best; —
E'en then, however keen the throe,
  'Tis easy for ourselves to die;
The deepest anguish is to know
  That grief will wring the mourner's sigh
    From those we love.

SONG OF THE SEA-GULLS.

Birds of the land, ye may carol and fly
O'er the golden corn 'neath a harvest sky;
Your portion is fair mid fields and flowers,
But it is not so broad or so free as ours.
Ye are content with the groves and the hills,
Ye feed in the valleys and drink at the rills;
But what are the joys of the forest and plain
To those we find on the fresh wide main?

Birds of the land, ye rear your broods
In the lofty tree or tangled woods,
Where the branch may be reft by the howling wind,
Or the prowling schoolboy seek and find;
But we roost high on the beetling rock,
That firmly stands the hurricane's shock.
Our callow young may rest in a home
Where no shot can reach and no footstep come.

Birds of the land, ye shrink and hide
As the tempest-cloud spreads black and wide;
Your songs are hushed in cowering fear
As the startling thunder-clap breaks near;
But the brave gull soars while the deluge pours,
While the stout ship groans and the keen blast roars.
Oh! the sea-gull leads the gayest life
While the storm-fiends wage their fiercest strife.

We lightly skim o'er the breaker's dash,
Where timbers strike with parting crash;
We play round the dark hull, sinking fast,
And find a perch on the tottering mast;
More loud and glad is our shrieking note
As the planks and spars of the wrecked bark float.
There live we in revelling glee,
Mid the whistling gale and raging sea.

We are not caught and caged to please
The fondled heirs of wealth and ease:
The hands of beauty never come
With soft caress or dainty crumb;
We are not the creatures of petted love,
We have not the fame of the lark or dove;
But our screaming tone rings harsh and wild,
To glad the ears of the fisher's child.

He hears our pinions flapping by,
And follows our track with wistful eye,
As we leave the clouds with rapid whirl
To dive 'neath the water's sweeping curl.
He laughs to see us plunge and lave
While the northern gale is waking the wave

And dances about, mid sand and spray,
To mimic the sea-gull's merry play.

We hold our course o'er the deep or the land,
O'er the swelling tide or weed-grown strand;
We are safe and joyous when mad waves roll,
We sport o'er the whirlpool, the rock, and the shoal;
Away on the winds we plume our wings,
And soar the freest of all free things.
Oh! the sea-gull leads a merry life
In the glassy calm or tempest strife.

SONG OF THE MARINERS.

The miser will hold his darling gold
Till his eyes are glazed and his hands are cold;
The minstrel one to his wild lyre clings
As though its chords were his own heart-strings;
No dearer boon will the reveller ask
Than the draught that deepens the purple flask;
But the firmest love-link that can be
Chains the mariners bold to the pathless sea.

Choose ye who will earth's dazzling bowers,
But the great and glorious sea be ours;
Give us, give us the dolphin's home,
With the speeding keel and splashing foam:
Right merry are we as the sound bark springs
On her lonely track like a creature of wings.

Oh, the mariner's life is blithe and gay,
When the sky is fair and the ship on her way.

We love the perilous sea, because
It will not bend to man or his laws;
It ever hath rolled the uncontrolled,
It cannot be warped to fashion or mould:
Now quiet and fair as a sleeping child;
Now rousing in tempests madly wild;
And who shall wean the mighty flood
From its placid dream, or passionate mood?

We are not so apt to forget our God
As those who dwell on the dry safe sod;
For we know each leaping wave we meet
May be a crystal winding-sheet;
We know each blustering gale that blows
May requiem to a last repose;
And the chafing tide, as it roars and swells,
Hath as solemn a tone as the calling bells.

The land has its beauty, its sapphire and rose;
But look on the colors the bright main shows,
While each billow flings from its pearly fringe
The lucid jewels of rainbow tinge.
Go, mark the waters at sunny noon,
Go, float beneath the full clear moon,
And cold is the spirit that wakes not there
With wondering praise and worshipping prayer.

'Tis true, we may sink mid deluge and blast,
But we cope with the strong, we are quelled by the vast;
And a noble urn is the foundered wreck,

Though no incense may burn, and no flower may deck.
We need no stately funeral car;
But, tangled with salt-weeds and lashed to a spar,
Down, down below the mariners go,
While thunders volley and hurricanes blow.

But little do we bold mariners care
What hour we fall, or what risk we dare,
For the groan on the struggling sailor's lip
Is less for himself than his dying ship.
Oh! ours is the life for the free and the brave;
We dance o'er the planks that may yawn as a grave,
We laugh mid the foam of our perilous home,
And are ready for death whene'er it may come

LOVE.

'Tis well to wake the theme of love
When chords of wild ecstatic fire
Fling from the harp, and amply prove
The soul as joyous as the lyre.

Such theme is blissful when the heart
Warms with the precious name we pour;
When our deep pulses glow and start
Before the idol we adore.

Sing ye, whose doating eyes behold,
Whose ears can drink the dear one's tone.

Whose hands may press, whose arms may fold,
  The prized, the beautiful, thine own.

But, should the ardent hopes of youth
  Have cherished dreams that darkly fled;
Should passion, purity, and truth,
  Live on, despairing o'er the dead;

Should we have heard some sweet voice hushed,
  Breathing our name in latest vow;
Should our fast heavy tears have gushed
  Above a cold, yet worshipped brow;

Oh! say, then can the minstrel choose
  The themes that gods and mortals praise?
No, no; the spirit will refuse,
  And sadly shun such raptured lays.

For who can bear to touch the string
  That yields but anguish in its strain;
Whose lightest notes have power to wring
  The keenest pangs from breast and brain?

"Sing ye of love in words that burn,"
  Is what full many a lip will ask;
But love the dead, and ye will learn
  Such bidding is no gentle task.

Oh! pause in mercy, ere ye blame
  The one who lends not love his lyre;
That which *ye* deem ethereal flame
  May be to *him* a torture pyre.

THE BOAT-CLOAK.

He is ready to sail, and he gazes with pride
On the bright buttoned jacket, the dirk by his side;
But the trappings of gold do not waken his joy
Like the boat-cloak his mother flings over her boy.
With graceful affection 'tis hung on his arm,
While he marks its full drapery, ample and warm.
"Thou'rt my shipmate," he cries, "'twill go hard if we part,"
And the boat-cloak seems linked to the sailor boy's heart.

Years brown his cheek, and far, far on the sea,
Carefully keeping the mid-watch is he.
The chill breeze is defied by his close-clinging vest,
For the weather-tanned boat-cloak encircles his breast.
The rocks are before and the sands are behind,
The wind mocks the thunder, the thunder the wind.
The noble ship founders — he leaps from the deck,
And his boat-cloak is all that he saves from the wreck.

Age comes, and he tells of his perils gone by,
Till the veteran lays him down calmly to die.
And soft is the pillow that bears his gray head,
And warm is the clothing that's heaped on his bed.
But "My boat-cloak!" he cries—"I am turning all cold,
Oh wrap me once more in its cherishing fold."
'Tis around him, he clasps it, he smiles, and he sighs,
He murmurs, "My boat-cloak, thou'rt warmest!" and dies.

THROUGH THE WATERS.

THROUGH the forest, through the forest, oh! who would not like to roam,
Where the squirrel leaps right gaily and the shy fawn makes a home;
Where branches, spreading high and wide, shut out the golden sun,
And hours of noontide steal away all shadowy and dun?
'Tis sweet to pluck the ivy sprigs or seek the hidden nest,
To track the spot where owlets hide and wild deer take their rest;
Through the forest, through the forest, oh, 'tis passing sweet to take
Our lonely way mid springy moss, thick bush, and tangled brake.

Through the valley, through the valley, where the glittering harebells peep,
Where laden bees go droning by, and hum themselves to sleep;
Where all that's bright with bloom and light springs forth to greet the day,
And every blade pours incense to the warm and cloudless ray;
Where children come to laugh away their happy summer hours,
To chase the downy butterfly, or crown themselves with flowers:

Through the valley, through the valley, oh! who does not like to bask
Amid the fairest beauties Heaven can give or man can ask?

Through the desert, through the desert, where the Arab takes his course,
With none to bear him company except his gallant horse;
Where none can question will or right, where landmarks ne'er impede,
But all is wide and limitless to rider and to steed.
No purling streamlet murmurs there, no checkered shadows fall;
'Tis torrid, waste, and desolate, but free to each and all.
Through the desert, through the desert! Oh, the Arab wonld not change
For purple robes or olive trees his wild and burning range.

Through the waters, through the waters, ah! be this the joy for me,
Upon the flowing river or the broad and dashing sea;
Of all that wealth could offer me the choicest boon I'd crave
Would be a bold and sturdy bark upon the open wave.
I love to see the wet sails fill before the whistling breath,
And feel the ship cleave on as though she spurned the flood beneath.

Through the waters, through the waters, can ye tell
me what below
Is freer than the wind lashed main, or swifter than the
prow?

I love to see the merry craft go running on her side;
I laugh to see her splashing on before the rapid tide;
I love to mark the white and hissing foam come
boiling up,
Fresh as the froth that hangs about the Thunderer's
nectar cup.
All sail away: ah! who would stay to pace the dusty
land
If once they trod a gallant ship, steered by a gallant
band.
Through the waters, through the waters, oh! there's
not a joy for me
Like racing with the gull upon a broad and dashing
sea!

A HOME IN THE HEART.

Oh! ask not a home in the mansions of pride,
Where marble shines out in the pillars and walls;
Though the roof be of gold it is brilliantly co'd,
And joy may not be found in its torch-lighted halls.
But seek for a bosom all honest and true,
Where love once awakened will never depart;
Turn, turn to that breast like the dove to its nest,
And you'll find there's no home like a home in the heart.

Oh! link but one spirit that's warmly sincere,
That will heighten your pleasure and solace your care;
Find a soul you may trust as the kind and the just,
And be sure the wide world holds no treasure so rare.
Then the frowns of misfortune may shadow our lot,
The cheek-searing tear-drops of sorrow may start,
But a star never dim sheds a halo for him
Who can turn for repose to a home in the heart.

THE SMUGGLER BOY.

We stole away at the fall of night,
When the red round moon was deepening her light,
But none knew whither our footsteps bent,
Nor how those stealthy hours were spent;
For we crept away to the rocky bay,
Where the cave and craft of a fierce band lay;
We gave the signal-cry, "Ahoy!"
And found a mate in the smuggler boy,

His laugh was deep, his speech was bold,
And we loved the fearful tales he told
Of the perils he met in his father's bark,
Of the chase by day and the storm by dark;
We got him to take the light boat out,
And gaily and freshly we dashed about,
And naught of pleasure could ever decoy
From the moonlight sail with the smuggler boy.

We caught his spirit, and learnt to love
The cageless eagle more than the dove;
And wild and happy souls were we,
Roving with him by the heaving sea.
He whispered the midnight work they did,
And showed us where the kegs were hid:
All secrets were ours — a word might destroy —
But we never betrayed the smuggler boy.

We sadly left him, bound to range
A distant path of care and change;
We have sought him again, but none could relate
The place of his home, or a word of his fate:
Long years have sped, but we dream of him now,
With the red cap tossed on his dauntless brow;
And the world hath never given a joy
Like the moonlight sail with the smuggler boy

THE HOMES OF THE DEAD.

We must not make a home for the dead,
  Nor raise an osiered mound,
Till the eloquent prayer and priestly tread
  Have sanctified the ground.

But there are those who fall and die
  Upon the desert land,
With no pall above but the torrid sky,
  No bier but the scorching sand.

No turf is laid, no sexton's spade
  Chimes in with the mourner's groans;
But the prowling jackal finds a feast,
  And the red sun crumbles the bones.

There are those who go down in the dark wild sea,
  When storms have wrecked proud ships,
With none to heed what the words may be
  That break from their gurgling lips.

No anthem peal flows sweet and loud,
  No tablets mark their graves;
But they soundly sleep in a coral shroud,
  To the dirge of the rolling waves.

There are those who sink on the mountain path,
  With cold and curdling blood;
With the frozen sleet for a funeral sheet,
  And no mates but the vulture brood:

No tolling bell proclaims their knell,
  No memory stone is found;
But the snow-drift rests on their skeleton breasts
  And the bleaching winds sweep round.

There are those who fall on the purple field,
  In glory's mad career;
Their dying couch — a battered shield,
  Their cross of faith — a spear:

No priest has been there with robes and prayer
  To consecrate the dust;
Where the soldier sleeps his steed sleeps too,
  And his gore-stained weapons rust.

No cypress waves, no daisy grows,
  Above such pillows of rest;
Yet say, are the riteless graves of those
  Unholy or unblest?

'Tis well to find our last repose
  'Neath the churchyard's sacred sod;
But those who sleep in the desert or deep
  Are watched by the self-same God.

MY BIRTHDAY.

Mother, there's no soft hand comes now
To smooth the dark curls o'er my brow;
I hear no voice so low and mild
As that which breathed " my own loved child."
No smile will greet, no lips will press,
No prayer will rise, no words will bless,
So fond, so dear, so true for me
As those I ever met from thee.

Oh! that my soul could melt in tears,
And die beneath the pain it bears;
The grief that springs, the thoughts that goad,
Become a heavy maddening load;
For all that heart and memory blends
But hotly scathes and sorely rends;
And feeling, with its biting fangs,
Tortures with sharp and bleeding pangs.

My Mother! thou did'st prophesy
With sighing tone and weeping eye
That the cold world would never be
A kindred resting-place for me.
Oh, thou wert right! I cannot find
One sympathetic link to bind,
But where some dark alloy comes in
To mar with folly, wrong, or sin.

My Mother! thou did'st know full well
My spirit was not fit to dwell
With crowds who dream not of the ray
That burns the very soul away.
That ray is mine; 'tis held from God,
But scourges like a blazing rod.
And never glows with fiercer flame
Than when 'tis kindled at thy name.

My Mother! thou art remembered yet
With doting love and keen regret;
My birthday finds me once again
In fervent sorrow, deep as vain.
Thou art gone for ever, I must wait
The will of Heaven, the work of fate
And faith can yield no hope for me
Brighter than that of meeting thee.

PRAYER.

How purely true, how deeply warm,
  The inly-breathed appeal may be,
Though adoration wears no form,
  In upraised hand or bended knee.
One Spirit fills all boundless space,
  No limit to the when or where;
And little recks the time or place
  That leads the soul to praise and prayer.

Father above, Almighty one,
  Creator, is that worship vain
That hails each mountain as thy throne,
  And finds a universal fane?
When shining stars, or spangled sod,
  Call forth devotion, who shall dare
To blame, or tell me that a God
  Will never deign to hear such prayer?

Oh, prayer is good when many pour
  Their voices in one solemn tone;
Conning their sacred lessons o'er
  Or yielding thanks for mercies shown.
'Tis good to see the quiet train
  Forget their worldly joy and care,
While loud response and choral strain
  Re-echo in the house of prayer.

But often have I stood to mark
  The setting sun and closing flower,

When silence and the gathering dark
  Shed holy calmness o'er the hour.
Lone on the hills, my soul confessed
  More rapt and burning homage there,
And served the Maker it addressed
  With stronger zeal and closer prayer.

When watching those we love and prize,
  Till all of life and hope be fled;
When we have gazed on sightless eyes,
  And gently stayed the falling head;
Then what can soothe the stricken heart,
  What solace overcome despair;
What earthly breathing can impart
  Such healing balm as lonely prayer?

When fears and perils thicken fast,
  And many dangers gather round;
When human aid is vain and past,
  No mortal refuge to be found;
Then can we firmly lean on heaven,
  And gather strength to meet and bear;
No matter where the storm has driven,
  A saving anchor lives in prayer.

Oh, God! how beautiful the thought,
  How merciful the blessed decree,
That grace can e'er be found when sought,
  And naught shut out the soul from Thee.
The cell may cramp, the fetters gall,
  The flame may scorch, the rack may tear;
But torture-stake, or prison wall,
  Can be endured with faith and prayer.

In desert wilds, in midnight gloom,
  In grateful joy, in trying pain;
In laughing youth, or nigh the tomb;
  Oh when is prayer unheard or vain?
The Infinite, the King of kings,
  Will never heed the when or where;
He'll ne'er reject a heart that brings
  The offering of fervent prayer.

SONNET,

WRITTEN AT THE COUCH OF A DYING PARENT.

'Tis midnight! and pale Melancholy stands
  Beside me, wearing a funereal wreath
  Of yew and cypress; the faint dirge of death
Moans in her breathing, while her withered hands
  Fling corse-bedecking rosemary around.
She offers nightshade, spreads a winding-sheet,
Points to the clinging clay upon her feet,
  And whispers tidings of the charnel ground.
Oh! pray thee, Melancholy, do not bring
  These bitter emblems with thee; I can bear
With all but these, — 'tis these, oh God! that wring
  And plunge my heart in maddening despair,
Hence, for awhile, pale Melancholy, go!
And let sweet slumber lull my weeping wo,

SONG OF THE IMPRISONED BIRD.

Ye may pass me by with pitying eye,
  And cry, "Poor captive thing!"
But I'll prove ye are caged as safely as I,
  If ye'll hearken the notes I sing.

I flutter in thrall, and so do all; —
  Ye have bonds ye cannot escape,
With only a little wider range,
  And bars of another shape.

The noble ranks of fashion and birth
  Are fettered by courtly rule;
They dare not rend the shackles that tend
  To form the knave and fool,

The parasite, bound to kiss the hand
  That, perchance, he may lothe to touch;
The maiden, high-born, wedding where she may scorn,
  Oh! has earth worse chains than such?

The one who lives but to gather up wealth,
  Though great his treasures may be,
Yet, guarding with care and counting by stealth, —
  What a captive wretch is he!

The vainly proud, who turn from the crowd,
  And tremble lest they spoil
The feathers of the peacock plume
  With a low plebeian soil; —

Oh! joy is mine to see them strut
  In their chosen narrow space;
They mount a perch, but ye need not search
  For a closer prison place.

The being of fitful curbless wrath
  May fiercely stamp and rave;
He will call himself free, but there cannot be
  More mean and piteous slave; —

For the greatest victim, the fastest bound,
  Is the one who serves his rage:
The temper that governs will ever be found
  A fearful torture cage.

Each breathing spirit is chastened down
  By the hated or the dear;
The gentle smile or tyrant frown
  Will hold ye in love or fear.

How much there is self-will would do,
  Were it not for the dire dismay
That bids ye shrink, as ye suddenly think
  Of "What will my neighbor say?"

Then pity me not; for mark mankind
  Of every rank and age;
Look close to the heart, and ye'll ever find,
  That each is a bird in a cage.

THE HEART — THE HEART!

THE heart — the heart! oh! let it be
  A true and bounteous thing;
As kindly warm, as nobly free,
  As eagle's nestling wing.
Oh! keep it not, like miser's gold,
  Shut in from all beside;
But let its precious stores unfold,
  In mercy, far and wide.
The heart — the heart, that's truly blest,
  Is never all its own;
No ray of glory lights the breast
  That beats for self alone.

The heart — the heart! oh! let it spare
  A sigh for other's pain;
The breath that soothes a brother's care
  Is never spent in vain.
And though it throb at gentlest touch,
  Or sorrow's faintest call,
'Twere better it should ache too much,
  Than never ache at all.
The heart — the heart, that's truly blest,
  Is never all its own;
No ray of glory lights the breast
  That beats for self alone.

GALLA BRAE.

O, TELL me did ye ever see
  Sweet Galla on a simmer night,
When ilka star had oped his e'e,
  An' tipped the broom wi' saft pale light?
Ye'd never gang toward the town,
  Ye wadna like the flauntie day,
If ance ye saw the moon blink down
  Her bonnie beams on Galla Brae.

A' silent, save the wimpling tune,
  The win's asleep, nae leaflet stirs;
O' gie me Galla neath the moon,
  Its siller birk an' goudon furze.
There's monie another leesome glen;
  But let 'em talk o' wilk they may,
O' a' the rigs an' shaws I ken
  There's nane sae fair as Galla Brae.

I crept a wee thing on its sod,
  A laughing laddie there I strayed;
I roved beside its burnie's tide
  In morning air an' gloaming shade:
Its gowans were the first I pu'd,
  An' still my leal heart loves it sae
That when I dee nae grave would be
  Sic hallowed earth as Galla Brae

THE KING'S OLD HALL.

FEW ages since, and wild echoes awoke
In thy sweeping dome and panelling oak;
Thy seats were filled with a princely band,
Rulers of men and lords of the land.
Loudly they raved, and gaily they laughed,
O'er the golden chalice and sparkling draught;
And the glittering board and gem-studded plume
Proclaimed thee a monarch's revelling room.

But now the spider is weaving his woof,
Making his loom of thy sculptured roof;
The slug is leaving his slimy stain,
Trailing his way o'er thy Gothic pane;
Weeds have gathered and moss hath grown
On thy topmost ridge and lowest stone;
And the wheeling bat comes flapping his wing
On the walls that circled a banqueting king.

The idle stare and vulgar tread
May fall where the regal train was spread;
The gloomy owl may hide its nest,
And the speckled lizard safely rest.
Who were the revellers? where are their forms?
Go to the charnel, and ask of the worms.
They are low in the dust, forgotten and passed,
And the pile they raised is following fast.

Oh, man, vain man! how futile your aim,
When building your temples to pleasure and fame

Go, work for heaven with faith and care;
Let good works secure thee a mansion there.
For the palace of pageantry crumbles away;
Its beauty and strength are mocked by decay;
And a voice from the desolate halls of kings
Cries, "Put not your trust in corrupted things!"

THE WILLOW-TREE.

Tree of the gloom, o'erhanging the tomb,
  Thou seem'st to love the churchyard sod;
Thou ever art found on the charnel ground,
  Where the laughing and happy have rarely trod.
When thy branches trail to the wintry gale,
  Thy wailing is sad to the hearts of men:
When the world is bright in a summer's light,
  'Tis only the wretched that love thee then.
The golden moth and the shining bee
Will seldom rest on the willow-tree.

The weeping maid comes under thy shade,
  Mourning her faithful lover dead;
She sings of his grave in the crystal wave,
  Of his sea-weed shroud and coral bed.
A chaplet she weaves of thy downy leaves,
  And twines it round her pallid brow;
Sleep falls on her eyes while she softly sighs,
  "My love, my dearest, I come to thee now"

She sits and dreams of the moaning sea,
While the night wind creeps through the willow-tree.

The dying one will turn from the sun,
The dazzling flowers, and luscious fruit,
To set his mark in thy sombre bark,
And find a couch at thy moss-clad root.
He is fading away like the twilight ray,
His cheek is pale and his glance is dim;
But thy drooping arms, with their pensive charms,
Can yield a joy till the last for him;
And the latest words on his lips shall be,
"Oh, bury me under the willow-tree!"

SONG OF THE SUN.

SUPREME of the sky — no throne so high —
I reign a monarch divine;
What have ye below that doth not owe
Its glory and lustre to mine?
Has beauty a charm I have not helped
To nurture in freshness and bloom?
Can a tint be spread — can a glance be shed
Like those I deign to illume?
Though ye mimic my beams, as ye do and ye will,—
Let all galaxies meet, I am mightiest still!

The first red ray that heralds my way,
Just kisses the mountain top;

And splendor dwells in the cowslip bells
  While I kindle each nectar drop:
I speed on my wide refulgent path,
  And nature's homage is given;
All tones are poured to greet me adored
  As I reach the blue mid-heaven,
And the sweetest and boldest, the truly free,
The lark and the eagle come nearest to me.

The glittering train so praised by man,
  The moon, night's worshipped queen,
The silvery scud, and the rainbow's span,
  Snatch from me their colors and sheen.
I know when my radiant streams are flung,
  Creation shows all that is bright,
But I'm jealous of naught save the face of the young,
  Laughing back my noontide light:
I see nothing so pure or so dazzling on earth,
As childhood's brow with its halo of mirth.

My strength goes down in the crystal caves,
  I gem the billow's wide curl,
I paint the dolphin and burnish the waves,
  I tinge the coral and pearl.
Love ye the flowers? What power, save mine,
  Can the velvet rose unfold?
Who else can purple the grape on the vine,
  Or flush the wheat-ear with gold?
Look on the beam-lit wilderness spot —
'Tis more fair than the palace, where I come not.

Though giant clouds ride on the whirlwind's tide,
  And gloom on the world may fall,

I yet flash on in gorgeous pride,
  Untarnished above them all.
So the pure warm heart for a while may appear,
  In probations of sorrow and sin,
To be dimmed and obscured, but trial or tear
  Cannot darken the spirit within.
Let the breast keep its truth, and life's shadows may roll,
But they quench not, they reach not the sun nor the soul.

WHILE THE CHRISTMAS LOG IS BURNING.

Hail to the night when we gather once more
  All the forms we love to meet;
When we've many a guest that's dear to our breast,
  And the household dog at our feet.
Who would not be in the circle of glee
  When heart to heart is yearning—
When joy breathes out in the laughing shout
  While the Christmas log is burning?

'Tis one of the fairy hours of life,
  When the world seems all of light;
For the thought of wo, or the name of a foe,
  Ne'er darkens the festive night.
When bursting mirth rings round the hearth,
  Oh! where is the spirit that's mourning,
While merry bells chime with the carol rhyme,
  And the Christmas log is burning?

Then is the time when the gray old man
  Leaps back to the days of youth;
When brows and eyes bear no disguise,
  But flush and gleam with truth.
Oh! then is the time when the soul exults,
  And seems right heavenward turning;
When we love and bless the hands we press,
  While the Christmas log is burning.

THE ACORN.

Beautiful germ! I have set thee low
In the dewy earth — strike, spring, and grow.
Oh! cleave to the soil, and thou mayst be
The king of the woods, a brave rare tree.
Acorn of England, thou mayst bear
Thy green head high in the mountain air.
Another age, and thy mighty form
May scowl at the sun and mock the storm.

A hundred years, and the woodman's stroke
May fiercely fall on thy heart of oak;
Let time roll on, and thy planks may ride
In glorious state o'er the fathomless tide.
Thou mayst baffle the waters, and firmly take
The winds that sweep and waves that break;
And thy vaunted strength shall as nobly stand
The rage of the sea as the storm on the land.

A hundred years, and in some fair hall
Thou mayst shine as the polished wainscot wall;
And ring with the laugh and echo the jest
Of the happy host and the feasting guest.
Acorn of England! deep in the earth
Mayst thou live and burst in flourishing birth;
May thy root be firm and thy broad arms wave,
When the hand that plants thee is cold in the grave.

FIRE.

Blandly glowing, richly bright,
Cheering star of social light;
While I gently heap it higher,
How I bless thee, sparkling fire!
Who loves not the kindly rays
Streaming from the tempered blaze?
Who can sit beneath his hearth
Dead to feeling, stern to mirth?
Who can watch the crackling pile
And keep his breast all cold the while.

Fire is good, but it must *serve:*
Keep it thralled — for if it swerve
Into freedom's open path,
What shall check its maniac wrath?
Where's the tongue that can proclaim
The fearful work of curbless flame?

Darting wide and shooting high,
It lends a horror to the sky;
It rushes on to waste, to scare,
Arousing terror and despair;
It tells the utmost earth can know
About the demon scenes below;
And sinks at last, all spent and dead,
Among the ashes it has spread.

Sure the poet is not wrong
To glean a moral from the song.
Listen, youth! nor scorn, nor frown,
Thou must chain thy passions down.
Well to serve, but ill to sway,
Like the fire they must *obey.*
They are good in subject state
To strengthen, warm, and animate;
But if once we let them *reign,*
They sweep with desolating train,
Till they but leave a hated name,
A ruined soul, and blackened fame.

A SUMMER SKETCH.

'Tis June, 'tis merry smiling June;
'Tis blushing summer now:
The rose is red — the bloom is dead —
The fruit is on the bough.

Flora, with Ceres, hand in hand,
  Bring all their smiling train:
The yellow corn is waving high,
  To gild the earth again.

The bird-cage hangs upon the wall,
  Amid the clustering vine:
The rustic seat is in the porch,
  Where honeysuckles twine.

The rosy ragged urchins play
  Beneath the glowing sky;
They scoop the sand, or gaily chase
  The bee that buzzes by.

The household spaniel flings his length
  Along the stone-paved hall:
The panting sheep-dog seeks the spot
  Where leafy shadows fall.

The petted kitten frisks among
  The bean-flowers' fragrant maze;
Or, basking, throws her dappled form
  To court the warmest rays.

The opened casement, flinging wide,
  Geraniums give to view;
With choicest posies ranged between,
  Still wet with morning dew.

'Tis June, 'tis merry laughing June;
  There's not a cloud above;
The air is still, o'er heath and hill,
  The bulrush does not move.

The pensive willow bends to kiss
  The stream so deep and clear;
While dabbling ripples gliding on,
  Bring music to mine ear.

The mower whistles o'er his toil,
  The em'rald grass must yield;
The scythe is out, the swarth is down.
  There's incense in the field.

Oh! how I love to calmly muse
  In such an hour as this;
To nurse the joy creation gives,
  In purity and bliss!

There is devotion in my soul
  My lip can ne'er impart;
But thou, oh God! wilt deign to read
  The tablet of my heart.

And if that heart should e'er neglect
  The homage of its prayer,
Lead it to nature's altar-piece,—
  'Twill always worship there.

SONG OF OLD TIME.

I WEAR not the purple of earth-born kings,
Nor the stately ermine of lordly things;
But monarch and courtier, though great they be,
Must fall from their glory and bend to me.
My sceptre is gemless; yet who can say
They will not come under its mighty sway?
Ye may learn who I am,—there's the passing chime,
And the dial to herald me, Old King Time!

Softly I creep, like a thief in the night,
After cheeks all blooming and eyes all light;
My steps are seen on the patriarch's brow,
In the deep-worn furrows and locks of snow.
Who laughs at my power? the young and the gay,
But they dream not how closely I track their way.
Wait till their first bright sands have run,
And they will not smile at what Time hath done.

I eat through treasures with moth and rust;
I lay the gorgeous palace in dust;
I make the shell-proof tower my own,
And break the battlement, stone from stone.
Work on at your cities and temples, proud man,
Build high as ye may, and strong as ye can;
But the marble shall crumble, the pillar shall fall,
And Time, Old Time, will be king after all.

THE BONNIE SCOT.

THE bonnie Scot! he hath nae got
  A hame o' sun an light;
His clime hath aft a dreary day
  An' mony a stormy night.
He hears the blast gae crooning past,
  He sees the snowflake fa':
But what o' that? He'll tell ye still,
  His land is best o' a':
He wadna' tine, for rose or vine,
  The gowans round his cot;
There is nae bloom like heath an' broom,
  To charm the bonnie Scot.

The roarin' din o' flood an' linn
  Is music unco sweet;
He loves the pine aboon his head,
  The breckans 'neath his feet:
The lavrock's trill, sae clear an' shrill,
  Is matchless to his ear;
What joy for him like bounding free
  To hunt the fleet dun deer?
Nae wonder he sae proudly scorns
  A safter, kinder lot;
He kens his earth gave Wallace birth.
  That brave and bonnie Scot.

THE OLD CLOCK.

Clock of the household, the sound of thy bell
Tells the hour, and to many 'tis all thou canst tell;
But to me thou canst preach with the tongue of a sage,
And whisper old tales from life's earliest page.
Thou bringest back visions of heart-bounding times,
When thy midnight stroke chorused the loud-carolled chimes;
When our Christmas was noticed for festival mirth,
And the merry New Year had a boisterous birth.

Thou hast broke on my ear through the dead of the night,
Till my spirit, out-wearied, has prayed for the light;
When thy echoing tone, and a mother's faint breath,
Seemed the sepulchre tidings that whispered of death.
I have listened to thee, when my own pillowed brow
Was wild in its throbbing and deep in its glow;
When the madness of fever, and anguish of pain,
Left a doubt if I ever should hear thee again.

Thou hast always been nigh: thou hast looked upon all,
On the birth—on the bridal—the cradle—and pall:
To the infant at play and the sire turning gray,
Thou hast spoken the warning of "passing away."
My race may be run, when thy musical chime
Will be still ringing out in the service of Time;
And the clock of the household will chime in the room,
When I, the forgotten one, sleep in the tomb!

WASHINGTON.

LAND of the west! though passing brief the record of
thine age,
Thou hast a name that darkens all on history's wide
page!
Let all the blasts of fame ring out — thine shall be
loudest far:
Let others boast their satellites — thou hast the planet
star.
Thou hast a name whose characters of light shall ne'er
depart;
'Tis stamped upon the dullest brain, and warms the
coldest heart;
A war-cry fit for any land where freedom's to be won.
Land of the west! it stands alone — it is thy Wash
ington!

Rome had its Cæsar, great and brave; but stain was
on his wreath;
He lived the heartless conquerer, and died the tyrant's
death.
France had its Eagle; but his wings, though lofty they
might soar,
Were spread in false ambition's flight, and dipped in
murder's gore.
Those hero-gods, whose mighty sway would fain have
chained the waves —
Who fleshed their blades with tiger zeal, to make a
world of slaves —

Who, though their kindred barred the path, still fiercely waded on —
Oh, where shall be *their* "glory" by the side of Washington?

He fought, but not with love of strive; he struck but to defend;
And ere he turned a people's foe, he sought to be a friend.
He strove to keep his country's right by reason's gentle word,
And sighed when fell injustice threw the challenge — sword to sword.
He stood the firm, the calm, the wise, the patriot and sage;
He showed no deep, avenging hate — no burst of despot rage.
He stood for liberty and truth, and dauntlessly led on,
Till shouts of victory gave forth the name of Washington.

No car of triumph bore him through a city filled with grief;
No groaning captives at the wheels proclaimed him victor chief:
He broke the gyves of slavery with strong and high disdain,
And cast no sceptre from the links when he had crushed the chain.
He saved his land, but did not lay his soldier trappings down
To change them for the regal vest, and don a kingly crown.

Fame was too earnest in her joy — too proud of such a
son —
To let a robe and title mask a noble Washington.

England, my heart is truly thine — my loved, my native
earth! —
The land that holds a mother's grave, and gave that
mother birth!
Oh, keenly sad would be the fate that thrust me from
thy shore,
And faltering my breath that sighed, "Farewell for
evermore!"
But did I meet such adverse lot, I would not seek to
dwell
Where olden heroes wrought the deeds for Homer's
song to tell.
Away, thou gallant ship! I'd cry, and bear me swiftly
on:
But bear me from my own fair land to that of Wash-
ington!

THE LAST GOOD-BYE.

FAREWELL! Farewell! is often heard
From the lips of those who part:
'Tis a whispered tone, 'tis a gentle word,
But it springs not from the heart.
It may serve for the lover's lay,
To be sung 'neath a summer sky ·

But give me the lips that say
  The honest words, "Good-bye!"

Adieu! Adieu! may greet the ear
  In the guise of courtly speech;
But when we leave the kind and dear,
  'Tis not what the soul would teach.
Whene'er we grasp the hands of those
  We would have for ever nigh,
The flame of friendship burns and glows
  In the warm, frank words, "Good-bye!"

The mother sending forth her child
  To meet with cares and strife,
Breathes through her tears her doubts and fears
  For the loved one's future life.
No cold "adieu," no "farewell" lives
  Within her choking sigh;
But the deepest sob of anguish gives,
  "God bless thee, boy! — good-bye!"

Go, watch the pale and dying one,
  When the glance has lost its beam —
When the brow is cold as the marble-stone,
  And the world a passing dream;
And the latest pressure of the hand,
  The look of the closing eye,
Yield what the heart *must* understand —
  A long, a last "Good-bye."

THE OLD BARN.

THE barn, the old barn, oh! its dark walls were rife
With the records most fair in my tablet of life;
And a rare barn it was, for, search twenty miles round
Such another brave building was not to be found.

'Twas large as an ark, 'twas strong as a church,
'Twas the chicken's resort, 'twas the young raven's perch;
There the bat flapped his wing, and the owlet migh screech,
Secure in the gable-ends, far out of reach.

It was evident Time had been playing his pranks
With the moss-garnished roof and the storm-beaten planks;
For many a year had the harvest-home wain
Creaked up to its door with the last load of grain

A wee thing, they tumbled me into its mow,
And left me to scramble out, Heaven knows how;
A wild, merry girl, the old barn was the spot
Which afforded delight that is still unforgot.

'Twas a birthday, one scion was walking life's stage,
In youth's proudest of characters — just come of age;
Many plans were devised — but the chosen of all
Was to clear out the old barn, and "get up a ball."

We had prayed, we had hoped that the lanes might be
dry,
That no cloud would come over the moon-lighted sky;
But, alas! 'twas November, and fog, sleet, and gloom,
Made night of our jubilee dark as the tomb.

The rain fell in torrents — the wind roared along —
The watch-dog howled back to the rude tempest song;
And we trembled and feared lest the merriest set
Should be scared by that true English sunshine — the
wet.

But, hark! what loud voices, what rumbling of wheels,
What stepping in puddles, what tragical "squeals!"
While close-tilted wagons and mud-spattered carts
Set down a rare cargo of happy young hearts.

What a dance was the first — with what pleasure we
went
Down the middle and up till our breathing was spent!
Though Musard might have shrugged at a bit of a
strife
'Twixt the notes of the fiddle and key of the fife.

Our flooring was rugged, our sconces had rust;
There was falling of grease—there was raising of dust,
But Terpsichore published a *Morning Post* "yarn"
On the Almacks we held in the noble old barn.

Then the rat-hunt! oh, mercy! we hear poets speak
Of the tug of fierce battle when "Greek joins with
Greek;"
But war held as wild and as deadly a reign
When the terriers met the destroyers of grain.

The smith left his bellows — the miller his sack —
'Twas fortunate business grew suddenly slack:
The thatcher was there, and the thatcher's boy too,
And, somehow, the butcher had nothing to do.

The 'Squire lent his stick and his voice to the fray, —
He, of course, only "chanced to be riding that way;"
And the master — the ploughman — the rich and the poor,
Stood Equality's jostling about the barn-door.

There was bustling old Pincher, all fierceness and bark,
And even fat Dido as gay as a lark;
Snap, Vixen, and Bob, and another full score,
For though rats might be many — the dogs were oft more.

'Twas sport, I dare say, but such works were torn down,
That the sapient "master" looked on with a frown;
And saw, without aid of astrologer's star,
That the hunters were worse than the hunted by far.

Full well I remember our taking the ale
To the good-natured fellow who toiled at the flail;
When the boy who now sleeps with a stone at his feet
Would fain try his hand as a thrasher of wheat.

'Twas agreed to — and boldly he swung the bright staff,
With an awkwardness raising a tittering laugh,
Which strengthened to bursting Vulgarity's tone,
When, instead of on wheat-ears, it fell on his own.

Ever luckless in daring, 'twas he who slipped down,
With a broken-out tooth and a broken-in crown —
When he clambered up high on the cross-beams to feed
The unhappy stray cat and her tortoise-shell breed.

'Twas he who, in petulance, sulked to his home,
And packed up his bundle the wide world to roam;
But, with penitent heart and a shelterless head,
He came back to the sheaves in the barn for a bed.

'Twas a bitter cold night, when I heard, with a pout,
That the stables were full and old Dobbin turned out:
Old Dob who had seen a score miles since the morn;
'Twas a shame and a cruelty not to be borne.

A brother was ready — the pony was caught —
Brought in he *must* be — yet where *could* he be brought;
But short was the parley, and, munching away,
He was warm in the barn with his oats and his hay.

The barn was the place where the beams and the rope
Gave our mischievous faculties plenty of scope;
And when rick lines were found, knotted, severed, and frayed,
Not a word did we breathe of the swings we had made.

"Hide and seek" was the game that delighted us most,
When we stealthily crept behind pillar and post;
When the law was enforced that "Home" should not be won,
Till we'd circled the barn in our scampering run.

I'd a merry heart then — but I scarcely know why
I should look into Memory's page with a sigh;
'Tis ungrateful to turn to the past with regret,
When we hold a fair portion of happiness yet.

My laugh in that day was a spirited shout,
But still it is heard to ring joyously out;
My friends were the warmest that childhood could find,
But those round me still are endearingly kind.

"Long ago," has too often awakened my soul,
Till my pale brow would sink and the tear-drop would roll:
Down, down, busy thought, for the future may be
As bright as the time of the old barn for me.

SONG OF THE DYING OLD MAN TO HIS YOUNG WIFE.

KATE, there's a trembling at my heart, a coldness at my brow,
My sight is dim, my breath is faint, I feel I'm dying now;
But ere my vision fadeth quite, ere all of strength be o'er,
Oh! let me look into thy face and press thy hand once more.

would my latest glance should fall on what I hold
most dear:
But, ah! thy cheek is wet again—wipe, wipe away the
tear.
Such tears of late have often gemmed thy drooping
eyelid's fringe,
Such tears of late have washed away thy young cheek's
ruddy tinge.

I brought thee from a simple home to be an old man's
bride,
Thou wert the altar where I laid affection, joy, and
pride;
My heart's devotion, like the sun, shone forth with dim-
less power,
And kept its brightest glory rays to mark its setting
hour.

I brought thee from a simple home, when early friends
had met,
And something filled thy farewell tone that whispered
of regret.
Oh! could I wonder, when you left warm spirits like
your own,
To dwell upon far distant earth with age and wealth
alone?

I gazed with holy fondness on thy meek retiring eye,
Soft in its beaming as the first fair star of evening's
sky;
I marked the dimpled mirth around thy sweet lips when
they smiled,
And while I loved thee as a bride I blest thee as
child.

But, oh! thy young and glowing heart could not respond
to mine,
My whitened hairs seemed mocked by those rich sunny
curls of thine;
And though thy gentle faith was kind as woman's faith
can be,
'Twas as the spring-flower clinging round the winter-
blighted tree.

My speech is faltering and low — the world is fading
fast —
The sands of life are few and slow — this day will be
my last;
I've something for thine ear — bend close — list to my
failing word,
Lay what I utter to thy soul, and start not when 'tis
heard.

There's one who loves thee — though his love has never
lived in speech —
He worships as a devotee the star he cannot reach;
He strives to mask his throbbing breast and hide its
burning glow;
But I have pierced the veil and seen the struggling
heart below.

Nay, speak not. I alone have been the selfish and un-
wise;
Young hearts will nestle with young hearts, young eyes
will meet young eyes.
And when I saw his earnest glance turn hopelessly
away,
I thanked the hand of Time that gave me warning of
decay.

I question not thy bosom, Kate — I cast upon thy name
No memory of jealous fear, no lightest shade of blame.
I know that he has loved thee long, with deep and secret truth;
I know he is a fitting one to bless thy trusting youth.

Weep not for me with bitter grief; I would but have thee tell,
That he who bribed thee to his heart has cherished thee right well.
I give thee to another, Kate — and may that other prove
As grateful for the blessing held, as doting in his love.

Bury me in the churchyard where the dark yew branches wave,
And promise thou wilt come sometimes to weed the old man's grave;
'Tis all I ask! I'm blind — I'm faint — take, take my parting breath —
I die within thy arms, my Kate, and feel no sting of death.

THE INDIAN HUNTER.

Oh, why does the white man follow my path,
  Like the hound on the tiger's track ?
Does the flush on my dark cheek waken his wrath ?
  Does he covet the bow on my back ?
He has rivers and seas, where the billows and breeze
  Bear riches for him alone ;
And the sons of the wood never plunge in the flood
  Which the white man calls his own.

Why, then, should he come to the streams where none
  But the red-skin dare to swim ?
Why, why should he wrong the hunter one,
  Who never did harm to him ?
The Father above thought fit to give,
  The white men corn and wine :
There are golden fields where they may live,
  But the forest shades are mine.

The eagle hath its place of rest,
  The wild-horse where to dwell ;
And the Spirit that gave the bird its nest,
  Made me a home as well.
Then back, go back from the red-man's track,
  For the hunter's eye grows dim
To find that the white man wrongs the one
  Who never did harm to him.

THE POOR MAN'S FRIEND.

No sable pall, no waving plume,
No thousand torch-lights to illume;
No parting glance, no struggling tear,
Is seen to fall upon the bier.

There is not one of kindred clay,
To watch the coffin on its way;
No mortal form, no human breast,
Cares where the poor man's bones may rest.

But one deep mourner follows there,
Whose grief outlives the funeral prayer:
He does not sigh, he does not weep,
But will not leave the sodless heap.

No! he who was the poor man's mate,
And made him more content with fate —
The old gray dog that shared his crust,
Is all that stands beside his dust.

He bends his listening head, as though
He thought to hear a voice below;
He pines to miss that voice so kind,
And wonders why he's left behind.

The sun goes down, the night is come
He needs no food, he seeks no home,
But, stretched upon the dreamless bed,
With doleful howl calls back the dead.

The passing gaze may coldly dwell
On all that polished marbles tell,
For temples built on churchyard earth
Are claimed by riches more than worth.

But who would mark with undimmed eyes,
The mourning dog that starves and dies?
Who would not ask, who would not crave,
Such love and faith to guard his grave?

HARVEST SONG.

I LOVE, I love to see
  Bright steel gleam through the land;
'Tis a goodly sight, but it must be
  In the reaper's tawny hand.

The helmet and the spear
  Are twined with laurel wreath;
But the trophy is wet with the orphan's tear,
  And blood-spots rest beneath.

I love to see the field
  That is moist with purple stain;
But not where bullet, sword, and shield,
  Lie strown with the gory slain.

No, no: 'tis when the sun
  Shoots down his cloudless beams,

Till the rich and bursting juice-drops run
  On the vineyard earth in streams.

My glowing heart beats high
  At the sight of shining gold;
But it is not that which the miser's eye
  Delighteth to behold.

A brighter wealth by far
  Than the deep mine's yellow vein,
Is seen around, in the fair hills crowned
  With sheaves of burnished grain.

Look forth, ye toiling men;
  Though little ye possess,
Be glad that dearth is not on earth,
  To leave that little less.

Let the song of praise be poured,
  In gratitude and joy,
By the rich man, with his garners stored,
  And the ragged gleaner boy.

The feast *that* warfare gives
  Is not for one alone —
'Tis shared by the meanest slave that lives,
  And the tenant of a throne.

Then glory to the steel
  That shines in the reaper's hand;
And thanks to God, who has blessed the sod,
  And crowns the harvest land!

SONG OF THE SPIRIT OF POVERTY.

A song, a song, for the beldame Queen,
  A Queen that the world knows well,
Whose portal of state is the workhouse gate,
  And throne the prison cell.

I have been crowned in every land,
  With nightshade steeped in tears,
I've a dog-gnawn bone for my sceptre wand
  Which the proudest mortal fears.

No gem I wear in my tangled hair,
  No golden vest I own,
No radiant glow tints cheek or brow,
  Yet say, who dares my frown?

Oh! I am Queen of a ghastly court,
  And tyrant sway I hold,
Baiting human hearts for my royal sport
  With the bloodhounds of Hunger and Cold.

My power can change the purest clay
  From its first and beautiful mould,
Till it hideth from the face of day,
  Too hideous to behold.

Mark ye the wretch who has cloven and cleft
  The skull of the lonely one,
And quailed not at purpling his blade to the heft,
  To make sure that the deed was done:

Fair seeds were sown in his infant breast,
 That held goodly blossom and fruit,
But I trampled them down — Man did the rest —
 And God's image grew into the brute.

He hath been driven, and hunted, and scourged,
 For the sin I bade him do,
He hath wrought the lawless work I urged
 Till blood seemed fair to his view.

I shriek with delight to see him bedight
 In fetters that chink and gleam,
"He is mine!" I shout as they lead him out,
 From the dungeon to the beam.

See the lean boy clutch his rough-hewn crutch,
 With limbs all warped and worn,
While hurries along through a noisy throng,
 The theme of their gibing scorn.

Wealth and care would have reared him straight
 As the towering mountain pine,
But I nursed him into that halting gait,
 And withered his marrowless spine.

Pain may be heard on the downy bed,
 Heaving the groan of despair,
For Suffering shuns not the diademed head,
 And abideth everywhere.

But the shortened breath and parching lip
 Are watched by many an eye,
And there is balmy drink to sip,
 And tender hands to ply.

Come, come with me, and ye shall see
   What a child of mine can bear,
Where squalid shadows thicken the light,
   And foulness taints the air.

He lieth alone to gasp and moan,
   While the cancer eats his flesh,
With the old rags festering on his wound,
   For none will give him fresh.

Oh, carry him forth in a blanket robe,
   The lazar house is nigh,
The careless hand shall cut and probe,
   And strangers see him die.

Where's the escutcheon of blazoned worth?
   Who is heir to the famed rich man?
Ha! ha! he is mine — dig a hole in the earth,
   And hide him as soon as ye can.

Oh, I am Queen of a ghastly Court,
   And the handmaids that I keep
Are such phantom things as Fever brings
   To haunt the fitful sleep.

See, see, they come in my haggard train,
   With jagged and matted locks
Hanging round them as rough as the wild steed's mane,
   Or the black weed on the rocks.

They come with broad and horny palms,
   They come in maniac guise,
With angled chins, and yellow skins,
   And hollow staring eyes.

They come to be girded with leather and link,
  And away at my bidding they go,
To toil where the soulless beast would shrink,
  In the deep, damp caverns below.

Daughters of beauty, they, like ye,
  Are of gentle womankind,
And wonder not if little there be,
  Of angel form and mind.

If I'd held your cheeks by as close a pinch,
  Would that flourishing rose be found?
If I'd doled you a crust out, inch by inch,
  Would your arms have been so round?

Oh, I am Queen with a despot rule,
  That crushes to the dust;
The laws I deal, bear no appeal,
  Though ruthless and unjust.

I deaden the bosom and darken the brain,
  With the might of the demon's skill;
The heart may struggle, but struggle in vain,
  As I grapple it harder still.

Oh, come with me, and ye shall see
  How well I begin the day,
For I'll hie to the hungriest slave I have,
  And snatch his loaf away.

Oh, come with me, and ye shall see
  How my skeleton victims fall;
How I order the graves without a stone,
  And the coffins without a pall.

Then a song, a song for the beldame Queen —
  A Queen that ye fear right well;
For my portal of state is the workhouse gate,
  And my throne the prison cell.

THE OLD MILL-STREAM.

Beautiful streamlet! how precious to me
Was the green-swarded paradise watered by thee;
I dream of thee still, as thou wert in my youth,
Thy meanderings haunt me with freshness and truth.

I had heard of full many a river of fame,
With its wide-rolling flood and its classical name;
But the Thames of Old England, the Tiber of Rome,
Could not peer with the mill-streamlet close to my home.

Full well I remember the gravelly spot,
Where I slyly repaired, though I knew I ought not;
Where I stood with my handful of pebbles to make
That formation of fancy, a duck and a drake.

How severe was the scolding, how heavy the threat,
When my pinafore hung on me dirty and wet!
How heedlessly silent I stood to be told
Of the danger of drowning, the risk of a cold!

"Now mark!" cried a mother, "the mischief done there
Is unbearable — go to that stream if you dare;

But I sped to that stream like a frolicsome colt,
For I knew that her thunder-cloud carried no bolt.

Though puzzled with longitude, adverb, and noun,
Till my forehead was sunk in a studious frown;
Yet that stream was a Lethe that swept from my soul
The grammar, the globes, and the tutor's control.

I wonder if still the young anglers begin,
As I did, with willow-wand, packthread, and pin;
When I threw in my line, with expectancy high
As to perch in my basket and eels in a pie.

When I watched every bubble that broke on a weed,
Yet found I caught nothing but lily and reed;
Till time and discernment began to instil
The manœuvres of Walton with infinite skill.

Full soon I discovered the birch-shadowed place
That nurtured the trout and the silver-backed dace;
Where the coming of night found me blest and content,
With my patience unworn and my fishing-rod bent.

How fresh were the flags on the stone-studded ridge,
That rudely supported the narrow oak bridge!
And that bridge, oh! how boldly and safely I ran
On the thin plank that now I should timidly scan!

I traversed it often at fall of the night,
When the clouds of December shut out the moon's
light;
A mother might tremble, but I never did,
For my footing was sure, though the pale stars were
hid.

When the breath of stern winter had fettered the tide,
What joy to career on its feet-warming slide;
With mirth in each eye and bright health on each cheek,
While the gale in our faces came piercing and bleak!

The snow-flakes fell fast on our wind-roughened curls,
But we laughed as we shook off the feathery pearls;
And the running, the tripping, the pull and the haul
Had a glorious end in the slip and the sprawl.

Oh! I loved the wild place where clear ripples flowed
On their serpentine way o'er the pebble-strewn road,
Where, mounted on Dobbin, we youngsters would dash,
Both pony and rider enjoying the splash.

How often I tried to teach Pincher the tricks
Of diving for pebbles and swimming for sticks!
But my doctrines could never induce the loved brute
To consider hydraulics a pleasant pursuit.

Did a *forcible* argument sometimes prevail,
What a woful expression was seen in his tail;
And though bitterly vexed, I was made to agree
That Dido, the spaniel, swam better than he.

What pleasure it was to spring forth in the sun
When the school-door was ope'd and our lessons were done;
When "Where shall we play?" was the doubt and the call,
And "Down by the mill-stream" was echoed by all;

When tired of childhood's rude boisterous pranks,
We pulled the tall rushes that grew on its banks·

And, busily quiet, we sat ourselves down
To weave the rough basket or plait the light crown.

I remember the launch of our fairy-built ship,
How we set her white sails, pulled her anchor atrip;
Till mischievous hands, working hard at the craft,
Turned the ship to a boat, and the boat to a raft.

The first of my doggerel breathings was there,
'Twas the hope of a poet, "An Ode to Despair."
I won't vouch for its metre, its sense, or its rhyme,
But I know that I then thought it truly sublime.

Beautiful streamlet! I dream of thee still,
Of thy pouring cascade, and the tic-tac-ing mill;
Thou livest in memory, and wilt not depart,
For thy waters seem blent with the streams of my heart.

Home of my youth! if I go to thee now,
None can remember my voice or my brow;
None can remember the sunny-faced child,
That played by the water-mill joyous and wild.

The aged, who laid their thin hands on my head
To smooth my dark shining curls, rest with the dead;
The young, who partook of my sports and my glee,
Can see naught but a wandering stranger in me.

Beautiful streamlet! I sought thee again,
But the changes that marked thee awakened deep pain,
Desolation had reigned, thou wert not as of yore—
Home of my childhood, I'll see thee no more!

OLD STORY BOOKS.

OLD story books! old story books! we owe ye much,
old friends,
Bright-colored threads in Memory's warp, of which
Death holds the ends.
Who can forget ye? — who can spurn the ministers of
joy
That waited on the lisping girl and petticoated boy?
I know that ye could *win* my heart when every bribe
or threat
Failed to allay my stamping rage, or break my sullen
pet:
A "promised story" was enough—I turned with eager
smile,
To learn about the naughty "pig that would not mount
the stile."

There was a spot in days of yore whereon I used to
stand,
With mighty question in my head and penny in my
hand;
Where motley sweets and crinkled cakes made up a
goodly show,
And "story books" upon a string, appeared in brilliant
row.
What should I have? the peppermint was incense in
my nose,
But I had heard of "hero Jack" who slew his giant
foes:

My lonely coin was balanced long before the tempting stall,
'Twixt book and bull's eye, but, forsooth! "Jack" got it after all.

Talk of your "vellum, gold embossed," "morocco," "roan," and "calf,"
The blue and yellow wraps of old were prettier by half:
And as to pictures! well we know that never one was made
Like that where "Bluebeard" swings aloft his wife-destroying blade.
"Hume's England!"— pshaw! what history of battles, states and men
Can vie with Memoirs "all about sweet little Jenny Wren?"
And what are all the wonders that e'er struck a nation dumb,
To those recorded as performed by "Master Thomas Thumb?"

"Miss Riding Hood," poor luckless child! my heart grew big with dread,
When the grim "wolf," in grandmamma's best bonnet, showed his head;
I shuddered when, in innocence, she meekly peeped beneath,
And made remarks about "great eyes," and wondered at "great teeth."
And then the "House that Jack built," and the "Beanstalk Jack cut down,"
And "Jack's eleven brothers," on their travels of renown;

And "Jack," whose cracked and plastered head insured him lyric fame,
These, these, methinks, make "vulgar Jack" a rather classic name.

Fair "Valentine," I loved him well; but, better still the bear
That hugged his brother in her arms with tenderness and care.
I lingered spell-bound o'er the page, though even-tide wore late,
And left my supper all untouched to fathom "Orson's" fate.
Then "Robin with his merry men," a noble band were they,
We'll never see the like again, go hunting where we may.
In Lincoln garb, with bow and barb, rapt Fancy bore me on,
Through Sherwood's dewy forest-paths, close after "Little John."

"Miss Cinderella" and her "shoe" kept long their reigning powers,
Till harder words and longer themes beguiled my flying hours;
And "Sinbad," wondrous sailor he, allured me on his track,
And set me shouting when he flung the old man from his back.
And oh! that tale—the matchless tale, that made me dream at night
Of "Crusoe's" shaggy robe of fur, and "Friday's" death-spurred flight;

Nay, still I read it, and again, in sleeping visions, see
The savage dancers on the sand — the raft upon the sea.

Old story books! old story books! I doubt if "Reason's Feast"
Provides a dish that pleases more than "Beauty and the Beast;"
I doubt if all the Ledger-leaves that bear a sterling sum,
Yield happiness like those that told of "Master Horner's plum."
Old story books! old story books! I never pass ye by
Without a sort of furtive glance — right loving, though 'tis sly;
And fair suspicion may arise — that yet my spirit grieves
For dear "Old Mother Hubbard's Dog" and "Ali Baba's Thieves."

THE

POETICAL WORKS

OF

MISS LANDON.

A NEW EDITION.

BOSTON:
PHILLIPS, SAMPSON, & CO.,
110 Washington Street.
1853.

MISCELLANEOUS POEMS.

ROSALIE.

'Tis a wild tale—and sad, too, as the sigh
That young lips breathe when Love's first dreamings fly:
When blights and cankerworms, and chilling showers,
Come withering o'er the warm heart's passion-flowers.
Love! gentlest spirit! I do tell of thee,—
Of all thy thousand hopes, thy many fears,
Thy morning blushes, and thy evening tears;
What thou hast ever been, and still will be,
Life's best, but most betraying witchery!
It is a night of summer,—and the sea
Sleeps, like a child, in mute tranquility.
Soft o'er the deep-blue wave the moonlight breaks;
Gleaming, from out the white clouds of its zone,
Like beauty's changeful smile, when that it seeks
Some face it loves, yet fears to dwell upon.
The waves are motionless, save where the oar,
Light as Love's anger, and as quickly gone,
Has broken in upon their azure sleep.
Odors are on the air: — the gale has been
Wandering in groves where the rich roses weep,—
Where orange, citron, and the soft lime-flowers
Shed forth their fragrance to night's dewy hours.

Afar the distant city meets the gaze,
  Where tower and turret in the pale light shine,
Seen like the monuments of other days —
Monuments time half shadows, half displays.
And there are many, who, with witching song
  And wild guitar's soul-thrilling melody,
Or the lute's melting music, float along
  O'er the blue waters, still and silently.
That night had Naples sent her best display
Of young and gallant, beautiful and gay.

There was a bark a little way apart
  From all the rest, and there two lovers leant: —
One with a blushing cheek and beating heart,
  And bashful glance, upon the sea-wave bent;
  She might not meet the gaze the other sent
Upon her beauty; — but the half-breathed sighs
The deepening color, timid smiling eyes,
Told that she listened Love's sweet flatteries.
Then they were silent: — words are little aid
To love, whose deepest vows are ever made
By the heart's beat alone. O, silence is
Love's own peculiar eloquence of bliss! —

Music swept past: — it was a simple tone;
  But it has wakened heartfelt sympathies; —
It has brought into life things past and gone;
  Has wakened all those secret memories,
That may be smothered, but that still will be
Present within thy soul, young Rosalie!
The notes had roused an answering chord within:
In other days, that song her vesper hymn had been.
Her altered look is pale: — that dewy eye
  Almost belies the smile her rich lips wear; —

That smile is mocked by a scarce-breathing sigh
  Which tells of silent and suppressed care—
  Tells that the life is withering with despair,
More irksome from its unsunned silentness—
  A festering wound the spirit pines to bear;
A galling chain, whose pressure will intrude,
Fettering Mirth's step, and Pleasure's lightest mood.

Where are her thoughts thus wandering!—A spot,
  Now distant far, is pictured on her mind,—
A chestnut shadowing a low white cot,
  With rose and jasmine round the casement twined,
  Mixed with the myrtle-tree's luxuriant blind,
Alone, (O! should such solitude be here?)
  An aged form beneath the shade reclined,
Whose eye glanced round the scene — and then a tear
  Told that she missed one in her heart enshrined!
Then came rememberances of other times,
  When eve oped her rich bowers for the pale day;
When the faint, distant tones of convent chimes
Were answered by the lute and vesper lay; —
When the fond mother blest her gentle child,
And for her welfare prayed the Virgin mild.
And she has left the aged one to steep
  Her nightly couch with tears for that lost child,—
The Rosalie,—who left her age to weep,
  When that the tempter flattered her and wiled
  Her steps away, from her own home beguiled.
She started up in agony:—her eye
  Met Manfredi's. Softly he spoke, and smiled.
Memory is past, and thought and feeling lie
Lost in one dream—all thrown on one wild die.
They floated o'er the waters, till the moon
Looked from the blue sky in her zenith noon,—

Till each glad bark at length had sought the shore,
And the waves echoed to the lute no more;
Then sought their gay palazzo, where the ray
Of lamps shed light only less bright than day;
And there they feasted till the morn did fling
Her blushes o'er their mirth and revelling.
  And life was as a tale of faërie,—
As when some Eastern geni rears bright bowers,
And spreads the green turf and the colored flowers;
  And calls upon the earth, the sea, the sky,
To yield their treasures for some gentle queen,
Whose reign is over the enchanted scene.
And Rosalie had pledged a magic cup—
  The maddening cup of pleasure and of love!
There was for her one only dream on earth!
  There was for her one only star above!—
She bent in passionate idolatry
Before her heart's sole idol—Manfredi!

II.

'Tis night again—a soft and summer night;—
A deep-blue heaven, white clouds, moon and starlight;
So calm, so beautiful, that human eye
Might weep to look on such a tranquil sky:—
A night just formed for Hope's first dream of bliss,
Or for Love's yet more perfect happiness!

The moon is o'er a grove of cypress trees,
Weeping, like mourners, in the plaining breeze;
Echoing the music of a rill, whose song
Glided so sweetly, but so sad, along.
There is a little chapel in the shade,
Where many a pilgrim has knelt down and prayed

To the sweet saint, whose portrait, o'er the shrine,
The painter's skill has made all but divine.
It was a pale, a melancholy face,—
A cheek which bore the trace of frequent tears,
And worn by grief,—though grief might not efface
The seal that beauty set in happier years;
And such a smile as on the brow appears
Of one whose earthly thoughts, long since subdued
Past this life's joys and sorrows, hopes and fears—
The wordly dreams o'er which the many brood.—
The heart-beat hushed in mild and chastened mood.
It was the image of the maid who wept
Those precious tears that heal and purify.
Love yet upon her lip his station kept,
But heaven and heavenly thoughts were in her eye.
One knelt before the shrine, with cheek as pale
As was the cold white marble. Can this be
The young—the loved—the happy Rosalie?
Alas! alas! hers is a common tale:—
She trusted,—as youth ever has believed;—
She heard Love's vows—confided—was deceived!

Oh, Love! thy essence is thy purity!
Breathe one unhallowed breath upon thy flame,
And it is gone forever,—and but leaves
A sullied vase—its pure light lost in shame!

And Rosalie was loved,—not with that pure
And holy passion which can age endure;
But loved with wild and self-consuming fires,—
A torch which glares—and scorches—and expires.
A little while her dream of bliss remained,—
A little while Love's wings were left unchained.

But change came o'er the trusted Manfredi:
His heart forgot its vowed idolatry;
And his forgotten love was left to brood
O'er wrongs and ruin in her solitude!

How very desolate that breast must be,
Whose only joyance is in memory!
And what must woman suffer, thus betrayed!—
Her heart's most warm and precious feelings made
But things wherewith to wound: that heart—so weak,
So soft—laid open to the vulture's beak!
Its sweet revealings given up to scorn
It burns to bear, and yet that must be borne!
And, sorer, still, that bitterer emotion,
To know the shrine which had our soul's devotion
Is that of a false deity!—to look
Upon the eyes we worshipped, and brook
Their cold reply! Yet these are all for her!—
The rude world's outcast, and love's wanderer!
Alas! that love, which is so sweet a thing,
Should ever cause guilt, grief, or suffering!
Yet she upon whose face the sunbeams fall—
That dark-eyed girl—had felt their bitterest thrall!

She thought upon her love; and there was not
In passion's record one green sunny spot—
It had been all a madness and a dream,
The shadow of a flower on the stream,
Which seems, but is not; and then memory turned
To her lone mother. How her bosom burned
With sweet and bitter thoughts! There might be rest—
The wounded dove will flee into her nest—

That mother's arms might fold her child again,
The cold world scorn, the cruel smite in vain,
And falsehood be remembered no more
In that calm shelter:—and she might weep o'er
Her faults and find forgiveness. Had not she
  To whom she knelt found pardon in the eyes
  Of Heaven, in offering for sacrifice
A broken heart? And might not pardon be
Also for her? She looked up to the face
  Of that pale saint; and in that gentle brow,
Which seemed to hold communion with her thought,
  There was a smile which gave hope energy.
She prayed one deep, wild prayer,—that she might gain
The home she hoped;—then sought that home again.

A flush of beauty is upon the sky—
Eve's last warm blushes—like the crimson dye
The maiden wears, when first her dark eyes meet
The graceful lover's sighing at her feet.
And there were sounds of music on the breeze,
And perfume shaken from the citron trees;
While the dark chestnuts caught a golden ray
On their green leaves, the last bright gift of day;
And peasants dancing gayly in the shade
To the soft mandolin, whose light notes made
An echo fit to the glad voices singing.
The twilight spirit his sweet urn is flinging
Of dew upon the lime and orange stems,
And giving to the rose pearl diadems.

There is a pilgrim by that old gray tree,
With head upon her hand bent mournfully;
And looking round upon each lovely thing,
And breathing the sweet air, as they could bring

To her no beauty and no solacing.
'Tis Rosalie! Her prayer was not in vain,
The truant-child has sought her home again!

It must be worth a life of toil and care,—
Worth those dark chains the wearied one must bear
Who toils up fortune's steep,—all that can wring
The worn-out bosom with lone suffering,—
Worth restlessness, oppression, goading fears,
And long-deferred hopes of many years,—
To reach again that little quiet spot,
So well-loved once, and never quite forgot;—
To trace again the steps of infancy,
And catch their freshness from their memory!
And it is triumph, sure, when fortune's sun
Has shone upon us, and our task is done,
To show our harvest to the eyes which were
Once all the world to us! Perhaps there are
Some who had presaged kindly of our youth;
Feel we not proud their prophecy was sooth?

But how felt Rosalie?—The very air
Seemed as it brought reproach! there was no eye
To look delighted, welcome none was there!
She felt as feels an outcast wandering by
Where every door is closed! She looked around!—
She heard some voices' sweet familiar sound.
There were some changed, and some remembered things;
There were girls, whom she left in their first springs,
Now blushed into full beauty. There was one
Whom she loved tenderly in days now gone!
She was not dancing gayly with the rest;
A rose-cheeked child within her arms was prest.

And it had twined its small hands in the hair
That clustered o'er its mother's brow: as fair
As buds in spring. She gave her laughing dove
To one who clasped it with a father's love;
And if a painter's eye had sought a scene
  Of love in its most perfect loveliness—
  Of childhood, and of wedded happiness,—
He would have painted the sweet Madeline!
But Rosalie shrank from them, and she strayed
Through a small grove of cypresses, whose shade
Hung o'er a burying-ground, where the low stone
And the gray cross recorded those now gone!
There was a grave just closed. Not one seemed near
To pay the tribute of one long—last tear!
How very desolate must that one be
Whose more than grave has not a memory!

Then Rosalie thought on her mother's age,—
  Just such her end would be with her away:
No child the last cold death-pang to assuage—
  No child by her neglected tomb to pray!
She asked—and like a hope from heaven it came?—
To hear them answer with a stranger's name.

She reached her mother's cottage; by that gate
She thought how her once lover wont to wait
To tell her honeyed tales; and then she thought
On all the utter ruin he had wrought!
The moon shone brightly, as it used to do
Ere youth, and hope, and love, had been untrue;
But it shone o'er the desolate! The flowers
Were dead; the faded jessamine, unbound,
Trailed, like a heavy weed, upon the ground;

And fell the moonlight vainly over trees,
Which had not even one rose,—although the breeze,
Almost as if in mockery, had brought
Sweet tones it from the nightingale had caught!

She entered in the cottage. None were there!
The hearth was dark,— the walls looked cold and bare!
All—all spoke poverty and suffering!
All—all was changed! and but one only thing
Kept its old place! Rosalie's mandolin
Hung on the wall, where it had ever been.
There was one other room,—and Rosalie
Sought for her mother there. A heavy flame
Gleamed from a dying lamp; a cold air came
Damp from the broken casement. There one lay,
Like marble seen but by the moonlight ray!
And Rosalie drew near. One withered hand
Was stretched, as it would reach a wretched stand
Where some cold water stood! And by the bed
She knelt—and gazed—and saw her mother—dead!

THE BAYADERE.

AN INDIAN TALE.

THERE were seventy pillars around the hall,
Of wreathed gold was each capital,
And the roof was fretted with amber and gems,
Such as light kingly diadems ;
The floor was marble, white as the snow
Ere its pureness is stained by its fall below :
In the midst played a fountain, whose starry showers
Fell, like beams, on the radiant flowers,
Whose colors were gleaming, as every one
Burnt from the kisses just caught from the sun ;
And vases sent forth their silvery clouds,
Like those which the face of the young moon shrouds,
But sweet as the breath of the twilight hour
When the dew awakens the rose's power.
At the end of the hall was a sun-bright throne,
Rich with every glorious stone ;
And the purple canopy overhead
Was like the shade o'er the day-fall shed ;
And the couch beneath was of buds half blown,
Hued with the blooms of the rainbow's zone ;
And round, like festoons, a vine was rolled,
Whose leaf was of emerald, whose fruit was of gold.
But though graced as for a festival,
There was something sad in that stately hall :
There floated the breath of the harp and flute,—
But the sweetest of every music is mute :

There are flowers of light, and spiced perfume,—
But there wants the sweetest of breath and of bloom:
And the hall is lone, and the hall is drear,
For the smiling of woman shineth not here.
With urns of odor o'er him weeping,
Upon the couch a youth is sleeping:
His radiant hair is bound with stars,
  Such as shine on the brow of night,
Filling the dome with diamond rays,
  Only than his own curls less bright.
And such a brow, and such an eye
As fit a young divinity;
A brow like twilight's darkening line,
An eye like morning's first sunshine,
Now glancing through the veil of dreams
As sudden light at daybreak streams.
And richer than the mingled shade
By gem, and gold, and purple made,
His orient wings closed o'er his head;
  Like that bird's, bright with every dye,
Whose home, as Persian bards have said,
  Is fixed in scented Araby.
Some dream is passing o'er him now—
A sudden flash is on his brow;
And from his lip come murmured words,
Low, but sweet as the light lute chords
When o'er its strings the night winds glide
To woo the roses by its side.
He, the fair boy-god, whose nest
Is in the water-lily's breast;
He of the many-arrowed bow,
Of the joys that come and go
Like the leaves, and of the sighs
Like the winds of summer skies,

Blushes like the birds of spring,
Soon seen and soon vanishing;
He of hopes, and he of fears,
He of smiles, and he of tears—
Young Camdeo, he has brought
A sweet dream of colored thought,
One of love and woman's power,
To Mandalla's sleeping hour.

Joyless and dark was his jewelled throne,
When Mandalla awakened and found him alone.
He drank the perfume that around him swept,
'Twas not sweet as the sigh he drank as he slept;
There was music, but where was the voice at whose thrill
Every pulse in his veins was throbbing still?
And dim was the home of his native star,
While the light of woman and love was afar;
And lips of the rosebud, and violet eyes
Are the sunniest flowers in Paradise.
He veiled the light of his glorious race
In a mortal's form and a mortal's face;
And 'mid earth's loveliest sought for one
Who might dwell in his hall and share in his throne

The loorie brought to his cinnamon nest
The bee from the midst of its honey quest,
And open the leaves of the lotus lay
To welcome the noon of the summer day.
It was glory, and light, and beauty all,
When Mandalla closed his wing in Bengal.
He stood in the midst of a stately square,
As the waves of the sea rolled the thousands there;

Their gathering was round the gorgeous car
Where sat in his triumph the Subadar;
For his sabre was red with the blood of the slain,
And his proudest foes were slaves in his chain;
And the sound of the trumpet, the sound of his name,
Rose in shouts from the crowd as onwards he came.
With gems and gold on his ataghan,
A thousand warriors led the van,
Mounted on steeds black as the night,
But with foam and with stirrup gleaming in light;
And another thousand came in their rear,
On white horses, armed with bow and spear,
With quivers of gold on each shoulder laid,
And with crimson belt for each crooked blade.
Then followed the foot ranks,—their turbans showed
Like flashes of light from a mountain cloud,
For white were the turbans as winter snow,
And death-black the foreheads that darkened below;
Scarlet and white was each soldier's vest,
And each bore a lion of gold on his breast,
For this was the chosen band that bore
The lion standard,—it floated o'er
Their ranks like morning; at every wave
Of that purple banner, the trumpets gave
A martial salute to the radiant fold
That bore the lion king wrought in gold.
And last the elephant came, whose tower
Held the lord of this pomp and power:
And round that chariot of his pride,
  Like chains of white sea-pearls,
Or braids enwove of summer flowers,
  Glided fair dancing girls;
And as the rose leaves fall to earth,
  Their light feet touched the ground,—

But for the zone of silver bells
  You had not heard a sound,
As, scattering flowers o'er the way,
Whirled round the beautiful array.
But there was one who 'mid them shone
A planet lovely and alone,
A rose, one flower amid many,
But still the loveliest of any,
Though fair her arm as the moonlight,
Others might raise an arm as white;
Though light her feet as music's fall,
Others might be as musical;
But where were such dark eyes as hers?
  So tender, yet withal so bright,
As the dark orbs had in their smile
  Mingled the light of day and night.
And where was that wild grace which shed
A loveliness o'er every tread,
A beauty shining through the whole,
Something which spoke of heart and soul.
The Almas had passed lightly on,
The armed ranks, the crowd, were gone,
Yet gazed Mandalla on the square
As she he sought still glided there,—
O that fond look, whose eyeballs' strain,
And will not know its look in vain!
At length he turned,—his silent mood
Sought that impassioned solitude,
The Eden of young hearts, when first
Love in its loneliness is nurst.
He sat him by a little fount;
  A tulip-tree grew by its side,
A lily with its silver towers
  Floated in silence on the tide;

And far round a banana tree
Extended its green sanctuary;
And the long grass, which was his seat,
With every motion grew more sweet,
Yielding a more voluptuous scent
At every blade his pressure bent.
And there he lingered, till the sky
Lost somewhat of its brilliancy,
And crimson shadows rolled on the west,
And taised the moon her diamond crest,
And came a freshness on the trees,
Harbinger of the evening breeze,
When a sweet far sound of song,
Borne by the breath of flowers along,
A mingling of the voice and lute,
  Such as the wind-harp, when it makes
Its pleasant music to the gale
  Which kisses first the chords it breaks
He followed where the echo led,
  Till in a cypress-grove he found
A funeral train, that round a grave
  Poured forth their sorrows' wailing sound;
And by the tomb a choir of girls,
  With measured steps and mournful notes.
And snow-white robes, while on the air
Unbound their wreaths, each dark curl floats,
Paced round and sang to her who slept
Calm, while their young eyes o'er her wept.
And she, that loveliest one, is here,
The morning's radiant Bayadere:
A darker light in her dark eyes,—
  For tears there are,—a paler brow
Changed but to charm the morning's smile,
  Less sparkling, but more touching now.

And first her sweet lip prest the flute,
A nightingale waked by the rose,
And when that honey breath was mute,
Was heard her low song's plaintive close,
Wailing for the young blossom's fall,
The last, the most beloved of all.
As died in gushing tears the lay
The band of mourners passed away:
They left their wreaths upon the tomb,
As fading leaves, and long perfume
Of her were emblems; and unbound
Many a cage's gilded round,
And set the prisoners free, as none
Were left to love now she was gone,
And azure wings spread on the air,
And songs, rejoicing songs, were heard;
But, pining as forgotten now,
Lingered one solitary bird:
A beautiful and pearl-white dove,
Alone in its remembering love.
It was a strange and lovely thing
To mark the drooping of its wing,
And how into the grave it prest,
Till soiled the dark earth-stain its breast;
And darker as the night-shade grew,
Sadder became its wailing coo,
As if it missed the hand that bore,
As the cool twilight came, its store
Of seeds and flowers.—There was one
Who like that dove, was lingering lone,—
The Bayadere: her part had been
Only the hired mourner's part;
But she had given what none might buy,—
The precious sorrow of the heart.

She wooed the white dove to her breast;
It sought at once its place of rest:
Round it she threw her raven hair,—
It seemed to love the gentle snare,
And its soft beak was raised to sip
The honey-dew of her red lip.
Her dark eyes filled with tears, to feel
The gentle creature closer steal
Into her heart with soft caress,
As it would thank her tenderness;
To her 'twas strange and sweet to be
Beloved in such fond purity,
And sighed Mandalla to think that sin
Could dwell so fair a shrine within.
"O, grief to think that she is one
Who like the breeze is wooed and won!
Yet sure it were a task for love
To come like dew of the night from above
Upon her heart, and wash away,
Like dust from the flowers, its stain of clay
And win her back in her tears to heaven,
Pure, loved, and humble, and forgiven;
Yes! freed from the soil of her earthly thrall,
Her smile shall light up my starry hall!"

The moonlight is on a little bower,
With wall and with roof of leaf and of flower,
Built of that green and holy tree
Which heeds not how rude the storm may be.
Like a bridal canopy overhead
The jasmines their slender wreathings spread,
One with stars as ivory white,
The other with clusters of amber light;

Rose-trees four grew by the wall,
Beautiful each, but different all:
One with that pure but crimson flush
That marks the maiden's first love-blush;
By its side grew another one,
Pale as the snow of the funeral stone;
The next was rich with the damask dye
Of a monarch's purple drapery;
And the last had leaves like those leaves of gold,
Worked on that drapery's royal fold;
And there were four vases with blossoms filled,
Like censers of incense, their fragrance distilled:
Lilies, heaped like the pearls of the sea,
Peeped from their large leaves' security;
Hyacinths with their graceful bells,
Where the spirit of odor dwells
Like the spirit of music in ocean shells;
And tulips, with every color that shines
In the radiant gems of Serendib's mines;
One tulip was found in every wreath,
That one most scorched by the summer's breath,
Whose passionate leaves with their ruby glow
Hide the heart that lies burning and black below:
And there, beneath the flowered shade
By a pink acacia made,
Mandalla lay, and by his side,
With eyes, and breath, and blush that vied
With the star and with the flower
In their own and loveliest hour,
Was that fair Bayadere, the dove
  Yet nestling in her long black hair;
She has now more than that to love,
  And the loved one sat by her there.
And by the sweet acacia porch

They drank the softness of the breeze.—
O more than lovely are love's dreams,
'Mid lights and blooms and airs like these!
And sometimes she would leave his side,
And like a spirit round him glide;
A light shawl now wreathed round her brow,
Now waving from her hand of snow,
Now zoned around her graceful waist,
And now like fetters round her placed;
And then, flung suddenly aside,
Her many curls, instead, unbound,
Waved in fantastic braids, till loosed,
Her long dark tresses swept the ground:
Then, changing from the soft slow step,
Her white feet bounded on the wind
Like gleaming silver, and her hair
Like a dark banner swept behind;
Or with her sweet voice, sweet like a bird's
When it pours forth its first song in spring,
The one like an echo to the other,
She answered the sigh of her soft lute-string,
And with eyes that darkened in gentlest tears,
Like the dewy light in the dark-eyed dove,
Would she sing those sorrowing songs that breathe
Some history of unhappy love.
"Yes, thou art mine!" Mandalla said,—
"I have lighted up love in thy youthful heart;
I taught thee its tenderness, now I must teach
Its faith, its grief, and its gloomier part;
And then, from my earth stains purified,
In my star and my hall shalt thou reign my bride."

It was an evening soft and fair,
As surely those in Eden are,

When, bearing spoils of leaf and flower,
Entered the Bayadere her bower:
Her love lay sleeping, as she thought,
And playfully a bunch she caught
Of azure hyacinth bells, and o'er
  His face she let the blossoms fall:
"Why, I am jealous of thy dreams,
  Awaken at thy Aza's call."
No answer came from him whose tone
Had been the echo of her own.
She spoke again,— no words came forth;
  She clasped his hand,—she raised his head,—
One wild, loud scream, she sank beside,
  As pale, as cold, almost as dead!

By the Ganges raised, for the morning sun
To shed his earliest beams upon,
Is a funeral pile,—around it stand
Priests and the hired mourners' band.
But who is she that so wildly prays
To share the couch and light the blaze?
Mandalla's love, while scornful eye
And chilling jeers mock her agony!
An Alma girl! O shame, deep shame
To Brahma's race and Brahma's name!
Unmarked, unpitied, she turned aside,
For a moment, her bursting tears to hide.
None thought of the Bayadere, till the fire
Blazed redly and fiercely the funeral pyre;
Then like a thought she darted by,
And sprang on the funeral pile to die!

"Now thou art mine! away, away
To my own bright star, to my home of day!"

A dear voice sighed, as he bore her along
Gently as spring breezes bear the song,
"Thy love and thy faith have won for thee
The breath of immortality.
Maid of earth, Mandalla is free to call
Aza the queen of his heart and hall!"

LOVE, HOPE, AND BEAUTY.

Love may be increased by fears,
May be fanned with sighs,
Nursed by fancies, fed by doubts;
But without Hope it dies!
As in the far Indian isles
Dies the young cocoa tree,
Unless within the pleasant shade
Of the parent plant it be;
So Love may spring up at first
Lighted at Beauty's eyes:—
But Beauty is not all its life,
For without Hope it dies.

LINES OF LIFE.

Well, read my cheek, and watch my eye,
  Too strictly schooled are they
One secret of my soul to show,
  One hidden thought betray.

I never knew the time my heart
  Looked freely from my brow;
It once was checked by timidness,
  'Tis taught by caution now.

I live among the cold, the false,
  And I must seem like them;
And such I am, for I am false
  As those I most condemn.

I teach my lip its sweetest smile,
  My tongue its softest tone:
I borrow others' likeness, till
  Almost I lose my own.

I pass through flattery's gilded sieve,
  Whatever I would say;
In social life, all, like the blind,
  Must learn to feel their way.

I check my thoughts like curbed steeds
  That struggle with the rein;
I bid my feelings sleep, like wrecks
  In the unfathomed main.

I hear them speak of love, the deep,
The true, and mock the name;
Mock at all high and early truth,
And I too do the same.

I hear them tell some touching tale,
I swallow down the tear;
I hear them name some generous deed,
And I have learnt to sneer.

I hear the spiritual, the kind,
The pure, but named in mirth;
Till all of good, ay, even hope,
Seems exiled from our earth.

And one fear, withering ridicule,
Is all that I can dread;
A sword hung by a single hair
For ever o'er the head.

We bow to a most servile faith,
In a most servile fear;
While none among us dares to say
What none will choose to hear.

And if we dream of loftier thoughts,
In weakness they are gone;
And indolence and vanity
Rivet our fetters on.

Surely I was not born for this!
I feel a loftier mood
Of generous impulse, high resolve,
Steal o'er my solitude!

I gaze upon the thousand stars
  That fill the midnight sky;
And wish, so passionately wish,
  A light like theirs on high.

I have such eagerness of hope
  To benefit my kind;
And feel as if immortal power
  Were given to my mind.

I think on that eternal fame,
  The sun of earthly gloom,
Which makes the gloriousness of death
  The future of the tomb—

That earthly future, the faint sign
  Of a more heavenly one;
—A step, a word, a voice, a look,—
  Alas! my dream is done.

And earth, and earth's debasing stain,
  Again is on my soul;
And I am but a nameless part
  Of a most worthless whole.

Why write I this? because my heart
  Towards the future springs,
That future where it loves to soar
  On more than eagle wings.

The present, it is but a speck
  In that eternal time,
In which my lost hopes find a home,
  My spirit knows its clime.

O! not myself,—for what am I?
  The worthless and the weak,
Whose every thought of self should raise
  A blush to burn my cheek.

But song has touched my lips with fire,
  And made my heart a shrine
For what, although alloyed, debased,
  Is in itself divine.

I am myself but a vile link
  Amid life's weary chain;
But I have spoken hallowed words,
  O do not say in vain!

My first, my last, my only wish,
  Say will my charmed chords
Wake to the morning light of fame,
  And breathe again my words?

Will the young maiden, when her tears
  Alone in moonlight shine—
Tears for the absent and the loved—
  Murmur some song of mine?

Will the pale youth by his dim lamp,
  Himself a dying flame,
From many an antique scroll beside,
  Choose that which bears my name?

Let music make less terrible
  The silence of the dead;
I care not so my spirit last
  Long after life has fled.

NEW YEAR'S EVE.

There is no change upon the air,
No record in the sky:
No pall-like storm comes forth to shroud
The year about to die.

A few light clouds are on the heaven,
A few far stars are bright;
And the pale moon shines as she shines
On many a common night.

Ah, not in heaven, but upon earth,
Are signs of change exprest;
The closing year has left its mark
On human brow and breast.

How much goes with it to the grave
Of life's most precious things?
Methinks each year dies on a pyre,
Like the Assyrian kings.

Affections, friendships, confidence,—
There's not a year hath died
But all these treasures of the heart
Lie with it side by side.

The wheels of time work heavily;
We marvel day by day
To see how from the chain of life
The gilding wears away.

Sad the mere change of fortune's chance,
  And sad the friend unkind;
But what has sadness like the change
  That in ourselves we find?

I've wept my castle in the dust,
  Wept o'er an altered brow;
'Tis far worse murmuring o'er those tears,
  "Would I could weep them now!"

O, for mine early confidence,
  Which like that graceful tree
Bent cordial, as if each approach
  Could but in kindness be!

Then was the time the fairy Hope
  My future fortune told,
Or Youth, the alchymist, that turned
  Whate'er he touched to gold.

But Hope's sweet words can never be
  What they have been of yore:
I am grown wiser, and believe
  In fairy tales no more.

And Youth has spent his wealth, and bought
  The knowledge he would fain
Change for forgetfulness, and live
  His dreaming life again.

I'm weary, weary: day-dreams, years,
  I've seen alike depart,
And sullen Care and Discontent
  Hang brooding o'er my heart.

Another year, another year,—
  Alas! and must it be
That Time's most dark and weary wheel
  Must turn again for me?

In vain I seek from out the past
  Some cherished wreck to save;
Affection, feeling, hope, are dead,—
  My heart is its own grave!

HOME.

I LEFT my home;—'twas in a little vale
Sheltered from snow-storms by the stately pines;
A small clear river wandered quietly,
Its smooth waves only cut by the light barks
Of fishers, and but darkened by the shade
The willows flung, when to the southern wind
They threw their long green tresses. On the slope
Were five or six white cottages, whose roofs
Reached not to the laburnum's height, whose boughs
Shook over them bright showers of golden bloom.
Sweet silence reigned around:—no other sound
Came on the air, than when the shepherd made
The reed-pipe rudely musical, or notes
From the wild birds, or children in their play
Sending forth shouts of laughter. Strangers come
Rarely or never near the lonely place. . . .
I went into far countries. Years passed by,

But still that vale in silent beauty dwelt
Within my memory. Home I came at last.
I stood upon a mountain height, and looked
Into the vale below; and smoke arose,
And heavy sounds; and through the thick dim air
Shot blackened turrets, and brick walls, and roofs
Of the red tile. I entered in the streets:
There were ten thousand hurrying to and fro;
And masted vessels stood upon the river,
And barges sullied the once dew-clear stream:
Where were the willows, where the cottages?
I sought my home; I sought, and found a city,—
Alas! for the green valley!

THE BATTLE-FIELD.

He sleeps—the night wind o'er the battle-field
  Is gently sighing;
Gently, though each breeze bear away
  Life from the dying.

He sleeps,—though his dear and early friend
  A corpse lies by him;
Though the ravening vulture and screaming crow
  Are hovering nigh him.

He sleeps,—where blood has been poured like rain,
  Another field before him:

And he sleeps as calm as his mother's eyes
  Were watching o'er him.

To-morrow that youthful victor's name
  Will be proudly given,
By the trumpet's voice, and the soldier's shout,
  To the winds of heaven.

Yet life, how pitiful and how mean,
  Thy noblest story;
When the high excitement of victory,
  The fullness of glory,

Nor the sorrow felt for the friend of his youth,
  Whose corpse he is keeping,
Can give his human weakness force
  To keep from sleeping.

And this is the sum of our mortal state,
  The hopes we number,—
Feverish, waking, danger, death,
  And listless slumber.

MANMADIN, THE INDIAN CUPID,

FLOATING DOWN THE GANGES.

There is a darkness on the sky,
And the troubled waves run high,
And the lightning flash is breaking,
And the thunder peal is waking;
Reddening meteors, strange and bright,
Cross the rainbow's timid light,
As if mingled hope and fear,
Storm and sunshine, shook the sphere.
Tempest winds rush fierce along,
Bearing yet a sound of song,
Music's on the tempest's wing,
Wafting thee young Manmadin!
Pillowed on a lotus flower
Gathered in a summer hour,
Rides he o'er the mountain wave
Which would be a tall ship's grave!
At his back his bow is slung,
Sugar-cane, with wild bees strung,—
Bees born with the buds of spring,
Yet with each a deadly sting;
Grasping in his infant hand
Arrows in their silken band,
Each made of a signal flower,
Emblem of its varied power;
Some formed of the silver leaf
Of the almond, bright and brief.

Just a frail and lovely thing,
For but one hour's flourishing;
Others, on whose shaft there glows
The red beauty of the rose;
Some in spring's half-folded bloom,
Some in summer's full perfume;
Some with withered leaves and sere,
Falling with the falling year;
Some bright with the rainbow dyes
Of the tulip's vanities;
Some, bound with the lily's bell,
Breathe of love that dares not tell
Its sweet feelings; the dark leaves
Of the esignum, which grieves
Droopingly, round some were bound;
Others were with tendrils wound
Of the green and laughing vine,—
And the barb was dipped in wine.
But all these are summer ills,
Like the tree whose stem distils
Balm beneath its pleasant shade
In the wounds its thorns have made.
Though the flowers may fade and die,
'Tis but a light penalty.
All these bloom-clad darts are meant
But for a short-lived content!
Yet one arrow has a power
Lasting till life's latest hour—
Weary day and sleepless night,
Lightning gleams of fierce delight,
Fragrant and yet poisoned sighs,
Agonies and ecstacies;
Hopes, like fires amid the gloom,
Lighting only to consume!

Happiness one hasty draught,
And the lip has venom quaffed.
Doubt, despairing, crime, and craft,
Are upon that honeyed shaft!
It has made the crowned king
Crouch beneath his suffering;
Made the beauty's cheek more pale
Than the foldings of her veil:
Like a child the soldier kneel
Who had mocked at flame or steel;
Bade the fires of genius turn
On their own breasts, and there burn:
A wound, a blight, a curse, a doom,
Bowing young hearts to the tomb!
Well may storm be on the sky,
And the waters roll on high,
When Manmadin passes by.
Earth below, and heaven above,
Well may bend to thee, O Love!

THE FEMALE CONVICT.

She shrank from all, and her silent mood
Made her wish only for solitude:
Her eye sought the ground, as it could not brook,
For innermost shame, on another's to look;
And the cheerings of comfort fell on her ear
Like deadliest words, that were curses to hear!—

She still was young, and she had been fair;
But weather-stains, hunger, toil, and care,
That frost and fever that wear the heart,
Had made the colors of youth depart
From the sallow cheek, save over it came
The burning flush of the spirit's shame.

They were sailing o'er the salt sea-foam,
Far from her country, far from her home;
And all she had left for her friends to keep
Was a name to hide, and a memory to weep!
And her future held forth but the felon's lot,
To live forsaken—to die forgot!
She could not weep, and she could not pray,
But she wasted and withered from day to day,
Till you might have counted each sunken vein,
When her wrist was prest by the iron chain;
And sometimes I thought her large dark eye
Had the glisten of red insanity.

She called me once to her sleeping place,
A strange, wild look was upon her face,
Her eye flashed over her cheek so white,
Like a gravestone seen in the pale moonlight,
And she spoke in a low, unearthly tone—
The sound from mine ear hath never gone!
"I had last night the loveliest dream:
My own land shone in the summer beam,
I saw the fields of the golden grain,
I heard the reaper's harvest strain;
There stood on the hills the green pine tree,
And the thrush and the lark sang merrily.
A long and a weary way I had come;
But I stopped, methought, by mine own sweet home.

I stood by the hearth, and my father sat there,
With pale, thin face, and snow-white hair!
The Bible lay open upon his knee,
But he closed the book to welcome me.
He led me next where my mother lay,
And together we knelt by her grave to pray,
And heard a hymn it was heaven to hear,
For it echoed one to my young days dear.
This dream has waked feelings long, long since fled,
And hopes which I deemed in my heart were dead!
—We have not spoken, but still I have hung
On the northern accents that dwell on thy tongue
To me they are music, to me they recall
The things long hidden by Memory's pall!
Take this long curl of yellow hair,
And give it my father, and tell him my prayer,
My dying prayer, was for him." . . . .

Next day
Upon the deck a coffin lay;
They raised it up, and like a dirge
The heavy gale swept o'er the surge;
The corpse was cast to the wind and wave—
The convict has found in the green sea a grave.

THE OAK.

. . . . . It is the last survivor of a race
Strong in their forest pride when I was young.
I can remember when, for miles around,
In place of those smooth meadows and corn-fields,
There stood ten thousand stately trees,
Such as had braved the winds of March, the bolt
Sent by the summer lightning, and the snow
Heaping for weeks their boughs. Even in the depth
Of hot July the glades were cool; the grass,
Yellow and parched elsewhere, grew long and fresh,
Shading wild strawberries and violets,
Or the lark's nest; and overhead the dove
Had her lone dwelling, paying for her home
With melancholy songs; and scarce a beech
Was there without a honeysuckle linked
Around, with its red tendrils and pink flowers;
Or girdled by a brier-rose, whose buds
Yield fragrant harvest for the honey bee
There dwelt the last red deer, those antlered kings.
But this is a dream,—the plough has passed
Where the stag bounded, and the day has looked
On the green twilight of the forest trees.
This oak has no companion! . . . .

THE SOLDIER'S GRAVE.

THERE'S a white stone placed upon yonder tomb,
Beneath is a soldier lying:
The death-wound came amid sword and plume,
When banner and ball were flying.

Yet now he sleeps, the turf on his breast,
By wet wild flowers surrounded;
The church shadow falls o'er his place of rest,
Where the steps of his childhood bounded.

There were tears that fell from manly eyes,
There was woman's gentler weeping,
And the wailing of age and infant cries,
O'er the grave where he lies sleeping.

He had left his house in his spirit's pride,
With his father's sword and blessing;
He stood with the valiant side by side,
His country's wrongs redressing.

He came again in the light of his fame,
When the red campaign was over:
One heart that in secret had kept his name,
Was claimed by the soldier lover.

But the cloud of strife came upon the sky;
He left his sweet home for battle:
And his young child's lisp for the loud war-cry,
And the cannon's long death-rattle.

He came again,—but an altered man:
  The path of the grave was before him,
And the smile that he wore was cold and wan,
  For the shadow of death hung o'er him.

He spoke of victory,—spoke of cheer:—
  These are words that are vainly spoken—
To the childless mother or orphan's ear,
  Or the widow whose heart is broken.

A helmet and sword are engraved on the stone,
  Half hidden by yonder willow;
There he sleeps, whose death in battle was won,
  But who died on his own home-pillow!

SONG OF THE HUNTER'S BRIDE.

Another day—another day—
  And yet he comes not nigh;
I look amid the dim blue hills,
  Yet nothing meets mine eye.

I hear the rush of mountain streams
  Upon the echoes borne;
I hear the singing of the birds,
  But not my hunter's horn.

The eagle sails in darkness past,
  The watchful chamois bounds;

But what I look for comes not near,—
  My Ulric's hawk and hounds.

Three times I thus have watched the snow
  Grow crimson with the stain,
The setting sun threw o'er the rock,
  And I have watched in vain.

I love to see the graceful bow
  Across his shoulder slung,—
I love to see the golden horn
  Beside his baldric hung.

I love his dark hounds, and I love
  His falcon's sweeping flight;
I love to see his manly cheek
  With mountain colors bright.

I've waited patiently, but now
  Would that the chase was o'er:
Well may he love the hunter's toil,
  But he should love me more.

Why stays he thus?—he would be here,
  If his love equalled mine;
Methinks had I one fond caged dove,
  I would not let it pine.

But, hark! what are those ringing steps
  That up the valley come?
I see his hounds—I see himself,—
  My Ulric, welcome home!

THE VIOLET.

Violets !—deep-blue violets !
April's loveliest coronets !
There are no flowers grow in the vale,
Kissed by the dew, wooed by the gale,—
None by the dew of the twilight wet,
So sweet as the deep-blue violet ;
I do remember how sweet a breath
Came with the azure light of a wreath
That hung round the wild harp's golden chords,
Which rang to my dark-eyed lover's words.
I have seen that deep harp rolled
With gems of the East and bands of gold ;
But it never was sweeter than when set
With leaves of the deep-blue violet !
And when the grave shall open for me,—
I care not how soon that time may be,—
Never a rose shall grow on that tomb,
It breathes too much of hope and of bloom ;
But there be that flower's meek regret,
The bending and deep-blue violet !

LOVE.

SHE prest her slight hand to her brow, or pain
Or bitter thoughts were passing there. The room
Had no light but that from the fireside,
Which showed, then hid her face. How very pale
It looked, when over it the glimmer shone!
Is not the rose companion of the spring?
Then wherefore has the red-leaved flower forgotten
Her cheek? The tears stood in her large dark eyes—
Her beautiful dark eyes—like hyacinth stars,
When shines their shadowy glory through the dew
That summer nights have wept;—she felt them not,
Her heart was far away! Her fragile form,
Like the young willow when for the first time
The wind sweeps o'er it rudely, had not lost
Its own peculiar grace; but it was bowed
By sickness, or by worse than sickness—sorrow!
And this is Love!—O! why should woman love;
Wasting her dearest feelings, till health, hope,
Happiness, are but things of which henceforth
She'll only know the name? Her heart is seared:
A sweet light has been thrown upon its life,
To make its darkness the more terrible.
And this is Love!

THE SOLDIER'S FUNERAL.

And the muffled drum rolled on the air,
Warriors with stately step were there;
On every arm was the black crape bound,
Every carbine was turned to the ground;
Solemn the sound of their measured tread,
As silent and slow they followed the dead.
The riderless horse was led in the rear,
There were white plumes waving over the bier;
Helmet and sword were laid on the pall
For it was a soldier's funeral.

That soldier had stood on the battle-plain,
Where every step was over the slain:
But the brand and the ball had passed him by,
And he came to his native land to die.
'Twas hard to come to that native land,
And not clasp one familiar hand!
'Twas hard to be numbered amid the dead,
Or ere he could hear his welcome said!
But 'twas something to see its cliffs once more,
And to lay his bones on his own loved shore;
To think that the friends of his youth might weep
O'er the green grass turf of the soldier's sleep.

The bugles ceased their wailing sound
As the coffin was lowered into the ground;
A volley was fired, a blessing said,
One moment's pause—and they left they dead!—

I saw a poor and an aged man,
His step was feeble, his lip was wan :
He knelt him down on the new-raised mound,
His face was bowed on the cold damp ground,
He raised his head, his tears were done,—
The father had prayed o'er his only son!

LINES

WRITTEN UNDER THE PICTURE OF A GIRL BURNING A LOVE-LETTER.

I TOOK the scroll: I could not brook,
  An eye to gaze on it save mine ;
I could not bear another's look
  Should dwell upon one thought of thine.
My lamp was burning by my side,
  I held thy letter to the flame,
I marked the blaze swift o'er it glide,
  It did not even spare thy name
Soon the light from the embers past,
  I felt so sad to see it die,
So bright at first, so dark at last,
  I feared it was love's historv

THE FACTORY.

THERE rests a shade above yon town,
A dark funereal shroud:
'Tis not the tempest hurrying down,
'Tis not a summer cloud.

The smoke that rises on the air
Is as a type and sign;
A shadow flung by the despair
Within those streets of thine.

That smoke shuts out the cheerful day,
The sunset's purple hues,
The moonlight's pure and tranquil ray
The morning's pearly dews.

Such is the moral atmosphere
Around thy daily life;
Heavy with care, and pale with fear,
With future tumult rife.

There rises on the morning wind
A low appalling cry,
A thousand children are resigned
To sicken and to die!

We read of Moloch's sacrifice,
We sicken at the name,
And seem to hear the infant cries—
And yet we do the same;—

And worse—'twas but a moment's pain
 The heathen altar gave,
But we give years,—our idol, Gain,
 Demands a living grave!

How precious is the little one,
 Before his mother's sight,
With bright hair dancing in the sun,
 And eyes of azure light!

He sleeps as rosy as the south
 For summer days are long;
A prayer upon the little mouth,
 Lulled by his nurse's song.

Love is around him, and his hours
 Are innocent and free;
His mind essays its early powers
 Beside his mother's knee.

When after-years of trouble come,
 Such as await man's prime,
How will he think of that dear home,
 And childhood's lovely time!

And such should childhood ever be,
 The fairy well, to bring
To life's worn, weary memory
 The freshness of its spring.

But here the order is reversed,
 And infancy, like age,
Knows of existence but its worst,
 One dull and darkened page;—

Written with tears and stamped with toil,
  Crushed from the earliest hour:
Weeds darkening on the bitter soil,
  That never knew a flower.

Look on yon child, it droops the head,
  Its knees are bowed with pain;
It mutters from its wretched bed,
  "O, let me sleep again!"

Alas! 'tis time, the mother's eyes
  Turn mournfully away;
Alas! 'tis time, the child must rise,
  And yet it is not day.

The lantern's lit—she hurries forth,
  The spare cloak's scanty fold
Scarce screens her from the snowy north;
  The child is pale and cold.

And wearily the little hands
  Their task accustomed ply;
While daily, some 'mid those pale bands,
  Droop, sicken, pine, and die.

Good God! to think upon a child
  That has no childish days,
No careless play, no frolics wild,
  No words of prayer and praise!

Man from the cradle—'tis too soon
  To earn their daily bread,
And heap the heat and toil of noon
  Upon an infant's head.

To labor ere their strength be come,
Or starve,—is such the doom
That makes of many an English home
One long and living tomb?

Is there no pity from above,—
No mercy in those skies;
Hath then the heart of man no love,
To spare such sacrifice?

O, England! though thy tribute waves
Proclaim thee great and free,
While those small children pine like slaves,
There is a curse on thee!

WHEN SHOULD LOVERS BREATHE THEIR VOWS?

When should lovers breathe their vows?
When should ladies hear them?
When the dew is on the boughs,
When none else are near them;
When the moon shines cold and pale,
When the birds are sleeping,
When no voice is on the gale,
When the rose is weeping;
When the stars are bright on high
Like hopes in young Love's dreaming,

And glancing round the light clouds fly,
  Like soft fears to shade their beaming.
The fairest smiles are those that live
  On the brow by starlight wreathing;
And the lips their richest incense give
  When the sigh is at midnight breathing.
O, softest is the cheek's love-ray
  When seen by moonlight hours;
Other roses seek the day,
  But blushes are night-flowers.
O, when the moon and stars are bright,
  When the dew-drops glisten,
Then their vows should lovers plight,
  Then should ladies listen!

THE LOST STAR.

A LIGHT is gone from yonder sky,
  A star has left its sphere;
The beautiful—and do they die
  In yon bright world as here?
Will that star leave a lonely place,
  A darkness on the night?—
No; few will miss its lovely face,
  And none will think heaven less bright!

What wert thou star of?—vanished one,
  What mystery was thine?

Thy beauty from the east is gone:
  What was thy sway and sign?
Wert thou the star of opening youth?—
  And is it then for thee,
Its frank glad thoughts, its stainless truth,
  So early cease to be?

Of hope—and was it to express
  How soon hope sinks in shade;
Or else of human loveliness,
  In sign how it will fade?
How was thy dying—like the song,
  In music to the last,
An echo flung the winds among,
  And then for ever past?

Or didst thou sink as stars whose light
  The fair moon renders vain?
The rest shone forth the next dark night,
  Thou didst not shine again.
Didst thou fade gradual from the time
  The first great curse was hurled,
Till lost in sorrow and in crime,
  Star of our early world?

Forgotten and departed star!
  A thousand glories shine
Round the blue midnight's regal car,
  Who then remembers thine?
Save when some mournful bard like me
  Dreams over beauty gone,
And in the fate that waited thee,
  Reads what will be his own.

GLENCOE.

Lay by the harp, sing not that song,
  Although so very sweet;
It is the song of other years,
  For thee and me unmeet.

Thy head is pillowed on my arm,
  Thy heart beats close to mine;
Methinks it were unjust to heaven,
  If we should now repine.

I must not weep, you must not sing
  That thrilling song again,—
I dare not think upon the time
  When last I heard that strain.

It was a silent summer eve:
  We stood by the hill-side,
And we could see my ship afar
  Breasting the ocean tide.

Around us grew the graceful larch,
  A calm blue sky above,
Beneath were little cottages,
  The homes of peace and love.

Thy harp was by thee then, as now,
  One hand in mine was laid;
The other, wandering 'mid the chords,
  A soothing music made:

Just two or three sweet chords, that seemed
An echo of thy tone,—
The cushat's song was on the wind,
And mingled with thine own.

I looked upon the vale beneath,
I looked on thy sweet face;
I thought how dear, this voyage o'er,
Would be my resting place.

We parted; but I kept thy kiss,—
Thy last one,—and its sigh,
As safely as the stars are kept
In yonder azure sky.

Again I stood by that hill-side,
And scarce I knew the place,
For fire, and blood, and death, had left
On everything their trace.

The lake was covered o'er with weeds,
Choked was our little rill,
There was no sign of corn or grass,
The cushat's song was still:

Burnt to the dust, an ashy heap
Was every cottage round;—
I listened but I could not hear
One single human sound:

I spoke, and only my own words
Were echoed from the hill;
I sat me down to weep, and curse
The hand that wrought this ill.

We met again by miracle:
  Thou wert another one
Saved from this work of sin and death,—
  I was not quite alone.

And then I heard the evil tale
  Of guilt and suffering,
Till I prayed the curse of God might fall
  On the false-hearted king.

I will not think on this,—for thou
  Art saved, and saved for me!
And gallantly my little bark
  Cuts through the moonlight sea.

There's not a shadow in the sky,
  The waves are bright below;
I must not, on so sweet a night,
  Think upon dark Glencoe.

If thought were vengeance, then its thought
  A ceaseless fire should be,
Burning by day, burning by night,
  Kept like a thought of thee.

But I am powerless and must flee;—
  That e'er a time should come,
When we should shun our own sweet land,
  And seek another home!

This must not be,—yon soft moonlight
  Falls on my heart like balm;
The waves are still, the air is hushed,
  And I too will be calm.

Away! we seek another land
  Of hope, stars, flowers, sunshine;
I shall forget the dark green hills
  Of that which once was mine!

THE EMERALD RING.

A SUPERSTITION.

It is a gem which hath the power to show
If plighted lovers keep their vow or no:
If faithful, it is like the leaves of spring;
If faithless, like those leaves when withering.
  Take back again your emerald gem,
    There is no color in the stone;
  It might have graced a diadem,
    But now its hue and light are gone!
Take back your gift, and give me mine—
  The kiss that sealed our last love-vow;
Ah, other lips have been on thine,——
  My kiss is lost and sullied now!
The gem is pale, the kiss forgot,
  And, more than either, you are changed;
But *my* true love has altered not,
  My heart is broken—not estranged!

THE GRAY CROSS.

A GRAY cross stands beneath yon old beech tree;
It marks a soldier's and a maiden's grave:
Around it is a grove of orange trees,
With silver blossoms and with golden fruit.
It was a Spaniard, whom he saved from death,
Raised that cross o'er the gallant Englishman.

He left home a young soldier, full of hope
And enterprise!—he fell in his first field!
There came a lovely pilgrim to his tomb,
The blue-eyed girl, his own betrothed bride,—
Pale, delicate,—one looking as the gale
That bowed the rose could sweep her from the earth.
Yet she had left her home, where every look
Had been watched, O, so tenderly!—and miles,
Long weary miles had wandered. When she came
To the dim shadow of the aged beech,
She was worn to a shadow; colorless
The cheek once dyed by her own mountain rose.
She reached the grave and died upon the sod!
They laid her by her lover:—and her tale
Is often on the songs that the guitar
Echoes in the lime valleys of Castile!

THE CHANGE.

Thy features do not bear the light
They wore in happier days;
Though still there may be much to love,
There's little left to praise.

The rose has faded from thy cheek—
There's scarce a blush left now;
And there's a dark and weary sign
Upon thine altered brow.

Thy raven hair is dashed with gray,
Thine eyes are dim with tears;
And care, before thy youth is past,
Has done the work of years.

Beautiful wreck! for still thy face
Though changed, is very fair;
Like beauty's moonlight, left to show
Her morning sun was there.

Come, here are friends and festival,
Recall thine early smile;
And wear yon wreath, whose glad red rose
Will lend its bloom awhile.

Come, take thy lute, and sing again
The song you used to sing—
The birdlike song:—See, though unused,
The lute has every string.

What, doth thy hand forget the lute?
  Thy brow reject the wreath?
Alas! whate'er the change above,
  There's more of change beneath?

The smile may come, the smile may go,
  The blush shine and depart;
But farewell when their sense is quenched
  Within the breaking heart.

And such is thine: 'tis vain to seek
  The shades of past delight:
Fling down the wreath, and break the lute;
  They mock our souls to-night.

THE DANISH WARRIOR'S DEATH-SONG.

Away, away! your care is vain;
  No leech could aid me now;
The chill of death is at my heart,
  Its damp upon my brow.

Weep not—I shame to see such tears
  Within a warrior's eyes;
Away! how can ye weep for him
  Who in the battle dies?

If I had died with idle head
  Upon my lady's knee—

Had Fate stood by my silken bed,
  Then might ye weep for me.

But I lie on my own proud deck
  Before the sea and sky;
The wind that sweeps my gallant sails
  Will have my latest sigh.

My banner floats amid the clouds,
  Another droops below:
Well with my heart's best blood is paid
  Such purchase from a foe.

Go ye and seek my halls, there dwells
  A fair-haired boy of mine;
Give him my sword, while yet the blood
  Darkens that falchion's shine.

Tell him that only other blood
  Should wash such stains away;
And if he be his father's child,
  There needs no more to say.

Farewell, my bark! farewell, my friends
  Now fling me on the wave;
One cup of wine, and one of blood,
  Pour on my bounding grave.

THE WRECK.

The moonlight fell on the stately ship;
  It shone over sea and sky;
And there was nothing but water and air
  To meet the gazing eye.

Bright and blue spread the heaven above,
  Bright and blue spread the sea;
The stars from their home shone down on the wave,
  Till they seemed in the wave to be.

With silver foam like a cloud behind,
  That vessel cut her way;
But the shadow she cast, was the sole dark thing
  That upon the waters lay.

With steps of power, and with steps of pride,
  The lord of the vessel paced
The deck, as he thought on the wave below,
  And the glorious heaven he faced

One moment's pause, and his spirit fell
  From its bearing high and proud;
But yet it was not a thought of fear
  That the seaman's spirit bowed:

For he had stood on the deck when washed
  With blood, and that blood his own;
When the dying were pillowed upon the dead,
  And yet you heard not a groan—

For the shout of battle came on the wind,
  And the cannon roared aloud;
And the heavy smoke hung round each ship,
  Even like its death-shroud.

And he had guided the helm, when fate
  Seemed stepping every wave,
And the wind swept away the wreath of foam,
  To show a yawning grave.

But this most sweet and lighted calm,
  Its blue and midnight hour,
Wakened the hidden springs of his heart
  With a deep and secret power.

Is there some nameless boding sent,
  Like a noiseless voice from the tomb?—
A spirit note from the other world,
  To warn of death and doom!

He thought of his home, of his own fair land,
  And the warm tear rushed to his eye;
Almost with fear he looked around,
  But no cloud was on the sky.

He sought his cabin, and joined his band—
  The wine-cup was passing round;
He joined in their laugh, he joined in the song,
  But no mirth was in the sound.

Peaceful they sought their quiet sleep,
  In the soft and lovely night;
But, like life, the sea was false, and hid
  The cold dark rock from sight.

At midnight there came a sudden shock,
  And the sleepers sprang from bed;
There was one fierce cry of last despair—
  The waves closed over head.

There was no dark cloud on the morning sky,
  No fierce wind on the morning air;
The sun shone over the proud ship's track,
  But no proud ship was there!

THE LITTLE SHROUD.

She put him on a snow-white shroud,
  A chaplet on his head;
And gathered early primroses
  To scatter o'er the dead.

She laid him in his little grave—
  'Twas hard to lay him there,
When spring was putting forth its flowers,
  And everything was fair.

She had lost many children—now
  The last of them was gone;
And day and night she sat and wept
  Beside the funeral stone.

One midnight, while her constant tears
  Were falling with the dew

She heard a voice, and lo! her child
Stood by her weeping too!

His shroud was damp, his face was white,
He said,—"I cannot sleep,
Your tears have made my shroud so wet,
O, mother, do not weep!"

O, love is strong!—the mother's heart
Was filled with tender fears;
O, love is strong! and for her child
Her grief restrained its tears.

One eve a light shone round her bed,
And there she saw him stand—
Her infant in his little shroud,
A taper in his hand.

"Lo! mother, see my shroud is dry,
And I can sleep once more!"
And beautiful the parting smile
The little infant wore.

And down within the silent grave
He laid his weary head;
And soon the early violets
Grew o'er his grassy bed.

The mother went her household ways—
Again she knelt in prayer,
And only asked of Heaven its aid
Her heavy lot to bear.

THE FROZEN SHIP.

THE fair ship cut the billows,
And her path lay white behind,
And dreamily amid her sails
Scarce moved the sleeping wind.

The sailors sang their gentle songs,
Whose words were home and love;
Waveless the wide sea spread beneath—
And calm the heaven above.

But as they sung, each voice turned low,
Albeit they knew not why;
For quiet was the waveless sea,
And cloudless was the sky.

But the clear air was cold as clear;
'Twas pain to draw the breath;
And the silence and the chill around
Were e'en like those of death.

Colder and colder grew the air,
Spell-bound seemed the wave to be,
And ere night fell, they knew they were locked
In the arms of that icy sea.

Stiff lay the sail, chain-like the ropes,
And snow passed o'er the main;
Each thought, but none spoke, of distant home
They never should see again.

Each looked upon his comrade's face,
  Pale as funereal stone;
Yet none could touch the other's hand,
  For none could feel his own.

Like statues fixed, that gallant band
  Stood on the dread deck to die;
The sleet was their shroud, the wind their dirge,
  And their churchyard the sea and the sky.

Fond eyes have watched by their native shore,
  And prayers to the wild winds gave;
But never again came that stately ship
  To breast the English wave.

Hope grew fear, and fear grew hope,
  Till both alike were done:
And the bride lay down in her grave alone,
  And the mother without her son.

Years passed, and of that goodly ship
  Nothing of tidings came;
Till, in after-time, when her fate had grown
  But a tale of fear and a name—

It was beneath a tropic sky
  The tale was told to me;
The sailor who told, in his youth had been
  Over that icy sea.

He said it was fearful to see them stand,
  Nor the living, nor yet the dead,
And the light glared strange in the glassy eyes
  Whose human look was fled.

For frost had done one half life's part,
  And kept them from decay:
Those they loved had mouldered, but these
  Looked the dead of yesterday.

Peace to the souls of the graveless dead!
  'Twas an awful doom to dree;
But fearful and wondrous are thy works,
  O God! in the boundless sea!

REVENGE.

Ay, gaze upon her rose-wreathed hair,
  And gaze upon her smile:
Seem as you drank the very air
  Her breath perfumed the while;

And walk for her the gifted line,
  That wild and witching lay,
And swear your heart is as a shrine,
  That only owns her sway.

Tis well: I am revenged at last,—
  Mark you that scornful cheek,—
The eye averted as you passed,
  Spoke more than words could speak.

Ay, now by all the bitter tears,
  That I have shed for thee,—

The racking doubts, the burning fears,—
  Avenged they well may be—

By the nights passed in sleepless care,
  The days of endless wo;
All that you taught my heart to bear,
  All that yourself will know.

I would not wish to see you laid
  Within an early tomb;
I should forget how you betrayed,
  And only weep your doom:

But this is fitting punishment—
  To live and love in vain,—
O my wrung heart, be thou content,
  And feed upon his pain.

Go thou and watch her lightest sigh,
  Thine own it will not be;
And back beneath her sunny eye,—
  It will not turn on thee.

'Tis well: the rack, the chain, the wheel,
  Far better hadst thou proved;
Even I could almost pity feel,
  For thou art not beloved.

THE NAMELESS GRAVE.

A NAMELESS grave,—there is no stone
  To sanctify the dead:
O'er it the willow droops alone,
  With only wild flowers spread.

"O, there is naught to interest here,
  No record of a name,
A trumpet-call upon the ear,
  High on the roll of fame.

"I will not pause beside a tomb
  Where nothing calls to mind
Aught that can brighten mortal gloom,
  Or elevate mankind;—

"No glorious memory to efface
  The stay of meaner clay;
No intellect whose heavenly trace
  Redeemed our earth:—away!"

Ah, these are thoughts that well may rise
  On youth's ambitious pride;
But I will sit and moralize
  This lowly stone beside.

Here thousands might have slept, whose name
  Had been to thee a spell,
To light thy flashing eyes with flame,—
  To bid thy young heart swell.

Here might have been a warrior's rest,
Some chief who bravely bled,
With waving banner, sculptured crest,
And laurel on his head.

That laurel must have had its blood,
That blood have caused its tear,—
Look on the lovely solitude—
What! wish for warfare here!

A poet might have slept,—what! he
Whose restless heart first wakes
Its life-pulse into melody,
Then o'er it pines and breaks?—

He who hath sung of passionate love,
His life a feverish tale:—
O! not the nightingale, the dove
Would suit its quiet vale.

See, I have named your favorite two,-
Each had been glad to crave
Rest 'neath this turf's unbroken dew,
And such a nameless grave.

CAN YOU FORGET ME?

CAN you forget me?—I who have so cherished
The veriest trifle that was memory's link;
The roses that you gave me, although perished,
Were precious in my sight; they made me think.
You took them in their scentless beauty stooping
From the warm shelter of the garden wall;
Autumn, while into languid winter drooping,
Gave its last blossoms, opening but to fall.
Can you forget them?

Can you forget me? I am not relying
On plighted vows—alas! I know their worth:
Man's faith to woman is a trifle, dying
Upon the very breath that gave it birth.
But I remember hours of quiet gladness,
When, if the heart had truth, it spoke it then,
When thoughts would sometimes take a tone of sadness,
And then unconsciously grow glad again.
Can you forget them?

Can you forget me? My whole soul was blended;
At least it sought to blend itself with thine;
My life's whole purpose, winning thee, seemed ended;
Thou wert my heart's sweet home—my spirit's shrine
Can you forget me?—when the firelight burning,
Flung sudden gleams around the quiet room,
How would thy words, to long past moments turning,
Trust me with thoughts soft as the shadowy gloom!
Can you forget them?

There is no truth in love, whate'er its seeming,
And heaven itself could scarcely seem more true—
Sadly have I awakened from the dreaming,
Whose charmed slumber—false one!—was of you.
I gave mine inmost being to thy keeping—
I had no thought I did not seek to share;
Feelings that hushed within my soul were sleeping,
Waked into voice, to trust them to thy care.
Can you forget them?

Can you forget me? This is vainly tasking
The faithless heart where I, alas! am not.
Too well I know the idleness of asking—
The misery—of why am I forgot?
The happy hours that I have passed while kneeling
Half slave, half child, to gaze upon thy face.
—But what to thee this passionate appealing—
Let my heart break—it is a common case.
You have forgotten me.

THE WREATH.

Nay, fling not down those faded flowers,
Too late they're scattered round;
And violet and rose-leaf lie
Together on the ground.

How carefully this very morn
Those buds were culled and wreathed.

And, 'mid the cloud of that dark hair,
  How sweet a sigh they breathed!

And many a gentle word was said
  Above their morning dye,
How that the rose had touched thy cheek,
  The violet thine eye.

Methinks, if but for memory,
  I should have kept these flowers;
Ah! all too lightly does thy heart
  Dwell upon vanished hours.

Already has thine eager hand
  Stripped yonder rose-hung bough;
The wreath that bound thy raven curls
  Thy feet are on it now.

That glancing smile, it seems to say
  "Thou art too fanciful;"
What matters it what roses fade,
  While there are more to cull!

Ay, I was wrong to ask of thee
  Such gloomy thoughts as mine:
Thou in thy Spring, how shouldst thou dream
  Of Autumn's pale decline?

Young, lovely, loved,—O! far from thee
  Life's after-dearth and doom;
Long ere thou learn how memory clings
  To even faded bloom!

THE INDIAN GIRL.

She sat alone beside her hearth—
For many nights alone;
She slept not on the pleasant couch
Where fragrant herbs were strown.

At first she bound her raven hair
With feather and with shell;
But then she hoped; at length, like night,
Around her neck it fell.

They saw her wandering 'mid the woods,
Lone, with the cheerless dawn,
And then they said, "Can this be her
We called 'The Startled Fawn.'"

Her heart was in her large sad eyes,
Half sunshine and half shade;
And love, as love first springs to life,
Of everything afraid.

The red leaf far more heavily
Fell down to autumn earth,
Than her light feet, which seemed to move
To music and to mirth.

With the light feet of early youth,
What hopes and joys depart?
Ah! nothing like the heavy step
Betrays the heavy heart.

It is a usual history
  That Indian girl could tell;
Fate sets apart one common doom
  For all who love too well.

The proud—the shy—the sensitive,
  Life has not many such;
They dearly buy their happiness,
  By feeling it too much.

A stranger to her forest home,
  That fair young stranger came,
They raised for him the funeral song—
  For him the funeral flame.

Love sprang from pity,—and her arms
  Around his arms she threw;
She told her father, "If he dies,
  Your daughter dieth too."

For her sweet sake they set him free—
  He lingered at her side;
And many a native song yet tells
  Of that pale stranger's bride.

Two years have passed—how much two years
  Have taken in their flight!
They've taken from the lip its smile,
  And from the eye its light.

Poor child! she was a child in years—
  So timid and so young;
With what a fond and earnest faith
  To desperate hope she clung!

His eyes grew cold—his voice grew strange—
  They only grew more dear.
She served him meekly, anxiously,
  With love—half faith, half fear.

And can a fond and faithful heart
  Be worthless in those eyes
For which it beats?—Ah! wo to those
  Who such a heart despise.

Poor child! what lonely days she passed,
  With nothing to recall
But bitter taunts, and careless words,
  And looks more cold than all.

Alas! for love, that sits at home,
  Forsaken, and yet fond;
The grief that sits beside the hearth,
  Life has no grief beyond.

He left her, but she followed him—
  She thought he could not bear
When she had left her home for him
  To look on her despair.

Adown the strange and mighty stream
  She took her lonely way!
The stars at night her pilots were,
  As was the sun by day.

Yet mournfully—how mournfully!—
  The Indian looked behind,
When the last sound of voice or step
  Died on the midnight wind.

Yet still adown the gloomy stream
  She plied her weary oar;
Her husband—he had left their home,
  And it was home no more.

She found him—but she found in vain—
  He spurned her from his side;
He said, her brow was all too dark,
  For her to be his bride.

She grasped his hands,—her own were cold,—
  And silent turned away,
As she had not a tear to shed,
  And not a word to say.

And pale as death she reached her boat,
  And guided it along;
With broken voice she strove to raise
  A melancholy song.

None watched the lonely Indian girl,—
  She passed unmarked of all,
Until they saw her slight canoe
  Approach the mighty Fall!

Upright, within that slender boat
  They saw the pale girl stand,
Her dark hair streaming far behind-
  Upraised her desperate hand.

The air is filled with shriek and shout—
  They call, but call in vain;
The boat amid the waters dashed—
  'Twas never seen again!

THE SNOWDROP.

THOU beautiful new comer,
  With white and maiden brow;
Thou fairy gift from summer,
  Why art thou blooming now?
This dim and sheltered alley
  Is dark with winter green;
Not such as in the valley
  At sweet spring-time is seen.

The lime-tree's tender yellow,
  The aspen's silvery sheen,
With mingling colors mellow
  The universal green.
Now solemn yews are bending
  'Mid gloomy fires around;
And in long dark wreaths descending
  The ivy sweeps the ground.

No sweet companion pledges
  Thy health as dewdrops pass;
No rose is on the hedges,
  No violet in the grass.
Thou art watching, and thou only,
  Above the earth's snow tomb;
Thus lovely, and thus lonely,
  I bless thee for thy bloom.

Though the singing rill be frozen,
  While the wind forsakes the west;

Though the singing birds have chosen
  Some lone and silent rest;
Like thee, one sweet thought lingers
  In a heart else cold and dead,
Though the summer's flowers, and singers,
  And sunshine long hath fled:

'Tis the love for long years cherished,
  Yet lingering, lorn, and lone;
Though its lovelier lights have perished,
  And its earlier hopes are flown.
Though a weary world hath bound it,
  With many a heavy thrall;
And the cold and changed surround it,
  It blossometh o'er all.

KALENDRIA;

A PORT IN CILICIA.

Do you see yon vessel riding,
  Anchored in our island bay,
Like a sleeping sea-bird biding
  For the morrow's onward way?
See her white wings folded round her,
  As she rocks upon the deep;
Slumber with a spell hath bound her,
  With a spell of peace and sleep.

Seems she not as if enchanted
  To that lone and lovely place,
Henceforth ever to be haunted
  By that sweet ship's shadowy grace?
Yet, come here again to-morrow,
  Not a vestige will remain,
Though those sweet eyes strain in sorrow,
  They will search the sea in vain.

'Twas for this I bade thee meet me,
  For a parting word and tear;
Other lands and lips may greet me;
  None will ever seem so dear.
Other lands—I may say, other—
  Mine again I shall not see;
I have left mine aged mother,
  She has other sons than me.

Where my father's bones are lying,
  There mine own will never lie;
Where the myrtle groves are sighing,
  Soft beneath our summer sky.
Mine will be a wilder ending,
  Mine will be a wilder grave,
Where the shriek and shout are blending,
  Or the tempest sweeps the wave.

Mine may be a fate more lonely,
  In some sick and foreign ward,
Where my weary eyes meet only
  Hired nurse or sullen guard.
Dearest maiden, thou art weeping;
  Must I from those eyes remove?

Hath thy heart no soft pulse sleeping
  Which might ripen into love?

No! I see thy brow is frozen,
  And thy look is cold and strange;
Ah! when once the heart has chosen,
  Well I know it cannot change.
And I know that heart has spoken,
  That another's it must be.
Scarce I wish that pure faith broken,
  Though the falsehood were for me.

No: be still the guileless creature
  That upon my boyhood shone;
Couldst thou change thy angel nature,
  Half my faith in heaven were gone.
Still thy memory shall be cherished,
  Dear as it is now to me;
When all gentler thoughts have perished,
  One shall linger yet for thee.

Farewell!—With those words I sever
  Every tie of youth and home;
Thou, fair isle! adieu for ever!
  See a boat cuts through the foam.
Wind, time, tide, alike are pressing,
  I must hasten from the shore.
One first kiss, and one last blessing—
  Farewell, love! we meet no more.

INFANTICIDE IN MADAGASCAR.

A LUXURY of summer green
 Is on the southern plain,
And water-flags, with dewy screen,
 Protect the ripening grain.
Upon the sky is not a cloud
 To mar the golden glow,
Only the palm-tree is allowed
 To fling its shade below.

And silvery, 'mid its fertile brakes,
 The winding river glides,
And every ray in heaven makes
 Its mirror of its tides.
And yet it is a place of death—
 A place of sacrifice;
Heavy with childhood's parting breath,
 Weary with childhood's cries.

The mother takes her little child-
 Its face is like her own;
The cradle of her choice is wild—
 Why is it left alone?
The trampling of the buffalo
 Is heard among the reeds,
And sweeps around the carrion crow
 That amid carnage feeds.

O! outrage upon mother Earth
 To yonder azure sky;

A destined victim from its birth,
  The child is left to die.
We shudder that such crimes disgrace
  E'en yonder savage strand;
Alas! and hath such crime no trace
  Within our English land?

Pause, ere we blame the savage code
  That such strange horror keeps;
Perhaps within her sad abode
  The mother sits and weeps,
And thinks how oft those eyelids smiled
  Whose close she may not see,
And says, "O, would to God, my child,
  I might have died for thee!"

Such law of bloodshed to annul
  Should be the Christian's toil;
May not such law be merciful,
  To that upon our soil?
Better the infant eyes should close
  Upon the first sweet breath,
Than weary for their last repose,
  A living life in death!

Look on the children of our poor,
  On many an English child:
Better that it had died secure
  By yonder river wild.
Flung careless on the waves of life,
  From childhood's earliest time,
They struggle, one perpetual strife,
  With hunger and with crime.

Look on the crowded prison-gate—
Instructive love and care
In early life had saved the fate
That waits on many there.
Cold, selfish, shunning care and cost,
The poor are left unknown;
I say, for every soul thus lost,
We answer with our own.

ALEXANDER AND PHILIP.

He stood by the river's side,
A conqueror and a king,
None matched his step of pride
Amid the armed ring.
And a heavy echo rose from the ground,
As a thousand warriors gathered round.

And the morning march had been long,
And the noontide sun was high,
And weariness bowed down the strong,
And heat closed every eye;
And the victor stood by the river's brim,
Whose coolness seemed but made for him.

The cypress spread their gloom
Like a cloak from the noontide beam
He flung back his dusty plume,
And plunged in the silver stream;

He plunged like the young steed fierce and wild,
He was borne away like the feeble child.

They took the king to his tent
From the river's fatal banks;
A cry of terror went
Like a storm through the Grecian ranks:
Was this the fruit of their glories won,
Was this the death for Ammon's son?

Many a leech heard the call,
But each one shrank away;
For heavy upon all
Was the weight of fear that day:
When a thought of treason, a word of death,
Was in each eye and on each breath.

But one with the royal youth
Had been from his earliest hour,
And he knew that his heart was truth,
And he knew that his hand was power;
He gave what hope his skill might give,
And bade him trust to his faith, and live.

Alexander took the cup,
And from beneath his head a scroll,
He drank the liquor up,
And bade Philip read the roll;
And Philip looked on the page, where shame,
Treason, and poison were named with his name

An angry flush rose on his brow,
And anger darkened his eye

What I have done I would do again now,
If you trust my fidelity.
The king watched his face, he felt he might dare
Trust the faith that was written there.

Next day the conqueror rose
From a greater conqueror free;
And again he stood amid those
Who had died his death to see:
He stood there proud of the lesson he gave
That faith and trust were made for the brave.

THE CASTLE OF CHILLON.

Fair lake, thy lovely and thy haunted shore
Has only echoes for the poet's lute;
None may tread there save with unsandalled foot,
Submissive to the great that went before,
Filled with the mighty memories of yore.
And yet how mournful are the records there—
Captivity, and exile, and despair,
Did they endure who now endure no more.
The patriot, the woman, and the bard,
Whose names thy winds and waters bear along;
What did the world bestow for their reward
But suffering, sorrow, bitterness, and wrong?—
Genius!—a hard and weary lot is thine—
The heart thy fuel—and the grave thy shrine.

THE RIVER WEAR.

COME back, come back, my childhood,
  To the old familiar spot,
Whose wild flowers, and whose wild wood
  Have never been forgot.
It is the shining river,
  With the bulrush by its tide,
Where I filled my green rush quiver
  With arrows at its side ;

And deemed that knightly glories
  Were honored as of old ;
My head was filled with stories
  My aged nurse had told.
The Douglas and the Percy
  Alike were forced to yield ;
I had but little mercy
  Upon the battle-field.

Ah! folly of the fancies,
  That haunt our childhood's hour,
And yet those old romances
  On after life have power ;
When the weight appears too weary
  With which we daily strive,
'Mid the actual and the dreary,
  How much they keep alive !

How often, amid hours
  By life severely tried,

Have I thought on those wild flowers
  On the sweet Wear's silver tide.
Each ancient recollection
  Brought something to subdue;
I lived in old affection,
  And felt the heart was true.

I am come again with summer,
  It is lovely to behold,
Will it welcome the new comer,
  As it seemed to do of old?
Within those dark green covers,
  Whose shade is downward cast,
How many a memory hovers
  Whose light is from the past!

I see the bright trout springing,
  Where the wave is dark yet clear,
And a myriad flies are winging,
  As if to tempt him near.
With the lucid waters blending,
  The willow shade yet floats,
From beneath whose quiet bending
  I used to launch my boats.

Over the sunny meadows,
  I watch them as of old,
Flit soft and sudden shadows
  That leave a greener gold;
And a faint south wind is blowing
  Amid the cowslip beds,
A deeper glow bestowing
  To the light around their heads.

Farewell, sweet river! ever
  Wilt thou be dear to me;
I can repay thee never
  One half I owe to thee.
Around thy banks are lying
  Nature's diviner part,
And thou dost keep undying
  My childhood at my heart.

DEATH OF LOUIS OF BOURBON,

BISHOP OF LIEGE.

How actual, through the lapse of years,
That scene of death and dread appears,
The maiden shrouded in her veil,
The burghers half resolved, half pale;
And the young archer leant prepared,
With dagger hidden, but still bared—
Are real, as if that stormy scene
In our own troubled life had been.
Such is the magic of the page
That brings again another age.
Such, Scott, the charms thy pages cast,
O, mighty master of the past!

ETTY'S ROVER.

Thou lovely and thou happy child,
  Ah, how I envy thee!
I should be glad to change our state,
  If such a thing might be.

And yet it is a lingering joy
  To watch a thing so fair,
To think that in our weary life
  Such pleasant moments are.

A little monarch thou art there,
  And of a fairy realm,
Without a foe to overthow,
  A care to overwhelm.

Thy world is in thy own glad will,
  And in each fresh delight,
And in thy unused heart, which makes
  Its own, its golden light.

With no misgivings in thy past,
  Thy future with no fear;
The present circles thee around,—
  An angel's atmosphere.

How little is the happiness
  That will content a child—
A favorite dog, a sunny fruit,
  A blossom growing wild.

A word will fill the little heart
With pleasure and with pride;
It is a harsh, a cruel thing,
That such can be denied.

And yet how many weary hours
Those joyous creatures know;
How much of sorrow and restraint
They to their elders owe!

How much they suffer from our faults!
How much from our mistakes!
How often, too, mistaken zeal
An infant's misery makes!

We overrule, and overteach,
We curb and we confine,
And put the heart to school too soon
To learn our narrow line.

No; only taught by love to love,
Seems childhood's natural task;
Affection, gentleness, and hope,
Are all its brief years ask.

Enjoy thy happiness, sweet child,
With careless heart and eye;
Enjoy those few bright hours which now,
E'en now, are hurrying by;—

And let the gazer on thy face
Grow glad with watching thee,
And better, kinder;—such at least
Its influence on me.

DISENCHANTMENT.

Do not ask me why I loved him,
Love's cause is to love unknown;
Faithless as the past has proved him,
Once his heart appeared mine own.
Do not say he did not merit
All my fondness, all my truth;
Those in whom love dwells, inherit
Every dream that haunted youth.

He might not be all I dreamed him,
Noble, generous, gifted, true,
Not the less I fondly deemed him,
All those flattering visions drew.
All the hues of old romances
By his actual self grew dim;
Bitterly I mock the fancies
That once found their life him.

From the hour by him enchanted,
From the moment when we met,
Henceforth with one image haunted,
Life may never more forget.
All my nature changed—his being
Seemed the only source of mine,
Fond heart, hadst thou no foreseeing
Thy sad future to divine?

Once, upon myself relying,
All I asked were words and thought;

Many hearts to mine replying,
  Owned the music that I brought.
Eager, spiritual, and lonely
  Visions filled the fairy hour,
Deep with love—though love was only
  Not a presence, but a power.

But from that first hour I met thee,
  All caught actual life from you,
Alas! how can I forget thee,
  Thou who mad'st the fancied true?
Once my wide world was ideal,
  Fair it was—ah! very fair:
Wherefore hast thou made it real?
  Wherefore is thy image there?

Ah! no more to me is given
  Fancy's far and fairy birth;
Chords upon my lute are riven,
  Never more to sound on earth.
Once, sweet music could it borrow
  From a look, a word, a tone;
I could paint another's sorrow—
  Now I think but of mine own.

Life's dark waves have lost the glitter
  Which at morning-tide they wore,
And the well within is bitter;
  Naught its sweetness may restore:
For I know how vainly given
  Life's most precious things may be,
Love that might have looked on heaven,
  Even as it looked on thee.

Ah, farewell!—with that word dying,
  Hope and love must perish too:
For thy sake themselves denying,
  What is truth with thee untrue?
Farewell!—'tis a dreary sentence,
  Like the death-doom of the grave,
May it wake in thee repentance,
  Stinging when too late to save!

THE HINDOO GIRL'S SONG.

Float on—float on—my haunted bark,
  Above the midnight tide;
Bear softly o'er the waters dark
  The hopes that with thee glide.

Float on—float on—thy freight is flowers,
  And every flower reveals
The dreaming of my lonely hours,
  The hope my spirit feels.

Float on—float on—thy shining lamp,
  The light of love is there;
If lost beneath the waters damp,
  That love must then despair.

Float on—beneath the moonlight float,
  The sacred billows o'er:
Ah, some kind spirit guards my boat,
  For it has gained the shore.

SASSOOR, IN THE DECCAN.

It is Christmas, and the sunshine
  Lies golden on the fields,
And flowers of white and purple,
  Yonder fragrant creeper yields.

Like the plumes of some bold warrior,
  The cocoa-tree on high,
Lifts aloft its feathery branches,
  Amid the deep blue sky.

From yonder shadowy peepul,
  The pale fair lilac dove,
Like music from a temple,
  Sings a song of grief and love.

The earth is bright with blossoms,
  And a thousand jewelled wings,
'Mid the green boughs of the tamarind
  A sudden sunshine flings.

For the East is earth's first-born,
  And hath a glorious dower,
As nature there had lavished
  Her beauty and her power.

And yet I pine for England,
  For my own—my distant home;
My heart is in that island,
  Where'er my steps may roam.

It is merry there at Christmas—
We have no Christmas here;
'Tis a weary thing, a summer
That lasts throughout the year.

I remember how the banners
Hung round our ancient hall,
Bound with wreaths of shining holly,
Brave winter's coronal.

And above each rusty helmet
Waved a new and cheering plume,
A branch of crimson berries,
And the latest rose in bloom.

And the white and pearly misletoe
Hung half concealed o'er head,
I remember one sweet maiden,
Whose cheek it dyed with red.

The morning waked with carols,
A young and joyous band
Of small and rosy songsters,
Came tripping hand in hand.

And sang beneath our windows,
Just as the round red sun
Began to melt the hoar-frost,
And the clear cold day begun.

And at night the aged harper
Played his old tunes o'er and o'er;
From sixteen up to sixty,
All were dancing on that floor

Those were the days of childhood,
  The buoyant and the bright;
When hope was life's sweet sovereign,
  And the heart and step were light.

I shall come again—a stranger
  To all that once I knew,
For the hurried steps of manhood
  From life's flowers have dashed the dew.

I yet may ask their welcome,
  And return from whence I came;
But a change is wrought within me,
  They will not seem the same.

For my spirits are grown weary,
  And my days of youth are o'er,
And the mirth of that glad season
  Is what I can feel no more.

THE DESERTER.

'Twas a sweet summer morn, the lark had just
Sprung from the clover bower around her nest,
And poured her blithe song to the clouds: the sun
Shed his first crimson o'er the dark gray walls
Of the old church, and stained the sparkling panes
Of ivy-covered windows. The damp grass,
That waved in wild luxuriance round the graves,
Was white with dew, but early steps had been
And left a fresh green trace round yonder tomb:
'Twas a plain stone, but graven with a name
That many stopped to read—a soldier's name—
And two were kneeling by it, one who had
Been weeping; she was widow to the brave
Upon whose quiet bed her tears were falling.
From off her cheek the rose of youth had fled,
But beauty still was there, that softened grief,
Whose bitterness is gone, but which was felt
Too deeply for forgetfulness; her look,
Fraught with high feelings and intelligence,
And such as might beseem the Roman dame
Whose children died for liberty, was made
More soft and touching by the patient smile
Which piety had given the unearthly brow,
Which Guido draws when he would form a saint
Whose hopes are fixed on Heaven, but who has yet
Some earthly feelings binding them to life.
Her arm was leant upon a graceful youth,
The hope, the comfort of her widowhood;
He was departing from her, and she led

The youthful soldier to his father's tomb—
As in the visible presence of the dead
She gave her farewell blessing; and her voice
Lost its so tremulous accents as she bade
Her child tread in that father's steps, and told
How brave, how honored he had been. But when
She did entreat him to remember all,
Her hopes were centred in him, that he was
The stay of her declining years, that he
Might be the happiness of her old age,
Or bring her down with sorrow to the grave,
Her words grew inarticulate, and sobs
Alone found utterance; and he, whose cheek
Was flushed with eagerness, whose ardent eye
Gave animated promise of the fame
That would be his, whose ear already rang
With the loud trumpet's war-song, felt these dreams
Fade for a moment, and almost renounced
The fields he panted for, since they must cost
Such tears as these. The churchyard left, they passed
Down by a hawthorn hedge, where the sweet May
Had showered its white luxuriance, intermixed
With crimson clusters of the wilding rose,
And linked with honeysuckle. O'er the path
Many an ancient oak and stately elm
Spread its green canopy. How Edward's eye
Lingered on each familiar sight, as if
Even to things inanimate he would bid
A last farewell! They reached the cottage gate,
His horse stood ready; many, too, were there,
Who came to say good-bye, and kindly wish
To the young soldier health and happiness.
It is a sweet, albeit most painful, feeling
To know we are regretted. "Farewell" said

And oft repeated, one last wild embrace
Given to his pale mother, who stood there,
Her cold hands pressed upon a brow as cold,
In all the bursting heart's full agony—
One last, last kiss,—he sprang upon his horse
And urged his utmost speed with spur and rein.
He is past . . . out of sight. . .

The muffled drum is rolling, and the low
Notes of the death-march float upon the wind,
And stately steps are pacing round that square
With slow and measured tread; but every brow
Is darkened with emotion, and stern eyes,
That looked unshrinking on the face of death,
When met in battle, are now moist with tears.
The silent ring is formed, and in the midst
Stands the deserter! Can this be the same,
The young, the gallant Edward? and are these
The laurels promised in his early dreams?
Those fettered hands, this doom of open shame.
Alas! for young and passionate spirits! Soon
False lights will dazzle. He had madly joined
The rebel banner! O 'twas pride to link
His fate with Erin's patriot few, to fight
For liberty or the grave! But he was now
A prisoner: yet there he stood, as firm
As though his feet were not upon the tomb:
His cheek was pale as marble, and as cold;
But his lip trembled not, and his dark eyes
Glanced proudly round. But when they bared his breast
For the death-shot, and took a portrait thence,
He clenched his hands, and gasped, and one deep sob
Of agony burst from him; and he hid

His face awhile—his mother's look was there.
He could not steel his soul when he recalled
The bitterness of her despair. It passed—
That moment of wild anguish; he knelt down;
That sunbeam shed its glory over one,
Young, proud, and brave, nerved in deep energy,
The next fell over cold and bloody clay.

There is a deep voiced sound from yonder vale,
Which ill accords with the sweet music made
By the light birds nestling by those green elms;
And, a strange contrast to the blossomed thorns,
Dark plumes are waving, and a silent hearse
Is winding through that lane. They told it bore
A widow, who died of a broken heart:
Her child, her soul's last treasure,—he had been
Shot for desertion!

CONISTON WATER.

Thou lone and lovely water, would I were
A dweller by thy deepest solitude!
How weary am I of my present life,
Its falsehoods, and its fantasies—its noise
And the unkindly hurry of the crowd,
'Mid whom my days are numbered! I would watch
The tremulous vibration of the rays
The moon sends down to kiss thy quiet waves;

And when they died, wish I could die like them,
Melting upon the still and silvery air:
Or when the autumn scatters the wan leaves
Like ghosts, I'd meditate above their fall,
And say "So perish all our earthly hopes."
So is the heart left desolate and bare,
And on us falls the shadow of the tomb,
Before we rest within it.

EXPECTATION.

SHE looked from out the window
With long and asking gaze,
From the gold-clear light of morning
To the twilight's purple haze.
Cold and pale the planets shone,
Still the girl kept gazing on.
From her white and weary forehead
Droopeth the dark hair,
Heavy with the dews of evening,
Heavier with her care;
Falling as the shadows fall,
Till flung round her like a pall.

When from the carved lattice
First she leant to look,
Her bright face was written
Like some pleasant book·

Her warm cheek the red air quaffed,
And her eyes looked out and laughed.
She is leaning back now languid,
  And her cheek is white;
Only on the drooping eyelash
  Glistens tearful light.
Color, sunshine hours are gone,
  Yet the lady watches on.

Human heart, this history
  Is thy faded lot;
Even such thy watching,
  For what cometh not,
Till with anxious waiting dull,
Round thee fades the beautiful,
Still thou seekest on, though weary,
  Seeking still in vain:
Daylight deepens into twilight,
  What has been thy gain?
Death and night are closing round,
All that thou hast sought unfound.

WARNING.

Pray thee, maiden, hear him not!
Take thou warning by my lot;
Read my scroll, and mark thou all
I can tell thee of thy thrall.

Thou hast owned that youthful breast
Treasures its most dangerous guest;
Thou hast owned that love is there:
Though no features he may wear,
Such as would a saint deceive,
Win a skeptic to believe,
Only for a time that brow
Will seem what 'tis seeming now.
I have said, heart, be content!
For Love's power o'er thee is spent.
That I love not now, O true!—
I have bade such dreams adieu:
Therefore deemest thou my heart
Saw them tranquilly depart;
That they past, nor left behind,
Wreck and ruin in my mind.
Thou art in the summer hour
Of first passion's early power;
I am in the autumn day
Of its darkness and decay.
—Seems thine idol now to thee
Even as a divinity?
Such the faith that I too held;
Not the less am I compelled
All my heart-creed to gainsay,
Own my idol gilded clay,
And yet pine to dream again
What I know is worse than vain.
Ay, I did love, and how well,
Let thine own fond weakness tell:
Still upon the softened mood
Of my twilight solitude,
Still upon my midnight tear
Rises image all too dear

Dark and starry eyes, whose light
Make the glory of the night;
Brow like ocean's morning foam,
For each noble thought a home.
Well such temple's fair outline
Seemed the spirit's fitting shrine.
—Is he hero, who hath won
Fields we shrink to think upon?
Patriot, on whose gifted tongue
Senates in their wonder hung?
Sage, before whose gifted eyes
Nature spreads her mysteries?
Bard, to whose charmed lute is given
All that earth can breathe of heaven?—
Seems thy lover these to thee?
Even more seemed mine to me.
Now, my fond belief is past;
Strange, methinks, if thine should last.
"Be content, thou lovest not now:"
Free, thou sayest,—dream'st thou how?
Loathing wouldst thou shun dismayed
Freedom by such ransom paid.
—Girl, for thee I'll lay aside
Veil of smiles and mask of pride;
Shrouds that only ask of Fate
Not to seem so desolate.
—I am young—but age's snow
Hides not colder depths below;
I am gay,—but such a light
Shines upon the grave by night.
Yet mine is a common tale;
Hearts soon changed, and vows were frail;
Each one blamed the other's deed,
Yet both felt they were agreed

Ne'er again might either prove
Those sweet fallacies of love.
Still for what so vain I hold
Is my wasted heart grown cold.
Can hopes be again believed,
When their sweetest have deceived?
Can affection's chain be trusted,
When its dearest links have rusted?
Can life's dreams again be cherished,
When its dearest one's have perished?
I know Love will not endure;—
Nothing now to me seems sure.
—Maiden, by the thousand tears,
Lava floods on my first years;
By the nights, when burning pain
Fed upon my heart and brain;
By the wretched days now past,
By the weary days to last;
Be thou warned, for still the same
Is Love, beneath whatever name.
Keep thy fond faith like a thing
Where Time never change may bring.
Vow thee to thy idol's shrine,—
Then, maiden! read thy fate in mine.

THE VISIONARY.

I PRAY thee do not speak to me
  As you are speaking now;
It brings the color to my cheek,
  The shadow to my brow.

I pray thee do not look at me,
  I cannot bear that gaze;
Though downcast be my eye, it still
  Too much my heart betrays.

I feel the past is written there,
  The past, long since gone by—
The past, where feelings, fancies, hopes,
  Alike unburied lie;—

Unburied, for their restless ghosts
  Still haunt the sad domain,
And mockeries of their former selves
  Come thronging back again.

But changed as I and thou art changed,
  Or rather me alone,
I never had your heart—but mine,
  Alas! was all your own.

O, magic of a tone and word,
  Loved all too long and well,
I cannot close my heart and ear
  Against their faithless spell—

I know them false, I know them vain,
And yet I listen on—
And say them to myself again,
Long after thou art gone.

I make myself my own deceit,
I know it is a dream,
But one that from my earliest youth
Has colored life's deep stream.—

Frail colors flung in vain, but yet
A thousand times more dear
Than any actual happiness
That ever brightened here.

The dear, the long, the dreaming hours
That I have passed with thee,
When thou hadst not a single thought
Of how thou wert with me—

I heard thy voice—I spoke again—
I gazed upon thy face;
And never scene of breathing life
Could leave a deeper trace,

Than all that fancy conjured up,
And made thee look and say,
Till I have loathed reality,
That chased such dream away.

Now, out upon this foolishness,
Thy heart it is not mine;
And, knowing this, how can I waste
My very soul on thine?

Alas! I have no power to choose,
  Love is not at my will;
I say I must be careless, cold,
  But find I love thee still.

I think upon my wasted life
  And on my wasted heart,
And turn, ashamed and sorrowful,
  From what will not depart.

Thy haunting influence, how it mocks
  My efforts to forget!
The stamp love only seals but once
  Upon my life is set.

I hear from others gentle words
  I scarcely heed the while;
Listened to, but with weariness,
  Forgotten with a smile.

But thine, though chance and usual words
  Are treasured, as we keep
Things lovely, precious, and beloved,
  O er which we watch and weep.

I scarcely wish to see thee now,
  It is too dear a joy:
It is such perfect happiness,
  It must have some alloy.

I dream of no return from thee—
  Enough for me to love;
I brood above my silent heart,
  As o'er its nest the dove

But speak not, look not, mock me not
  With light and careless words;
It wounds me to the heart, it jars
  My spirit's finest chords.

I'll not forget thee;—let me dream
  About thee as before.
But, farewell, dearest; yes, farewell,
  For we must meet no more.

THE COQUETTE.

She danced upon the waters,
  Beneath the morning sun,
Of all old Ocean's daughters
  The very fairest one.
An azure zone comprest her
  Round her white and slender side,
For her gallant crew had drest her
  Like a beauty and a bride.

She wore her trappings gaily,
  As a lady ought to do,
And the waves which kissed her daily
  Proud of their mistress grew.
They clung like lovers round her,
  And bathed her airy feet;
With white foam-wreaths they bound her,
  To grace her, and to greet.

She cut the blue wave, scorning
  Our dull and common land;
To the rosy airs of morning,
  We saw her sails expand.
How graceful was their drooping
  Ere the winds began to blow,
While the gay Coquette was stooping
  To her clear green glass below!

How gallant was their sweeping,
  While they swelled upon the air;
As the winds were in their keeping,
  And they knew they were so fair!
A shower of spray before her,
  A silvery wake behind,
A cloud of canvass o'er her,
  She sprang before the wind.

She was so loved, the fairy,
  Like a mistress or a child;
For she was so trim and airy,
  So buoyant and so wild.
And though so young a rover,
  She knew what life could be;
For she had wandered over
  Full many a distant sea.

One night, 'twas in September,
  A mist arose on high;
Not the oldest could remember
  Such a dense and darkened sky:

And small dusk birds came hovering
  The gloomy waters o'er;
The waves mocked their sweet sovereign,
  And would obey no more.

There was no wind to move them,
  So the sails were furled and fast,
And the gallant flag above them
  Drooped down upon the mast.
All was still as if death's shadow
  Were resting on the grave;
And the sea, like some dark meadow,
  Had not one rippling wave:

When the sky was rent asunder
  With a flood of crimson light,
And one single burst of thunder
  Aroused the silent night.
'Twas the signal for their waking!
  The angry winds arose,
Like giant captives breaking
  The chain of forced repose.

Yet bravely did she greet them,
  Those jarring winds and waves;
Ready with scorn to meet them,
  They who had been her slaves.
She faced the angry heaven,
  Our bold and fair Coquette;
Her graceful sides are riven,
  But she will brave it yet.

Like the old oak of the forest,
  Down comes the thundering mast;
Her need is at the sorest,
  She shudders in the blast.
Hark to that low quick gushing!
  The hold has sprung a-leak;
On their prey the waves are rushing
  The valiant one grows weak.

One cry, and all is quiet,
  There is nor sight nor sound;
Save the fierce gale at its riot,
  And the angry waters round.
The morn may come with weeping,
  And the storm may cease to blow:
But the fair Coquette is sleeping
  A thousand fathoms low.

THE ORPHAN BALLAD SINGERS.

O, WEARY, weary are our feet,
  And weary, weary is our way:
Through many a long and crowded street
  We've wandered mournfully to-day.
My little sister she is pale;
  She is too tender and too young
To bear the autumn's sullen gale,
  And all day long the child has sung.

She was our mother's favorite child,
  Who loved her for her eyes of blue,
And she is delicate and mild,—
  She cannot do what I can do.
She never met her father's eyes,
  Although they were so like her own,
In some far distant sea he lies,
  A father to his child unknown.

The first time that she lisped his name,
  A little playful thing was she;
How proud we were,—yet that night came
  The tale how he had sunk at sea.
My mother never raised her head;
  How strange, how white, how cold she grew!
It was a broken heart they said—
  I wish our hearts were broken too.

We have no home—we have no friends:
  They said our home no more was ours;
Our cottage where the ash-tree bends,
  The garden we had filled with flowers,
The sounding shell our father brought,
  That we might hear the sea at home;
Our bees, that in the summer wrought
  The winter's golden honeycomb.

We wandered forth 'mid wind and rain
  No shelter from the open sky;
I only wish to see again
  My mother's grave, and rest and die.

Alas! it is a weary thing
  To sing our ballads o'er and o'er;
The songs we used at home to sing—
  Alas! we have a home no more!

THE NIZAM'S DAUGHTER.

She is as yet a child in years,
  Twelve springs are on her face,
Yet in her slender form appears
  The woman's perfect grace.
Her silken hair, that glossy black,
  But only to be found
There, or upon the raven's back,
  Falls sweeping to the ground.

'Tis parted in two shining braids
  With silver and with gold,
And one large pearl by contrast aids
  The darkness of each fold.
And, for she is so young, that flowers
  Seem natural to her now,
There wreaths the champac's snowy showers
  Around her sculptured brow.

Close to her throat the silvery vest
  By shining clasps is bound;
Scarce may her graceful shape be guessed
  'Mid drapery floating round.

But the small curve of that veined throat,
Like marble, but more warm,
The fairy foot and hand denote
How perfect is the form.

Upon the ankle and the wrist
There is a band of gold;
No step by Grecian fountain kissed
Was of diviner mould.
In the bright girdle round her waist,
Where the red rubies shine,
The kandjar's glittering hilt is placed,
To mark her royal line.

Her face is like the moonlight pale,
Strangely and purely fair,
For never summer sun nor gale
Has touched the softness there.
There are no colors of the rose,
Alone the lip is red;
No blush disturbs the sweet repose
Which o'er that cheek is shed.

And yet the large black eyes, like night,
Have passion and have power;
Within their sleepy depths is light,
For some wild wakening hour.
A world of sad and tender dreams
'Neath those long lashes sleep,
A native pensiveness that seems
Too still and sweet to weep

Of such seclusion know we naught;
  Yet surely woman here
Grows shrouded from all common thought,
  More delicate and dear.
And love, thus made a thing apart,
  Must seem the more divine,
When the sweet temple of the heart
  Is a thrice-veiled shrine.

THE LAKE OF COMO.

Again I am beside the lake,
The lonely lake, which used to be
The wide world of the beating heart,
When I was, love, with thee.

I see the quiet evening lights
Amid the distant mountains shine;
I hear the music of a lute;
It used to come from thine.

How can another sing the song,
The sweet sad song that was thine own?
It is alike, yet not the same;
It has not caught thy tone.

Ah, never other lip may catch
The sweetness round thine own that clung;

To me there is a tone unheard,
There is a chord unstrung.

Thou loveliest lake, I sought thy shores,
That dreams from other days might cast
The presence elsewhere sought in vain,
The presence of the past.

I find the folly of the search,
Thou bringest but half the past again;
My pleasure calling faintly back
Too vividly my pain.

Too real the memories that haunt
The purple shadows round thy brink—
I only asked of thee to dream,
I did not ask to think.

False beauty haunting still my heart,
Though long since from that heart removed;
These waves but tell me how thou wert
Too well and vainly loved.

Fair lake, it is all vain to seek
The influence of thy lonely shore—
I ask of thee for hope and love-
They come to me no more.

THE NEGLECTED ONE.

And there is silence in that lonely hall,
Save where the waters of the fountains fall,
And the wind s distant murmuring, which takes
Sweet messages from every bud it wakes.
'Tis more than midnight; all the lamps are gone,
Their fragrant oils exhausted,—all but one,
A little silver lamp beside a scroll,
Where a young maiden leant, and poured her soul,
In those last words, the bitter and the brief:
How can they say confiding is relief?
Light are the woes that to the eyelids spring,
Subdued and softened by the tears they bring;
But there are some too long, too well concealed,
Too deeply felt,—that are but once revealed:
Like the withdrawing of the mortal dart,
And then the life-blood follows from the heart;
Sorrow, before unspoken by a sigh,
But which, once spoken, only hath to die.
Young, very young, the lady was, who now
Bowed on her slender hand her weary brow:
Not beautiful, save when the eager thought
In the soft eyes a sudden beauty wrought:
Not beautiful, save when the cheek's warm blush
Grew eloquent with momentary flush
Of feeling, that made beauty, not to last,
And scarcely caught, so quickly is it past.
—Alas! she knew it well; too early throw
'Mid a cold world, the unloved and the lone,

With no near kindred ties on whom could dwell
Love that so sought to be beloved as well,
Too sensitive for flattery, and too kind
To bear the loneliness by fate assigned,
Her life had been a struggle; long she strove
To fix on things inanimate her love;
On pity, kindness, music, gentle lore,
All that romance could yield of fairy store.
In vain! she loved:—she loved, and from that hour
Gone were the quiet loves of bird or flower;
The unread book dropped listless on her knee,
The untouched lute hung on the bending tree,
Whose unwreathed boughs no more a pleasant shade
For the lone dreamings of her twilight made.
—Well might she love him: every eye was turned
On that young knight, and bright cheeks brighter burned,
Save one, that grew the paler for his sake:
Alas! for her, whose heart but beat to break;
Who knew too well, not hers the lip or eye
For which the youthful lover swears to die.
How deep, how merciless, the love repressed,
That robs the silent midnight of its rest;
That sees in gathered crowds but one alone;
That hears in mingled footsteps only one;
That turns the poet's page, to only find
Some mournful image for itself designed;
That seeks in music but the plaining tone
Which secret sorrow whispers in its own!
Alas for the young heart, when love is there,
Its comrade and its confidant, despair!

How often leant in some unnoticed spot,
Her very being by the throng forgot,

Shrunk back to shun the glad lamp's mocking ray,
Passed many a dark and weary hour away,
Watching the young, the beautiful, the bright,
Seeming more lovely in that lonely light;
And as each fair face glided through the dance,
Stealing at some near mirror one swift glance,
Then, starting at the contrast, seek her room,
To weep, at least, in solitude and gloom!
And he, her stately idol, he, with eye
Dark as the eagle's in a summer sky,
And darker curls, amid whose raven shade
The very wild wind amorously delayed,
With that bright smile, which makes all others dim,
So proud, so sweet,—what part had she in him?
And yet she loved him: who may say, be still,
To the fond heart that beats not at our will?

'Twas too much wretchedness:—the convent cell,
There might the maiden with her misery dwell.
And that, to-morrow was her chosen doom:
There might her hopes, her feelings find a tomb.
Her feelings!—no—pray, struggle, weep, condemn—
Her feelings,—there was but one grave for them.
'Twas her last night, and she had looked her last,
And she must live henceforward in the past.
She lingered in the hall,—he had been there;
Her pale lips grew yet paler with the prayer
That only asked his happiness. She took
A blank leaf from an old emblazoned book,
Which told love's chronicles; a faint hope stole,—
A sweet light o'er the darkness of her soul—
Might she not leave remembrance, like the wreath
Whose dying flowers their scents on twilight breathe

Just one faint tone of music, low and clear,
Coming when other songs have left the ear?
Might she not tell him how she loved, and pray
A mournful memory for some distant day?
She took the scroll:—what? bare perhaps to scorn
The timid sorrow she so long had borne?
Silent as death, she hid her face, for shame
In rushing crimson to her forehead came;
Through the small fingers fell the bitter rain,
And tremblingly she closed the leaves again.
—The hall is lit with rose, that morning hour,
Whose lights are colored by each opening flower:
A sweet bird by the casement sat and sang
A song so glad, that like a laugh it rang,
While its wings shook the jessamine, till the bloom
Floated like incense round that joyous room.
—They found the maiden: still her face was bowed,
As with some shame that might not be avowed;
They raised the long hair which her face concealed,—
And she is dead,— her secret unrevealed.

THE CHURCH AT POLIGNAC.

Kneel down in yon chapel, but only one prayer
Should awaken the echoes its tall arches bear;
Pale mother, pray not for the child on the bed,
For the sake of the prisoner let matins be said;
Old man, though the shade of thy gravestone be nigh,
Yet not for thyself raise thy voice to the sky;

Young maiden there kneeling, with blush and with tear,
Name not the one name to thy spirit most dear.
The prayer for another, to Heaven addressed,
Comes back to the breather thrice blessing and blest.

Beside the damp marsh, rising sickly and cold,
Stand the bleak and stern walls of the dark prison-hold;
There fallen and friendless, forlorn and oppressed,
Are they—once the flattered, obeyed, and caressed.
From the blessings that God gives the poorest exiled;
His wife is a widow, an orphan his child.
For years there the prisoner has wearily pined,
Apart from his country, apart from his kind;
Amid millions of freemen, one last lonely slave,
He knoweth the gloom, not the peace of the grave.

I plead not their errors, my heart's in the cause,
Which bows down the sword with the strength of the laws;
But France, while within her such memories live,
With her triumphs around, can afford to forgive.
Let freedom, while raising her glorious brow,
Shake the tears from her laurels that darken there now;
Be the chain and the bar from yon prison removed,
Give the children their parents, the wife her beloved.
By the heart of the many is pardon assigned,
For, Mercy, thy cause is the cause of mankind.

THE PIRATE'S SONG.

To the mast nail our flag, it is dark as the grave,
Or the death which it bears while it sweeps o'er the wave.
Let our deck clear for action, our guns be prepared;
Be the boarding-axe sharpened, the cimetar bared;
Set the canisters ready, and then bring to me,
For the last of my duties, the powder-room key.
It shall never be lowered, the black flag we bear;
If the sea be denied us, we sweep through the air.

Unshared have we left our last victory's prey;
It is mine to divide it, and yours to obey.
There are shawls that might suit a sultana's white neck,
And pearls that are fair as the arms they will deck:
There are flasks which, unseal them, the air will disclose
Diametta's fair summer, the home of the rose.
I claim not a portion; I ask but as mine,
'Tis to drink to our victory—one cup of red wine.

Some fight, 'tis for riches; some fight, 'tis for fame;
The first, I despise, and the last is a name.
I fight, 'tis for vengeance. I love to see flow,
At the stroke of my sabre, the life of my foe.
I strike for the memory of long vanished years;
I only shed blood, where another sheds tears.
I come, as the lightning comes red from above,
O'er the race that I loathe, to the battle I love.

THE KNIGHT OF MALTA.

The vessel swept in with the light of the morn,
High on the red air its gonfalon borne;
The roofs of the dwellings, the sails of the mast,
Mixed in the crimson the daybreak had cast.

On came the vessel:—the sword in his hand,
At once from the deck leapt a stranger to land.
A moment he stood, with the wind in his hair,
The sunshine less golden—the silk was less fair.

He looked o'er the waters—what looked he to see?
What alone in the depths of his own heart could be.
He saw an old castle arise from the main,
The oak on its hills, and the dee on its plain.

He saw it no longer; the vision is fled;
Paler the pressed lip, and firmer the tread.
He takes from his neck a light scarf that he wore;
'Tis flung on the waters that bear it from shore.

'Twas the gift of a false one; and with it he flung
All the hopes and the fancies that round it had clung.
The shrine has his vow—the Cross has his brand;
He weareth no gift of a woman's white hand.

A seal on his lip, an oath at his heart,
His future a warfare—he knoweth his part.
The visions that haunted his boyhood are o'er,
The young knight of Malta can dream them no more.

CALDRON SNOUT,

WESTMORELAND.

Long years have past since last I stood
  Alone amid this mountain scene,
Unlike the future which I dreamed
  How like my future it has been!
A cold gray sky o'erhung with clouds,
  With showers in every passing shade,
How like the moral atmosphere
  Whose gloom my horoscope has made!

I thought if yet my weary feet
  Could rove my native hills again,
A world of feeling would revive,
  Sweet feelings wasted, worn in vain.
My early hopes, my early joys,
  I dreamed those valleys would restore,
I asked for childhood to return,
  For childhood, which returns no more.

Surely the scene itself is changed!
  There did not always rest as now
That shadow in the valley's depth,
  That gloom upon the mountain's brow.
Wild flowers within the chasms dwelt
  Like treasures in some fairy hold,
And morning o'er the mountains shed
  Her kindling world of vapory gold.

Another season of the year
  Is now upon the earth and me;
Another spring will light these hills—
  No other spring mine own may be:
I must retune my unstrung heart,
  I must awake the sleeping tomb;
I must recall the loved and lost,
  Ere spring again for me could bloom.

I've wandered, but it was in vain,
  In many a far and foreign clime,
Absence is not forgetfulness,
  And distance cannot vanquish time.
One face was ever in my sight,
  One voice was ever on my ear;
From all earth's loveliness I turned
  To wish, ah! that the dead were here!

O! weary wandering to no home,
  O! weary wandering alone;
I turned to childhood's once glad scenes
  And found life's last illusion flown.
Ah! those who left their childhood's scenes
  For after years of toil and pain,
Who but bring back the breaking heart,
  Should never seek those scenes again.

DERWENT WATER.

I KNEW her—though she used to make
Her dwelling by that lonely lake.
A little while she came to show
How lovely distant flowers can go.
The influence of that fairy scene
Made beautiful her face and mein.
I have seen faces far more fair,
But none that had such meaning there,
For to her downcast eyes were given
The azure of an April heaven;
The softening of those sunny hours,
By passing shadows and by showers

O'er her cheek the wandering red,
By the first wild rose was shed.
Evanescent, pure, and clear,
Just the heart's warm atmosphere.
Like the sweet and inner world,
In that early rosebud furled.
All whose rich revealings glow
Round the lovelier world below.
Light her step was, and her voice
Said unto the air, rejoice;
And her light laugh's silvery breaking
Sounded like the lark's first waking.

Return to that fair lake, return,
On whose green heathlands grows the fern;

And mountain heights of dark gray stone
Are bright with lichens overgrown.
Thou art too fay-like and too fair
For our more common clouded air,
Beauty such as thine belongs
To a world of dreams and songs;
Let thy image with us dwell,
Lending music to farewell.

THE WIDOW'S MITE.

It is the fruit of waking hours
When others are asleep,
When moaning round the low thatched roof
The winds of winter creep.

It is the fruit of summer days
Passed in a gloomy room,
When others are abroad to taste
The pleasant morning bloom.

'Tis given from a scanty store,
And missed while it is given;
'Tis given—for the claims of earth
Are less than those of heaven.

Few save the poor feel for the poor;
The rich know not how hard
It is to be of needful food
And needful rest debarred.

Their paths are paths of plenteousness;
  They sleep on silk and down,
And never think how heavily
  The weary head lies down.

They know not of the scanty meal
  With small pale faces round;
No fire upon the cold, damp hearth,
  When snow is on the ground.

They never by their window sit,
  And see the gay pass by;
Yet take their weary work again,
  Though with a mournful eye.

The rich, they give—they miss it not—
  A blessing cannot be
Like that which rests, thou widowed one,
  Upon thy gift and thee!

HEBE.

YOUTH! thou art a lovely time,
  With thy wild and dreaming eyes;
Looking onwards to their prime,
  Colored by their April skies.
Yet I do not wish for thee,
  Pass, O! quickly pass from me.

Thou hast all too much unrest,
  Haunted by vain hopes and fears;
Though thy cheek with smiles be drest,
  Yet that cheek is wet with tears.
Bitter are the frequent showers,
Falling in thy sunny hours.

Let my heart grow calm and cold,
  Calm to sorrow, cold to love:
Let affections loose their hold,
  Let my spirit look above.
I am weary—youth pass on,
All thy dearest gifts are gone.

She in whose sweet form the Greek
  Bade his loveliest vision dwell;
She of yon bright cup and cheek,
  From her native heaven fell.
Type of what may never last,
Soon the heaven of youth is past.

O! farewell—for never more
  Can thy dreams again be mine;
Hope and truth and faith are o'er,
  And the heart which was their shrine
Has no boon of thee to seek,
Asking but to rest or break.

COTTAGE COURTSHIP.

Now, out upon this smiling,
  No smile shall meet his sight;
And a word of gay reviling
  Is all he'll hear to-night;
For he'll hold my smiles too lightly,
  If he always sees me smile;
He'll think they shine more brightly,
  When I have frowned awhile

'Tis not kindness keeps a lover,
  He must feel the chain he wears:
All the sweet enchantment's over,
  When he has no anxious cares.
The heart would seem too common,
  If he thought that heart his own;
Ah! the empire of a woman
  Is still in the unknown.

Let change without a reason,
  Make him never feel secure;
For it is an April season
  That a lover must endure.
They are all of them so faithless,
  Their torment is your gain;
Would you keep your own heart scathless,
  Be the one to give the pain.

THE PHANTOM.

I COME from my home in the depth of the sea,
I come that thy dreams may be haunted by me;
Not as we parted, the rose on my brow,
But shadowy, silent, I visit thee now.
The time of our parting was when the moon shone,
Of all heaven's daughters the loveliest one;
No cloud in her presence, no star at her side,
She smiled on her mirror and vassal, the tide.

Unbroken its silver, undreamed of its swell,
There was hope, and not fear, in our midnight farewell;
While drooping around were the wings white and wild,
Of the ship that was sleeping, as slumbers a child.
I turned to look from thee, to look on the bower,
Which thou hast been training in sunshine and shower;
So thick were the green leaves, the sun and the rain
Sought to pierce through the shelter from summer in vain.

It was not its ash-tree, the home of the wren,
And the haunt of the bee, I was thinking of then;
Nor yet of the violets, sweet on the air,
But I thought of the true love who planted them there.
I come to thee now, my long hair on the gale,
It is wreathed with no red rose, is bound with no veil,
It is dark with the sea damps, and wet with the spray,
The gold of its auburn has long past away.

And dark is the cavern wherein I have slept,
There the seal and the dolphin their vigil have kept;

And the roof is incrusted with white coral cells,
Wherein the strange insect that buildeth them dwells.
There is life in the shells that are strewed o'er the sands,
Not filled but with music as on our own strands;
Around me are whitening the bones of the dead,
And a starfish has grown to the rock overhead.

Sometimes a vast shadow goes darkly along,
The shark or the sword-fish, the fearful and strong:
There is fear in the eyes that are glaring around,
As they pass like the spectres of death without sound:
Over rocks, without summer, the dull sea-weeds trail,
And the blossoms that hang there are scentless and pale;
Amid their dark garlands, the water-snakes glide,
And the sponge, like the moss, gathers thick at their side.

O! would that the sunshine could fall on my grave,
That the wild flower and willow could over it wave;
O! would that the daisies grew over my sleep,
That the tears of the morning could over me weep.
Thou art pale 'mid the dreams, I shall trouble no more,
The sorrow that kept me from slumber is o'er;
To the depths of the ocean in peace I depart,
For I still have a grave greener far in thy heart!

A LEGEND OF TEIGNMOUTH.

Some few brief hours, my gallant bark,
  And we shall see the shore;
My native, and my beautiful,
  That I will leave no more.

And gallantly the white sails swept
  On, on before the wind;
The prow dashed through the foam, and left
  A sparkling line behind.

The sun looked out through the blue sky,
  A gladsome summer sun;
The white cliffs like his mirrors show
  Their native land is won.

And gladly from the tall ship's side
  Sir Francis hailed the land,
And gladly in his swiftest boat,
  Rowed onward to the strand.

"I see my father's castle walls
  Look down upon the sea;
The red wine will flow there to-night,
  And all for love of me.

"I left a gentle maiden there;
  For all the tales they say
Of woman's wrong and faithlessness
  To him who is away:

"I'll wager on her lily hand,
  There's still a golden ring;
But, lady, 'tis a plainer one
  That o'er the seas I bring."

His bugle sound the turret swept,
  They met him in the hall;
But 'mid dear faces where is hers,
  The dearest of them all?

Ah! every brow is dark and sad,
  And every voice is low;
His bosom beats not as it beat
  A little while ago.

They lead him to a darkened room,
  A heavy pall they raise;
A face looks forth as beautiful
  As in its living days.

A ring is yet upon the hand,
  Sir Francis, worn for thee;
Alas! that such a clay-cold hand,
  Should true love's welcome be!

He kissed that pale and lovely mouth,
  He laid her in the grave;
And then again Sir Francis sailed
  Far o'er the ocean wave.

To east and west, to north and south,
  That mariner was known;
A wanderer bound to many a shore,
  But never to his own.

At length the time appointed came,
He knew that it was come;
With pallid brow and wasted frame,
That mariner sought home.

The worn-out vessel reached the shore,
The weary sails sank down;
The seamen cleared her of the spoils
From many an Indian town.

And then Sir Francis fired the ship
Yet tears were in his eyes,
When the last blaze of those old planks
Died in the midnight skies.

Next morning, 'twas a Sabbath morn,
They sought that church to pray;
And cold beside his maiden's tomb
The brave Sir Francis lay.

O, Death! the pitying, that restored
The lover to his bride;
Once more the marble was unclosed—
They laid him at her side.

And still the evening sunshine sheds
Its beauty o'er that tomb;
Like heaven's own hope, to mitigate
Earth's too unkindly doom.

THE CITY CHURCHYARD.

I PRAY thee lay me not to rest
  Among these mouldering bones,
Too heavily the earth is prest
  By all these crowded stones.

Life is too gay—life is too near—
  With all its pomp and toil;
I pray thee, do not lay me here,
  In such a world-struck soil.

The ceaseless roll of wheels would wake
  The slumbers of the dead;
I cannot bear for life to make
  Its pathway o'er my head.

The flags around are cold and drear,
  They stand apart, alone;
And no one ever pauses here,
  To sorrow for the gone.

No: lay me in the far green fields
  The summer sunshine cheers;
And where the early wild-flower yields
  The tribute of its tears;

Where shadows the sepulchral yew,
  Where droops the willow tree;
Where the long grass is filled with dew—
  O! make such grave for me!

And passers-by, at evening's close,
  Will pause beside the grave,
And moralize o'er the repose
  They fear, and yet they crave.

Perhaps some kindly hand may bring
  Its offering to the tomb;
And say, as fades the rose in spring,
  So fadeth human bloom.

But here there is no kindly thought
  To soothe, and to relieve;
No fancies and no flowers are brought,
  That soften while they grieve.

Here Poesy and Love come not—
  It is a world of stone;
The grave is bought—is closed—forgot!
  And then life hurries on.

Sorrow, and beauty—nature—love,
  Redeem man's common breath;
Ah! let them shed the grave above—
  Give loveliness to death.

THE UNKNOWN GRAVE.

There is a little lonely grave
  Which no one comes to see,
The foxglove and red orchis wave
  Their welcome to the bee.
There never falls the morning sun,
  It lies beneath the wall,
But there when weary day is done
  The lights of sunset fall;
Flushing the warm and crimson air
As life and hope were present there.

There sleepeth one who left his heart
  Behind him in his song;
Breathing of that diviner part
  Which must to heaven belong;
The language of those spirit chords,
  But to the poet known.
Youth, love, and hope yet use his words,
  They seem to be his own.
And yet he has not left a name,
The poet died without his fame.

How many are the lovely lays
  That haunt our English tongue,
Defrauded of their poet's praise,
  Forgotten he who sung.
Tradition only vaguely keeps
  Sweet fancies round this tomb;

Its tears are what the wild flower weeps,
  Its record is that bloom:
Ah, surely nature keeps with her
The memory of her worshipper.

One of her loveliest mysteries
  Such spirit blends at last,
With all the fairy fantasies
  Which o'er some scenes are cast.
A softer beauty fills the grove,
  A light is in the grass,
A deeper sense of truth and love
  Comes o'er us as we pass;
While lingers in the heart one line,
The nameless poet hath a shrine.

THE MISSIONARY.

It is a glorious task to seek,
  Where misery droops the patient head:
Where tears are on the widow's cheek,
  Where weeps the mourner o'er the dead.

These are the moments when the heart
  Turns from a world no longer dear;
These are the moments to impart
  The only hope still constant here.

That hope is present in our land,
For many a sacred shrine is there;
Time-honored old cathedrals stand;
Each village has its house of prayer.

O'er all the realm one creed is spread—
One name adored—one altar known.
If souls there be in doubt, or dread,
Alas! the darkness is their own.

The priest whose heart is in his toil
Hath here a task of hope and love;
He dwells upon his native soil,
He has his native sky above.

Not so beneath this foreign sky:
Not so upon this burning strand;
Where yonder giant temples lie,
The miracles of mortal hand.

Mighty and beautiful, but given
To idols of a creed profane,
That cast the shade of earth on heaven,
By fancies monstrous, vile, and vain.

The votary here must half unlearn
The accents of his mother tongue;
Must dwell 'mid strangers, and must earn
Fruits from a soil reluctant wrung.

His words on hardened hearts must fall,
Hardened till God's appointed hour;
Yet he must wait, and watch o'er all,
Till hope grows faith, and prayer has power.

And many a grave neglected lies,
  Where sleep the soldiers of the Lord;
Who perished 'neath the sultry skies,
  Where first they preached that sacred word.

But not in vain—their toil was blest;
  Life's dearest hope by them was won;
A blessing is upon their rest,
  And on the work which they begun.

Yon city, where our purer creed
  Was a thing unnamed, unknown,
Has now a sense of deeper need,
  Has now a place of prayer its own.

And many a darkened mind has light,
  And many a stony heart has tears;
The morning breaking o'er the night,
  So long upon those godless spheres.

Our prayers be with them—we who know
  The value of a soul to save,
Must pray for those, who seek to show
  The Heathen Hope beyond the grave.

THE WISHING GATE.

Wishes, no! I have not one,
Hope's sweet toil with me is done;
One by one have flitted by,
All the rainbows of the sky.
Not a star could now unfold
Aught I once wished to be told.
What have I to seek of thee?
Not a wish remains for me.

Let the soldier pause to ask,
Honor on his glorious task;
Let the parting sailor crave
A free wild wind across the wave;
Let the maiden pause to frame
Blessings on some treasured name;
Let them breathe their hopes in thee,
Not a wish remains for me.

Not a wish! beat not my heart,
Thou hast not bade thy dreams depart;
They have past, but left behind
Weary spirit, wasted mind.
Ah! if this old charm were sooth,
One wish yet might tax its truth;
I would ask, however vain,
Never more to wish again

THE SHEPHERD BOY.

Like some vision olden
  Of far other time,
When the age was golden,
  In the young world's prime
Is thy soft pipe ringing,
  O lonely shepherd boy,
What song art thou singing,
  In thy youth and joy?

Or art thou complaining
  Of thy lowly lot,
And thine own disdaining,
  Dost ask what thou hast not?
Of the future dreaming,
  Weary of the past,
For the present scheming,
  All but what thou hast.

No, thou art delighting
  In thy summer home,
Where the flowers inviting
  Tempt the bee to roam;
Where the cowslip bending,
  With its golden bells,
Of each glad hour's ending
  With a sweet chime tells.

All wild creatures love him
  When he is alone,
Every bird above him
  Sings its softest tone.
Thankful to high Heaven,
  Humble in thy joy,
Much to thee is given,
  Lowly shepherd boy.

THE WOODLAND BROOK.

Thou art flowing, thou art flowing,
  O small and silvery brook;
The rushes by thee growing,
  And with a patient look
The pale narcissus o'er thee bends
Like one who asks in vain for friends.

I bring not back my childhood,
  Sweet comrade of its hours;
The music of the wild wood,
  The color of the flowers;
Tney do not bring again the dream
That haunted me beside thy stream.

When black-lettered old romances
  Made a world for me alone;
O, days of lovely fancies,
  Are ye forever flown?

Ye are fled, sweet, vague, and vain,
So I cannot dream again.

I have left a feverish pillow
  For thy soothing song:
Alas, each fairy billow
  An image bears along!
Look where I will, I only see
One face too much beloved by me.

In vain my heart remembers
  What pleasure used to be;
My past thoughts are but embers
  Consumed by love for thee.
I wish to love thee less—and feel
A deeper fondness o'er me steal.

THE DANCING GIRL.

A LIGHT and joyous figure, one that seems
As if the air were her own element;
Begirt with cheerful thoughts, and bringing back
Old days, when nymphs upon Arcadian plains
Made musical the wind, and in the sun
Flashed their bright cymbals and their whitest hands
These were the days of poetry—the woods
Were haunted with sweet shadows; and the caves
Odorous with moss, and lit with shining spars,
Were homes where Naiades met some graceful youth

Beneath the moonlit heaven—all this is past;
Ours is a darker and a sadder age;
Heaven help us through it!—'tis a weary world,
The dust and ashes of a happier time.

DIRGE.

Lay her in the gentle earth,
Where the summer maketh mirth;
Where young violets have birth;
Where the lily bendeth.
Lay her there, the lovely one!
With the rose, her funeral stone;
And for tears, such showers alone
As the rain of April lendeth.

From the midnight's quiet hour
Will come dews of holy power,
O'er the sweetest human flower
That was ever loved.
But she was too fair and dear
For our troubled pathway here;
Heaven, that was her natural sphere,
Has its own removed.

SCENES IN LONDON.

Life in its many shapes was there,
The busy and the gay:
Faces that seemed too young and fair
To ever know decay.

Wealth, with its waste, its pomp, and pride,
Led forth its glittering train;
And poverty's pale face beside
Asked aid, and asked in vain.

The shops were filled from many lands—
Toys, silks, and gems, and flowers;
The patient work of many hands,
The hope of many hours.

Yet 'mid life's myriad shapes around,
There was a sigh of death;
There rose a melancholy sound—
The bugle's wailing breath.

They played a mournful Scottish air,
That on his native hill
Had caught the notes the night winds bear
From weeping leaf and rill.

'Twas strange to hear that sad wild strain
Its warning music shed,
Rising above life's busy train,
In memory of the dead.

There came a slow and silent band
  In sad procession by:
Reversed the musket in each hand,
  And downcast every eye.

They bore the soldier to his grave;
  The sympathizing crowd
Divided like a parted wave
  By some dark vessel ploughed.

A moment, and all sounds were mute,
  For awe was over all;
You heard the soldier's measured foot,
  The bugle's wailing call.

The gloves were laid upon the bier,
  The helmet and the sword;
The drooping war-horse followed near,
  As he, too, mourned his lord.

Slowly—I followed too—they led
  To where a church arose,
And flung a shadow o'er the dead
  Deep as their own repose.

Green trees were there—beneath the shade
  Of one was made a grave;
And there to his last rest was laid
  The weary and the brave.

They fired a volley o'er the bed
  Of an unconscious ear;
The birds sprang fluttering overhead,
  Struck with a sudden fear.

All left the ground; the bugles died
  Away upon the wind;
Only the tree's green branches sighed
  O'er him they left behind.

Again, all filled with light and breath,
  I passed the crowded street—
O, great extremes of life and death,
  How strangely do ye meet!

THE ALTERED RIVER.

Thou lovely river, thou art now
  As fair as fair can be;
Pale flowers wreathe upon thy brow,
  The rose bends over thee.
Only the morning sun hath leave
  To turn thy waves to light,
Cool shade the willow branches weave
  When noon becomes too bright.

The lilies are the only boats
  Upon thy diamond plain,
The swan alone in silence floats
  Around thy charmed domain.
The moss-bank's fresh embroidery,
  With fairy favors starred,
Seems made the summer haunt to be
  Of melancholy bard.

Fair as thou art, thou wilt be food
  For many a thought of pain;
For who can gaze upon thy flood,
  Nor wish it to remain
The same pure and unsullied thing
  Where heaven's face is as clear,
Mirrored in thy blue wandering
  As heaven's face can be here.

Flowers fling their sweet bonds on thy breast,
  The willows woo thy stay;
In vain,—thy waters may not rest,
  Their course must be away.
In yon wide world, what wilt thou find?
  What all find—toil and care:
Your flowers you have left behind,
  Far other weight to bear.

The heavy bridge confines your stream,
  Through which the barges toil;
Smoke has shut out the sun's glad beam,
  Thy waves have caught the soil.
On—on—though weariness it be,
  By shoal and barrier crossed,
Till thou hast reached the mighty sea,
  And there art wholly lost.

Bend thou, young poet, o'er the stream—
  Such fate will be thine own;
Thy lute's hope is a morning dream,
  And when have dreams not flown?

THE FORGOTTEN ONE.

No shadow rests upon the place
Where once thy footsteps roved;
Nor leaf, nor blossom, bear a trace
Of how thou wert beloved.
The very night-dew disappears
Too soon, as if it spread its tears.

Thou art forgotten!—thou, whose feet
Were listened for like song!
They used to call thy voice so sweet;—
It did not haunt them long.
Thou, with thy fond and fairy mirth—
How could they bear their lonely hearth?

There is no picture to recall
Thy glad and open brow;
No profiled outline on the wall
Seems like thy shadow now;
They have not even kept to wear
One ringlet of thy golden hair.

When here we sheltered last, appears
But just like yesterday;
It startles me to think that years
Since then are passed away.
The old oak tree that was our tent,
No leaf seems changed, no bough seems rent.

A shower in June—a summer shower,
  Drove us beneath the shade;
A beautiful and greenwood bower
  The spreading branches made:
The rain-drops shine upon the bough,
The passing rain—but where art thou?

But I forget how many showers
  Have washed this old oak tree,
The winter and the summer hours,
  Since I stood here with thee:
And I forget how chance a thought
Thy memory to my heart has brought.

I talk of friends who once have wept,
  As if they still should weep;
I speak of grief that long has slept,
  As if it could not sleep;
I mourn o'er cold forgetfulness,
Have I, myself, forgotten less?

I've mingled with the young and fair,
  Nor thought how there was laid,
One fair and young as any there,
  In silence and in shade.
How could I see a sweet mouth shine
With smiles, and not remember thine?

Ah! it is well we can forget,
  Or who could linger on,
Beneath a sky whose stars are set—
  On earth whose flowers are gone?
For who could welcome loved ones near,
Thinking of those once far more dear,

Our early friends, those of our youth?—
  We cannot feel again
The earnest love, the simple truth,
  Which made us such friends then.
We grow suspicious, careless, cold;
We love not as we loved of old.

No more a sweet necessity,
  Love must and will expand;
Loved and beloving we must be,
  With open heart and hand,
Which only ask to trust and share
The deep affections which they bear.

Our love was of that early time;
  And now that it is past,
It breathes as of a purer clime
  Than where my lot is cast;
My eyes fill with their sweetest tears
In thinking of those early years.

It shocked me first to see the sun
  Shine gladly o'er thy tomb;
To see the wild flowers o'er it run
  In such luxuriant bloom.
Now I feel glad that they should keep
A bright sweet watch above thy sleep.

The heaven whence thy nature came
  Only recalled its own;
It is Hope that now breathes thy name,
  Though borrowing Memory's tone.
I feel this earth could never be
The native home of one like thee.

Farewell! the early dews that fall
  Upon thy grass-grown bed,
Are like the thoughts that now recall
  Thine image from the dead.
A blessing hallows thy dark cell—
I will not stay to weep. Farewell!

THE LEGACY OF THE LUTE.

Come take the lute—the lute I loved—
  'Tis all I have to offer thee;
And may it be less fatal gift
  Than it has ever been to me.
My sigh yet lingers on the strings,
  The strings I have not heart to break:
Wilt thou not, dearest! keep the lute
  For mine—for the departed's sake?

But, pray thee, do not wake that lute;
  Leave it upon the cypress tree;
I would have crushed its charmed chords,
  But they so oft were strung to thee.
The minstrel-lute! O, touch it not,
  Or weary destiny is thine!
Thy life a twilight's haunted dream—
  Thou, victim, at an idol's shrine.

Thy breath but lives on others' lips—
  Thy hope, a thing beyond the grave,-

Thy heart, bare to the vulture's beak—
  Thyself a bound and bartered slave.
And yet a dangerous charm o'er all,
  A bright but ignis-fatuus flame.
Luring thee with a show of power,
  Dazzling thee with a blaze of flame.

It is to waste on careless hearts
  The throbbing music of thine own;
To speak love's burning words, yet be
  Alone—ay, utterly alone.
I sought to fling my laurel wreath
  Away upon the autumn wind:
In vain,—'twas like those poisoned crowns
  Thou may'st not from the brow unbind.

Predestined from my birth to feed
  On dreams, yet watch those dreams depart,
To bear through life—to feel in death—
  A burning and a broken heart.
Then hang it on the cypress bough,
  The minstrel-lute I leave to thee;
And be it only for the wind
  To wake its mournful dirge for me.

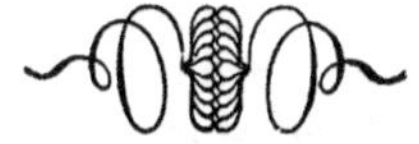

THE CITY OF THE DEAD.

I.

Laurel ! O, fling thy green boughs on the air,
There is dew on thy branches, what doth it do there ?
Thou that art worn on the conqueror's shield,
When his country receives him from glory's red field ;
Thou that art wreathed round the lyre of the bard,
When the song of its sweetness has won its reward.
Earth's changeless and sacred—thou proud laurel tree !
The tears of the midnight, why hang they on thee ?

II.

Rose of the morning, the blushing and bright,
Thou whose whole life is one breath of delight ;
Beloved of the maiden, the chosen to bind
Her dark tresses' wealth from the wild summer wind.
Fair tablet, still vowed to the thoughts of the lover,
Whose rich leaves with sweet secrets are written all
over ;
Fragrant as blooming—thou lovely rose tree !
The tears of the midnight, why hang they on thee ?

III.

Dark cypress ! I see thee—thou art my reply,
Why the tears of the night on thy comrade trees lie ;
That laurel it wreathed the red brow of the brave,
Yet thy shadow lies black on the warrior's grave ;
That rose was less bright than the lip which it prest,
Yet thy sad branches bend o'er the maiden's last rest ;

The brave and the lonely alike they are sleeping,
I marvel no more rose and laurel are weeping.

IV.

Yet sunbeam of heaven! thou fallest on the tomb;
Why pausest thou by such dwelling of doom?
Before thee the grove and the garden are spread—
Why lingerest thou round the place of the dead?
Thou art from another, a lovelier sphere,
Unknown to the sorrows that darken us here.
Thou art as a herald of hope from above;—
Weep, mourner, no more o'er thy grief and thy love!
Still thy heart in its beating; be glad of such rest,
Though it call from thy bosom its dearest and best.
Weep no more that affection thus loosens its tie;
Weep no more that the loved and the loving must die;
Weep no more o'er the cold dust that lies at your feet;
But gaze on yon starry world—there ye shall meet.

V.

O heart of mine! is there not one dwelling there
To whom thy love clings in its hope and its prayer?
For whose sake thou numberest each hour of the day,
As a link in the fetters that keep me away!
When I think of the glad and the beautiful home
Which oft in my dreams to my spirit hath come:
That when our last sleep on my eyelids hath prest,
That I may be with thee at home and at rest:
When wanderer no longer on life's weary shore,
I may kneel at thy feet, and part from thee no more:
While death holds such hope forth to soothe and to save,
O, sunbeam of heaven, thou may'st well light the grave!

THE IONIAN CAPTIVE.

SADLY the captive o'er her flowers is bending,
  While her soft eye with sudden sorrow fills:
They are not those that grew beneath her tending
  In the green valley of her native hills.

There is the violet—not from the meadow
  Where wandered carelessly her childish feet;
There is the rose—it grew not in the shadow
  Of her old home—it cannot be so sweet.

And yet she loves them—for those flowers are bringing
  Dreams of the home that she will see no more;
The languid perfumes are around her, flinging
  What almost for the moment they restore.

She hears her mother's wheel, that, slowly turning,
  Murmured unceasingly the summer day;
And the same murmur, when the pine boughs burning,
  Told that the summer hours had passed away.

She hears her young companions sadly singing
  A song they loved—an old complaining tune;
Then comes a gayer sound—the laugh is ringing
  Of the young children—hurrying in at noon.

By the dim myrtles, wandering with her sister,
  They tell old stories, broken by the mirth
Of her young brother: alas! have they missed her,
  She who was borne a captive from their hearth?

She starts—too present grows the actual sorrow,
  By her own heart she knows what they have borne;
Young as she is, she shudders at to-morrow,
  It can but find her prisoner and forlorn.

What are the glittering trifles that surround her—
  What the rich shawl—and what the golden chain?
Would she could break the fetters that have bound her,
  And see her household and her hills again!

THE CEDARS OF LEBANON.

Ye ancients of the earth, beneath whose shade
  Swept the fierce banners of earth's mightiest kings,
When millions for a battle were arrayed,
  And the sky darkened with the vulture's wings.

Long silence followed on the battle-cries;
  First the bones whitened, then were seen no more;
The summer grasses sprang for summer skies,
  And dim tradition told no tales of yore.

The works of peace succeeded those first wars,
  Men left the desert tents for marble walls;
Then rose the towers from whence they watched the stars,
  And the vast wonders of their kingly halls.

And they are perished—those imperial towers
  Read not amid the midnight stars their doom;
The pomp and art of all their glorious hours
  Lie hidden in the sands that are their tomb.

And ye, ancestral trees! are somewhat shorn
  Of the first strength that marked earth's earlier clime;
But still ye stand, stately and tempest-worn,
  To show how nature triumphs over time.

Much have ye witnessed—but yet more remains;
  The mind's great empire is but just begun;
The desert beauty of your distant plains
  Proclaim how much has yet been left undone.

Will not your giant columns yet behold
  The world's old age, enlightened, calm, and free;
More glorious than the glories known of old—
  The spirit's placid rule o'er land and sea.

All that the past has taught is not in vain—
  Wisdom is garnered up from centuries gone;
Love, Hope, and Mind prepare a nobler reign
  Than ye have known—Cedars of Lebanon!

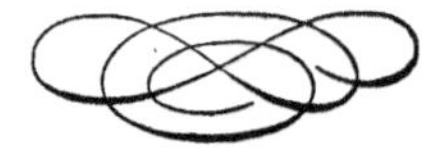

DEATH AND THE YOUTH.

"Not yet—the flowers are in my path,
  The sun is in the sky;
Not yet—my heart is full of hope—
  I cannot bear to die.

Not yet—I never knew till now
  How precious life could be;
My heart is full of love—O Death!
  I cannot come with thee!"

But Love and Hope, enchanted twain,
  Passed in their falsehood by;
Death came again and then he said—
  "I'm ready now to die!"

THE END.

www.ingramcontent.com/pod-product-compliance
Lightning Source LLC
LaVergne TN
LVHW021303110826
845150LV00003B/465

* 9 7 8 1 4 2 5 5 6 0 0 1 0 *